The Scale and Scope of Economics

Other titles by the same author

Democratic Systems

A Degree of Freedom

The Scale and Scope of Economics

A.C.Sturt

Churinga Publishing

First published in Great Britain in 1995

by Churinga Publishing

16 Horseshoe Lane, Guildford, Surrey GU1 2SX

© 1984 A.C.Sturt

A.C.Sturt has asserted his right
under the Copyright, Designs and Patents Act 1988
to be identified as the author of this work

A CIP catalogue record for this book
is available from the British Library

ISBN 0 9526736 2 2

Printed and bound in the UK
by Biddles Limited of Guildford

CONTENTS

List of Figures   ix

Table   x

PREFACE   xi

1 INTRODUCTION   1

2 THE ECONOMIC PROCESS   9
    2.1 Natural Living Resources 11
    2.2 Farming of Living Resources 12
    2.3 Industry and Manufacturing:
         the Non-living Resources 13
    2.4 The Categories of Goods, Utilities and Services 15
    2.5 The Special Role of Energy 19
    2.6 Time and Equilibrium 25
    2.7 Rules of the Economic Process 27
    2.8 Incentives as a Feedback Loop 28
    2.9 Use of Resources 29

3 THE PERFECT MARKET AS A SYSTEM   31
    3.1 Definition of a Perfect Market 33
    3.2 Mechanisms of Operation of a Perfect Market 34
    3.3 The Role of Information 37
    3.4 Examples of the Role of Information
         in Market Systems 44
    3.5 Time in the "Perfect Market" System 46
    3.6 Model of Operation of the Economic Process 48
    3.7 Example of an Economic Chain 51
    3.8 The Incentive Feedback Loop 52
    3.9 Markets and Competition 53
    3.10 Equilibrium and the Physical System Analogue 58

4 THE MARKET SYSTEM IN THE REAL WORLD 61
- 4.1 Flaws in the Basic Thesis 62
- 4.2 Flaws in the Mechanism of Operation 69
- 4.3 Exogenous Distortions of Markets 76
- 4.4 Interpretation of Price Signals from Markets 82
- 4.5 The Problem of Common Goods 93
- 4.6 Conclusions 96

5 THE COST BASIS OF ECONOMIC ACTIVITY 99
- 5.1 Scale-related Costs 103
- 5.2 Opportunity Costs 114

6 ECONOMIES OF SCOPE 118
- 6.1 The Scope of Labour 121
- 6.2 The Scope of Capital Investment 126
- 6.3 The Scope of Land 133
- 6.4 The Scope of Energy 143
- 6.5 The Effect of Information Technology 148
- 6.6 The Underlying Assumptions 149
- 6.7 Conclusions 155

7 THE PROCESS OF TECHNOLOGICAL INNOVATION 161
- 7.1 The Nature of Technological Innovation 165
- 7.2 The Stages of Innovation 169
- 7.3 Response Times in Technological Innovation 176
- 7.4 Costs and Risks in Technological Innovation 177
- 7.5 Rates of Innovation 183
- 7.6 Product Life Cycles 184
- 7.7 The Role of Competition 189
- 7.8 Rate of Return on Innovation 192
- 7.9 Cycles of Innovation 193
- 7.10 Conclusions 197

8 ORGANISATION AND INNOVATION IN THE ECONOMIC PROCESS 200
  8.1 The Individual 202
  8.2 Information Systems 204
  8.3 Levels of Abstraction 207
  8.4 Architectures 210
  8.5 Decision-making in Organisations 216
  8.6 Creative Problem Solving 220
  8.7 Strategic Planning 224
  8.8 Innovation and Organisation 228
  8.9 The Economic Costs of Behavioural Effects 231
  8.10 Conclusions 235

9 CONCLUSIONS 240

References 248

Index 255

List of Figures

2.1	Categorisation of Goods and Services	17
2.2	The Economic Process	19
2.3	Increase of Economic Energy Content with Stages of Production and Installation	23
2.4	Economic Energy Content of a Loaf of Bread	24
2.5	The Cycle of Production and Consumption	26
2.6	Economic Process with Incentive Feedback Loop	29
3.1	Representation of a Perfect Market	34
3.2	Supply and Demand Schedules	35
3.3	Progress of Bargaining between Two Independent Sellers and Two Independent Buyers	39
3.4	Progress of Bargaining between x Independent Sellers and y Independent Buyers	40
3.5	Alternative Interactions of Two Sellers with Three Buyers	40
3.6	Blackboard Display of Bargaining between Two Sellers and Two Buyers	41
3.7	Blackboard Display of Bargaining between x Sellers and y Buyers	43
3.8	Flow of a Commodity through a Market	46
3.9	Example of the Flow of Corn through a Market	47
3.10	Flow of Materials through a Conversion Process	47
3.11	Model of Operation of the Economic Process	49
3.12	Wear and Tear in a Conversion Process as a Leak to Earth	50
3.13	Feedback from Markets to Converters	53
4.1	Some Deviations from the "Perfect" Market	63
4.2	Product Differentiation	71
4.3	Representation of Stocks in the Conversion Process	73
4.4	Diagrammatic Representation of Trading	74
4.5	Diagrammatic Representation of Speculation	75
4.6	Net Revenue as Feedback	83
4.7	Effect of Stocks on Feedback System	85
4.8	Market Response to Change of Conditions	89
4.9	Price Response on Launching of British Telecom Shares	90
4.10	Response of Oil Product Market Prices to the Oil Price Shock of 1973	91
5.1	The Harvest	103

5.2	Increase of Market Revenues and Costs with Area Cultivated	104
5.3	Model of a Factory	105
5.4	Simple Production Curve for a Conversion Process with Fixed Costs	106
5.5	General Cost/Revenue Curve for a Conversion Process	107
6.1	Energy Intensities of GDP of the OECD and the LDCs 1950-1992	147
6.2	Optimum Size of a Firm	155
7.1	Inception of Innovation in a Subsystem of a System	170
7.2	Innovation Process Spreading through and between Systems over Time	172
7.3	Innovating System formed from Innovator System A and User System B	174
7.4	Cost Structures of Existing and Potential New Processes	179
7.5	Cost Structures of a Potential New and an Existing Product	181
7.6	Product Life Cycle	185
7.7	Reduction over Time of Unit Costs of Products A and B in Isolation	194
7.8	Reduction over Time of Unit Costs of Product A in Economic Synergy with Product B	195
8.1	Two Levels of Abstraction	208
8.2	Three Levels of Abstraction	209
8.3	Flow of Information into and between Levels of Abstraction	210
8.4	Elimination of Interactions	211
8.5	Flows of Information up a Hierarchical Organisation	212
8.6	Hierarchy with Five Flows into Some Nodes	213
8.7	Simple Matrix Organisation	214
8.8	Co-ordination Matrix	215
8.9	Establishing a Task Force	216
8.10	Information Flows for Strategic Planning Purposes	225

Table

2.1	Examples of the Elements of the Economic Process	21

PREFACE

This is a book for those who come to economics from outside, as well as economists by training who doubt the current efficacy of the solutions which their discipline traditionally prescribes, as economic dominance begins to move with the technology to parts of the world that only a short time ago were considered "less developed", and old assumptions of a given international economic pecking order fade.

Many at the growth points of our economies need a sound grasp of economic fundamentals in the course of their work: engineers, scientists, managers of all kinds of businesses, administrators, politicians, marketers, anyone concerned with research and development and anyone involved in the processes of innovation. Many more simply wish to understand the changes which are going on around them. But they are often confronted with problems which economics fails even to address, let alone solve. In particular for those who have perhaps had a systematic grounding in other, especially technical, disciplines, the assumptions and methods of textbook economics may seem rather like having to believe three impossible things before breakfast.

Yet this need not be so. This book presents an analysis of economic processes which does not require strained hypotheses. It shows how economies evolve through the deliberate action not only of individuals but also of firms, institutions and governments, and that waiting for the timeless equilibria of neoclassical economics to come to the rescue is a vain hope.

A century ago Marshall, one of the fathers of economics, described economic systems as "differentiated", by analogy with the biological world which was particularly catching the imagination of the time. Differentiation meant the complexity of a system as opposed to its size or "scale". The full implications of that distinction have not featured sufficiently in subsequent economic analysis, and treatment of economics as merely scalar has led many into false conclusions, as well as the confusion which was described above. The present analysis is intended to remedy that situation.

Here the "differentiation" of an economic system is termed its "scope", thus dispensing with the biological connotations. Economic

Preface

development is driven by man towards the goal of his own choice. Such development is brought about through "economies of scope", which are achieved through organisation and strategic management, ultimately expressed as investment, a far cry from the view of economic innovation as serendipity or some similarly haphazard occurrence.

This is made particularly clear by recognising that economics is about the behavioural systems by which we organise production and consumption. As such it obeys the rules of systems, which are simple but definite, and must include time, information and energy. It also requires an appreciation that technological innovations from flints and bronze axes to machine tools and microchips have always been an integral part of the economic process, and cannot be treated, as an "exogenous variable", some kind of analytical optional extra. The process of technological innovation is central to economics and to the analysis of this book.

For the sake of brevity, the word "man" which appears in the text from time to time is used in the sense of "mankind" or "people in general". All people, men and women, children and adults, taxpayers and non-taxpayers alike are part of the economic process. Indeed they are its raison d'être; to coin a phrase, there are no economic ends.

18th April 1994

Chapter One

INTRODUCTION

Few disciplines seem to impinge on the lives of ordinary people as much as economics. Yet for those who come to economics from outside, its theorems often seem to be much stronger on assertion than on evidence. Although it is now customary to omit the adjective "political", which used to be inseparable from the word economy, the two are still very much intertwined. Different schools of economics tend to interpret economic mechanisms according to their own particular inclinations. Indeed, economics sometimes seems to the lay person to be the embodiment of whichever political philosophy is being propounded at the time, rather than a discipline which stands alone on neutral, observable principles.

For the unconvinced it is the artificiality of some of the basic postulates that impedes acceptance. In the perfect economic world, for instance, markets are "cleared", i.e. everything is sold, at a price determined by all individuals acting freely and solely in their own interests (1). This price is unique, since it is the only price at which no one is prepared to buy or sell more. Supply and demand are then said to be in "equilibrium". Remarkably, "supply" and "demand" apply to everything bought and sold, including your work and mine, which is called labour. Since all markets are in "equilibrium", they must also be in "general equilibrium" with each other. If the markets are allowed to operate freely, according to this school of teaching, all available resources automatically become employed in the economic process, because everything will be sold; it is only a question of arriving at the right price. Thus the whole economy is said to be optimised by the self-interest of individuals, who make their way through life only colliding with others in markets as self-contained units, rather like economic billiard balls or molecules of inert gas. If the results turn out to be less than optimum, it must be because of "imperfections" in the market. Needless to say, other economists hold other views (2).

However, even those who regard the literal truth of such propositions with more than a little scepticism are in no doubt that economic forces, whatever their exact nature, are indeed very powerful. The difficulty is that the underlying model of much economic theory seems to be remote from the real world which we see around us. If prices are decided in this detached way, what is it that actually moves during the process of reaching equilibrium in markets? How do markets for, say, new industrial products come into being, when everything is in general economic equilibrium? How has it come about that some countries have become more developed industrially than others? Is there some kind of pre-ordained industrial pecking order, as seems to be the tacit assumption of many people? In which case, why do so many of the new high technology products flooding into our shops and our workplaces seem to come from a few countries which only decades ago were considered to be economically weak?

The process of technological innovation is the central theme of this book. It is a most important aspect of economic development, one which has a bearing on all the questions posed above. Some eminent economists have even considered it to be the crux of economics itself (3), although economic teaching traditionally finds technical change difficult to encompass, and therefore treats it as exogenous, something outside the system itself.

Technological innovation is the introduction into the industrial base of new products or processes, including modifications to existing process equipment which significantly reduce its cost of operation. The physical difference between the industrialised countries and the rest is the technological hardware which they have on the ground i.e. the factories, distribution systems and all the fixed capital investment which they have accumulated. Technological innovation is the mechanism by which this industrial base evolves.

Introduction

To make the mechanisms by which this evolution occurs as clear and as free from ambiguity as possible, the method we use is to analyse economic systems literally as such. The systems approach permits us to illuminate the dynamics of change in an industrial base in a way that is impossible with the essentially static "equilibrium" model. Systems are collections of things which relate to each other through some form of regular interaction or interdependence. They may be physical, like the solar system or an ecological system, or they may be simply behavioural, like an organisation. The term will come as nothing new to anyone with a background in scientific or engineering disciplines, though it is being used in a much wider context here. Those who require a fuller explanation of systems thinking should scan some of the well known books on the subject (e.g. 4, 5, 6).

Within broad limits we may define a system as best suits our purpose, but in doing so we also define the environment in which it functions. Our skill in doing this will determine the clarity, and hence usefulness, of the subsequent analysis. Here the simplest way is to give some examples from economics. A national economy is a system. Markets are systems. Firms and factories are systems. Families and, most important of all, individuals are economic systems. The economics of the largest systems, national economies, may be called macroeconomics, which deals in terms of national aggregates for output, income, productivity and so on. The economics of small systems, which are their parts or subsystems, may be called microeconomics.

All systems are governed by rules which are universal, and therefore permit us to make general observations about the conditions for successful operation of any particular system. These may be stated briefly as follows:

1. A whole system is more than the sum of its parts: it cannot be optimised by optimising its parts.

From this it can be concluded that optimisation of an economic system must take into account all parts of that system simultaneously, whether it is a firm, a country, or a community etc. If this is not done, it may well be that any action taken by one part for its own good will rebound against another part, and so negate the beneficial effects on the system as a whole. This may be important in considering the role of the individual in economics. And at a national level, it sometimes happens that governments tackle one economic problem, only to find that their very action gives rise to another problem elsewhere which may be just as bad. By analogy with medicine, a human being as a system is clearly more than just arms plus legs plus a head plus vital organs, and so on. The physician therefore considers the whole system, and does not try to treat one part of the body as if it were medically independent of the rest, or the cure might turn out to be worse than the disease.

A government is in a unique position in a national economy. It has a dual role; not only is it a subsystem of the whole national economic system, with all the preoccupations and constraints which that brings, but it is also the only body in a position to look at the national system as a whole. If a government does not address the optimisation of the national interest, no one else can.

2. A system transforms inputs into outputs.

An economic system is such a process. For example, factories as systems take in raw materials, services etc and turn them into goods for sale i.e. outputs. People buy goods, enjoy their use, which is the desired output, and consume them, thereby transforming them into rubbish, which is an additional, incidental but inevitable output. Countries consume their natural resources to enhance their standard of living, and in so doing turn them into waste products. And so on.

3. A system consists of a hierarchy of subsystems which interact: it is these interactions which make the whole system more than the sum of its parts.

If the system in question is a national economy, some of the subsystems one might consider to be: the government, which is what makes it a nation; the institutions; the firms; the banks; the consumers; the natural resources which it has at its disposal, and so on. Each subsystem is itself composed of subsystems of a lower order; thus a firm is composed of factories, offices, stocks etc, and each of these can be "decomposed" into further subsystems, depending on the purpose

Introduction

of the analysis. All subsystems interact with each other by definition, and the importance of the term "interaction" is that it means more than that one thing has an effect on another; it implies that the two together have a greater effect on the output of the whole system than would be expected from their individual characteristics i.e. they are synergistic. The interaction may be so large and so important that annihilation of one of the subsystems may, by removing the possibility of interaction, effectively render the other useless, even though it apparently survives intact. This is like removing one half of the male/female system.

4. An open system is a system which exchanges information, energy and materials with its environment. A closed system is one in which these exchanges do not take place.

All the systems which we examine in this book are open systems. (There is a good case to be made that all economic systems are open, but that debate may only divert us from our main consideration, which is the world of tangible things).

So for example, a factory will take in raw materials and convert them into output in the form of products for sale, using as energy electricity from power stations, heat from coal- fired boilers and so on. It will return energy to the environment as low grade heat in cooling water and hot air; indeed it could not function without disposing of waste energy in this way. It will receive information from outside as orders from customers, and give information itself, say as specifications of its products.

5. An open system orders and differentiates itself in response to its environment. If it becomes isolated from its environment, its entropy tends to a maximum i.e. internal disorder increases and the system atrophies.

It follows that an economic system must continually adapt and restructure to meet the challenges of a changing economic environment, if it is to prosper. For example, a firm must respond to its environment in the form of its customers' needs, threats from its competitors, government regulations etc, or else atrophy. Such a response will entail reordering and differentiation i.e. modification of its subsystems and their goals, and generation of new subsystems as appropriate. The same will be true of a country. The process of technological innovation is a fundamental part of such change. If the system loses touch with its environment, it has no criteria by which to adapt, and it becomes aimless. The concept of entropy meaning disorder is drawn from physics, but it is none the less apposite for that (7).

6. A system must have feedback from its output to its input to reach its goals.

Suppose we consider a system as a kind of black box with inputs and outputs, but we are not concerned with the process which actually goes on inside the box. First the system has to set itself a goal that it wishes to achieve in relation to its environment. Setting a meaningful goal clearly entails gathering appropriate information about the environment. Then it has to detect how nearly its output, which results from the process going on in the black box, is helping it to attain its goal, because that is the only reason for transforming inputs into outputs. Finally it has to adjust its inputs in order more closely to approach its goal. Information from the output is thus used to control the input, which is called feedback. This is exactly what individuals do in their daily lives, and what firms do when they control their stock levels etc. In our analysis of economic systems the feedback is essentially provided by money in all its related forms.

Economic systems, like any other, obey the laws of physical science. Time must be an explicit variable in economic systems, because by definition it is not possible to approach a goal or have feedback except in time. Understanding the mechanism of change requires us to follow each movement throughout time. Conventionally economics represents time by a succession of "equilibrium" diagrams, if this is not a contradiction in terms, but the problem with this approach is that it is like trying to ascertain the behaviour of a pendulum from a series of snapshots; the answer depends on how far apart in time the snapshots are taken. They may show it apparently swinging much less or much more slowly than it in fact does, and there is no possibility of determining in which direction it is moving at any particular time. Much the same may happen with the tides of the

Introduction

economy. Even when the picture is not downright misleading, the dynamics may still be unduly difficult to interpret.

The energy changes involved in economic systems require that the systems reach a steady state rather than an equilibrium. Systems are said to be in equilibrium if they return to their former states after small, temporary displacements. But consumption of energy means that economic systems can never return to their former states. Energy is always "consumed" in the course of a total process, though it would be more precise to say that the energy is downgraded, or that high intensity energy sources such as coal or oil are transformed into waste heat, because that is the overall effect. The process cannot therefore be put into exact reverse, any more than an egg can be unscrambled, which is another way of describing an increase in entropy, as referred to above, and shows the passage of time with entropy as time's arrow.

The concept of a steady state itself needs careful consideration in this context. Economic systems can remain in a steady state only so long as the inputs, including the cost of energy, remain constant. Then they must move on down the energy gradient. But even this is a dubious proposition for systems which are continuously learning and adapting. Most of the change which these bring about ultimately influences energy use in some form or other, and central to it is the process of technological innovation, which does not appear in classical economic theory at all.

People appear in all the systems of an economy. Everyone takes part in at least one, and most appear in more than one, i.e. as producer, consumer, buyer, seller etc. People are the motors of economic systems; they set goals, detect changes in the world around them and determine what response their systems make, though that is not to imply that they are the same people in each case. It is people that drive the innovation process.

Yet it is the nature of man to be wary of change; indeed this may be necessary to his survival. Consequently the evolution of the economic system through innovation is by no means a straightforward process. It is usually very different from the popular conception of some scientific discovery or technical invention. These may be necessary, but they are certainly not sufficient, because innovation ultimately means changing people's customs and practices, a far cry from small, reversible movements.

The Scale and Scope of Economics

To grasp the full extent of technological innovation, we need to understand the fundamental nature of the economic process itself. We begin, therefore, with an analysis of the economic process and the mechanisms of exchange through markets. We then set out the conditions necessary for successful innovation. Finally we examine the innovation process and the nature of the economic and social changes involved. The analysis shows that strategic management and organisation are the crux of technological innovation. It is these which are ultimately rendering the concept of economic equilibrium null and void in a modern industrial nation. Moreover, many of the shibboleths of classical, or perhaps by now neoclassical, economic theory fall by the way side as the argument proceeds.

Technological innovation concerns not only those who are directly engaged in bringing it about, but also the other organisations and institutions which are their environment. Complex organisations are among man's greatest achievements, but by their very nature they are inhibitors of innovation. In a changing world, change will occur whether we like it or not, either generated from within or imposed from without. The problem is how to manage the process and extend the benefits to all, while preserving what we want. But first we need to understand it.

Chapter Two

THE ECONOMIC PROCESS

For the errors of definitions multiply themselves as the reckoning proceeds, and lead men into absurdities ....
Thomas Hobbes

So then always that knowledge is worthiest .... which considereth the simple forms or differences of things, which are few in number, and the degrees and co-ordinations whereof make all this variety.
Francis Bacon

The economic process consists of the production and consumption of goods and services by man. It is a process devised by man for his own benefit; it has no other purpose. Though textbooks describe it in terms such as supply, demand, money, labour, capital and land, exclusive reliance on such abstract, derivative concepts may serve to obscure the underlying physical movement, which is from natural resources to consumption. It is salutary, therefore, to begin any discussion of the economic process with a reminder of the wider natural context into which it fits, whether we are conscious of it or not.

Man superimposes his economic activity on the thinnest of layers on the surface of the physical world around him. Even in the twentieth century he is only just beginning to move beyond the confinement of this layer. Outside this layer natural processes produce change on geological or solar scales in which man is scarcely discernible.

The Scale and Scope of Economics

Continents collide, rocks form, mountains rear up, volcanoes erupt. Winds and tides erode even rocky shores, rain falls, rivers cut their beds and sweep down their silt into the oceans.

This ceaseless process is driven by the great engines of nature on a scale which dwarfs, and will continue to dwarf, man. The earth's crust floats in continental lumps on the molten rock below and will continue to do so until the core solidifies, which is for man an infinity of time away. The spinning of the earth on its axis and the pull of the moon drive the great tides and winds circling around the globe. The sun and the declination of the earth's axis together give the climate, the rain and the daily winds, and the cycle of seasons in perpetuity. The whole earth, as the whole universe, is gradually cooling down to the coldest of temperatures, so that in the geological "long run" everything will be chilling waste and void.

On all this man has no influence and never will have. Not that this need concern us in this year, century or millennium. Man simply does not feature in this timescale. The engines of change, driven by their own sources of energy, steadily and relentlessly reform the shape and nature of the planet's surface, whatever he does. If man observes the change at all, it tends to be in retrospect, as he wonders at the remains of villages submerged beneath the sea, ports left high and dry inland and seabeds at the tops of mountains.

In the biosphere, the thin crust of the earth's surface and the air immediately above it, vegetation flourishes and decays and living creatures pass out their existence. Man produces some order out of the natural resources thrown up by these processes to satisfy his own needs. Making the order is called production, consumption is returning the spent resources to the general increasing disorder of the environment after use and enjoyment. The engine which drives the process for man is energy, just as in the natural processes, indeed as in all processes. The process of order/disorder contrived by man, i.e. production and consumption, is the economic process. This process has existed since the time when man first began to shape the world around him for his own purposes, rather than living off what it happened to provide. It began long before there was money. The catalyst was man's skills, knowledge, organisation and creativity, the facilitators of economic change.

If this seems trite, it should be remembered that many are under the illusion that the economic process is almost exclusively concerned with money, the medium of economic exchange, and is somehow regulated by divine laws. But money is a concept, an agreement between the members of society, and since it consumes no energy (except that which may be necessary to shift binary digits in a computer or to telephone a broker) it can produce nothing of itself. It is a device to assist man in the application of the aforesaid skills, knowledge, organisation and creativity, a co-catalyst. Indeed it is a product of them.

Seen from this vantage point the economic process may be likened to an unfolding tapestry of increasing complexity, and most would say richness and beauty, as more and more people are freed from the debilitating fight to survive. Its development is picked out in the weft of production and consumption in each age, and the warp, which runs through it from the beginning of time, energy.

2.1 Natural Living Resources

In his early days man lived off the resources of nature which surrounded him, gathering fruits and berries, and fishing and hunting for game. His influence on the living world was little more than that of any other animal, except that tools and weapons extended his armoury, and fire his comfort and digestion.

The economic process was therefore very simple. Man attached himself to the natural cycle which is driven by the energy of the sun, the moon and the rotation of the earth. The living things of nature which were produced by that energy provided his store of inner energy, which is food, and the external energy that he needed for cooking and warmth, which is fire. All production was through the biological processes of nature, all consumption through the biological processes of man. Both the natural resources and the driving force of energy were replenished daily. If his demands exceeded the capacity of the local environment to provide, he moved on or perished.

The slight exception to this process, but one with momentous implications, was the tools which he might have chipped out of flints or similar earth materials. This was the earliest manufacturing process. Flints were excavated and split to form knives and scrapers, which was production, and these were used until they were broken and discarded, which was consumption. The natural flint resource could not be replaced except by geological processes; it was consumption of a non-renewable resource.

The transformation energy of the economic processes was manpower, derived from food. But man would not have survived the strong competition from his fellow creatures, had it not been for his development of communal skills in the form of organisation, which was given cohesion and continuity by language. These skills increased production, and gradually became extended to the exchange of produce, the beginning of trading, the agreement of exchange values, and hence primitive markets. Organisation allowed the specialisation necessary to hunt and gather effectively, while avoiding the ever present dangers. Thus in this simple description we have identified the nature of the early economic process, the energy which drove it and the learning which catalysed it. The elements were materials and energy in simple forms, processed by the skills and co-operative behaviour of man.

2.2 Farming of Living Resources

The major disadvantage of living resources in their natural form is that they are scattered widely, with a low energy density, so that man needed much time and effort to gather them. Anyone who has picked wild fruit, except for passing enjoyment, can vouch for that. The natural consequence, therefore, is that man began to concentrate them, and this he did by farming.

Using manpower, accumulated knowledge and the tools of fire, he cleared the land of its natural vegetation, cultivated the crops he needed and farmed the animals he wanted for food. In this way the biological process of nature, still powered by the energy of the sun, was concentrated and extended for man's benefit. In effect he changed the scope of the natural process itself in his own interest, and reduced the effort needed to live, his "cost of living". To supplement his own labour he used the ox and the horse to work in the fields, and sent the dog to fetch the sheep, thus extending the process much further than his own efforts could have. These animals too derived their energy from their food, and so from the sun.

The Economic Process

Farming required a much greater degree of organisational skill than hunting and gathering, because of the continual battle against nature. The very processes of nature which he controlled to his advantage in farming were always trying to turn the land back into the natural state from which it came. His great achievements were continually being eroded by the forces of nature, and needed replenishing every year by ploughing and hoeing, irrigating and draining. Nature has its own views about the scope of the landscape.

The inestimable benefit of all this labour was that it created a stock of food, a store of personal energy for man. This stock permitted greatly increased specialisation and hence knowledge and skills, which reinforced the economic process in a virtuous circle to give still more food and prosperity. So great was the benefit that eventually such societies could even afford professional hierarchies to help the process along by enlisting the help of the gods, who might otherwise devote all their attention to the natural processes, and, no less important, by writing down what was learnt for posterity.

Thus we have an economic process as before, but much intensified by changing the scope of the landscape and other living things. The driving force was still the daily energy of the sun, but it was more efficiently harnessed for man's purpose. The knowledge and skills were embodied in the social development which was inherent in farming. They changed the scope of man's activity, and so permitted an increase in the scale of production to the point that a significant part of the surface of the globe was under his management.

2.3 Industry and Manufacturing: the Non-living Resources

Manufacturing is an activity which can begin only when the basic needs of man have already been met and a surplus is being produced; manufacturers must exchange at least part of their wares for some of that surplus in order to survive, because their own products could not alone sustain them. Moreover, there is a significant delay between investment of effort in the manufacturing process and the availability of product to exchange for food, often much longer than the lag between sowing and reaping. The investment of resources required for manufacturing processes of any sophistication requires a commitment which will only be repaid much later. In some way he must bridge the gap.

The implication of this is that the organisation of a society which is engaged in manufacturing must be much more complex still than that required for hunting or farming. Whole chains of supportive activity must be set up, while continuing to produce enough food for everyone, and the result is a far greater specialisation of labour. The scope of such a society, the specialisation and the learning systems, must embody a complex network of commitments and skills if it is not to regress into the more primitive states.

The manufacturing stage thus subsumes the farming that went before, but it extends the economic process into the processing of things as well as food. Things according to this definition are made from non-living resources, such as iron and copper ores, stone, clays and glazes. They have to be concentrated or brought together into a convenient place by extracting and refining, and then transformed by manufacturing processes into objects which are of value to society.

The knowledge and skills to do this are much more specialised again than the hunter's or farmer's, but the major characteristic of such processes is the concentration of energy which they require. In the early stages this may simply mean many people working in the same place, but it soon leads to machinery which requires energy in excess of manpower and animal power, and so in excess of what they can absorb of the daily dose from the sun through the food they eat.

They must therefore draw first on firewood from the forests, then on whole forests themselves, and eventually on the fossil fuels which are the remains of former living things, the stored energy of past light from the sun. For example, the Weald in southern England used to be dense forest which supplied wood to make charcoal for smelting iron, but in Elizabethan times, when England needed a much larger supply of cannonballs to defend its interests, so much charcoal was required that, together with wood for housebuilding, nearly all the forest was consumed. To meet the demand for iron the industry had to move to a new technology and a more concentrated energy source, coal, in a new location (1).

The increasing skills of manufacturing and the use of more intensive energy resources, such as coal and oil, gave man ever more power to modify the scope of the earth's surface and even to tap to a

The Economic Process

limited extent some of the resources hidden just below. They enabled him to develop new, more desirable objects of consumption and to turn energy into new, more convenient forms to be consumed, for example, as electric light and automotive power. The scale and scope of production and consumption grew to proportions which were unimaginable even a few decades before.

The inevitable and necessary concomitant of these economic processes was the development of mechanisms for suppliers to make contact with buyers of the products. Specialised factories greatly increased the number of commonly available products. Arrangements to dispose of them led inexorably to more trade and more sophisticated markets, as places for buyers and sellers to meet, and the increasing use of a medium of exchange, such as gold or money. The growing scope which these arrangements for supply and distribution permitted, at the same time enabled the scale of operations to be increased in even greater proportion.

Thus we have identified the earth resource base, the energy needed to transform it into products and the knowledge base which catalyses it.

2.4 The Categories of Goods, Utilities and Services

At this stage it is worth pausing to categorise the goods and services which are consumed in the economic process, because errors of definition may lead to confusion in the development of later arguments. The classification used here is not the broad aggregations used by economists and governments to keep track of flows of money in an economy, but a much more fundamental division by energy use. The resources available to man on earth then fall into two classes, material things and utilities (Figure 2.1). These, together with what is directly derived each day from the sun, form the supply of products which is also equal to what is consumed over the long term.

Material things are literally materials, whether they are copper, television sets or caviar. The matter of which they are made is present on earth in some dispersed form. Their production consists of bringing together the necessary elements of matter and assembling them into the required product, consuming energy in the process i.e. conversion. In economics, therefore, all products may be considered to have locked into them by man an energy content which depends on how they were put together. The various stages of production may be considered as adding to the energy content of the materials being processed or as "energy added". Consumption is then dissipation of that energy content into general or economically useless form in the environment i.e. conversion back to nature again by time.

Utilities as defined here are not material things but rather energy in a more convenient form. The most primitive form of utility is man or animal power, a more convenient form of energy than the food or feed which powers them. Heat, light, sound and motive power are other forms of energy which are more convenient than firewood, coal, oil etc. Utilities of this sort may only be made possible by materials, and so they are not completely distinct in everyday experience, but the consumption of energy in a utility may far exceed that which is inherent in the material. The ordered material (for example an electric motor) provides a mechanism for the convenient use of energy (electricity) which has relatively little effect on the consumption of materials in the motor itself (only wear and tear).

There are two other categories of human activity which are dear to economists, and which become confused with the fundamental physical nature of the economic process: services and incentives. Neither need involve the consumption of energy, and so neither forms part of the process of conversion and consumption. Instead they should be considered as facilitators of the economic process. The distinction may seem to be pedantic, but it is far from a merely academic concept when we come to consider economic growth, innovation and markets.

This use of the term "service" differs in important respects from that which is current in conventional economic thinking. Services in economists' terminology are a derivative concept which may involve not only person to person services, but also materials and utilities. Thus entertainment, planning, administration, and writing books are all included under the economists' heading of services together with painting the house and providing a taxi service. But the incremental energy required for planning, for example, in addition to what is expended during the normal course of day to day living is small. Both painting the house and driving a taxi on the other hand consume energy, either directly or by use of the materials which have an energy content, such as paint and tyres.

The Economic Process

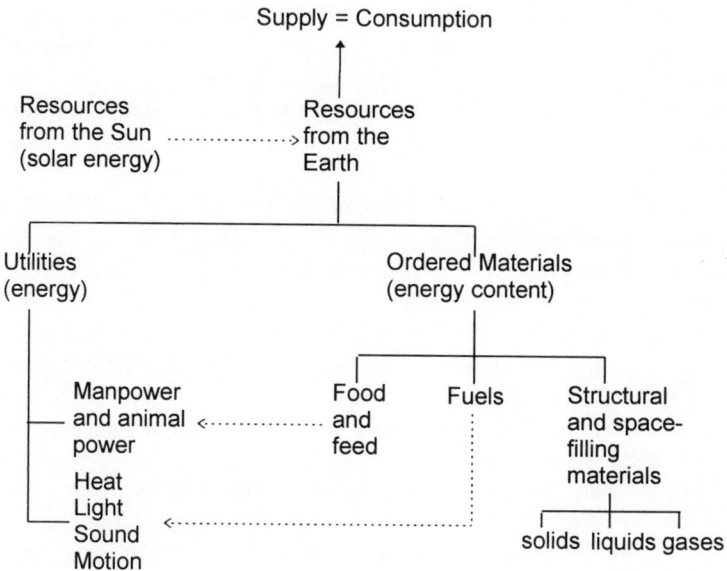

Figure 2.1 Categorisation Of Goods And Services

To make the classification clear and homogeneous we describe the contribution of mankind to the economic process in terms of energy. The simplest contribution is brute manpower which like animal power we have defined as a utility, a more convenient form of food or feed energy. Skills, knowledge, organisation and creativity, on the other hand need consume no energy, and do not play a direct part in the conversion process, however essential they may be. These we describe as catalysts of the economic process; they enable conversion processes to take place. The ultimate difference is that skills, knowledge, organisation and creativity endure; they can be stored for use later, within limits. But brute energy cannot be stored. One man delivers one man's work each day; he cannot store his energy for a month and deliver thirty times as much at the end of that period. Thus the term power in the term manpower is precise; it indicates the rate at which he can turn his stored energy into useful work.

The Scale and Scope of Economics

The other attribute of man is that he requires incentives to carry out the economic process at all i.e. apply his skills, knowledge, organisation, creativity and energy to the conversion process. At the basest level the incentive is the will to survive, but once that need has been met it is the desire to share in the consumption of what is produced.

In a modern industrial economy the incentive system is all that which is to do with the flow of money i.e. wages, banking, insurance, etc. It enables the exchange of goods, utilities, skills and creativity to take place in the present or by agreement in the future. In order to overcome the uncertainty relating to exchange, the incentive system requires to be underpinned by the State in two ways; first freedom of exchange of goods and utilities e.g. access to markets in a market economy, and secondly guaranteed acceptability and availability at all times of the medium of exchange, money. The incentive system needs a separate analysis, which is beyond the scope of this book. We simple take the existence of money in the form of costs and revenues as given.

The result of this analytical framework is that the physical economic process can be classified as conversion processes for the production of ordered materials (or goods) and utilities as in Figure 2.2. The physical process can then be put into the total context with: energy as the force of transformation which converts materials into what is required for consumption; skills, knowledge, organisation and creativity as the catalyst which makes it work; and the incentive in the form of participation in consumption, which encourages man to apply himself to the economic process.

Economists usually classify what they call factors of production into land, labour and capital. Leaving aside capital as part of the incentive system, we have described the contribution of people to the modern economy. The term labour is more appropriate to the eighteenth and nineteenth centuries when many of the concepts were developed, because it implies some sort of commodity, which of course farm labour very nearly was. Land, however, is more difficult. By using energy of conversion as in effect a factor of production we have subsumed what can be extracted from growth on it. Land as space or area, however, is not consumable by the definition which we have used. It owes its place in the economic system to the community in

The Economic Process

which it is located. We therefore classify it as part of the incentive system.

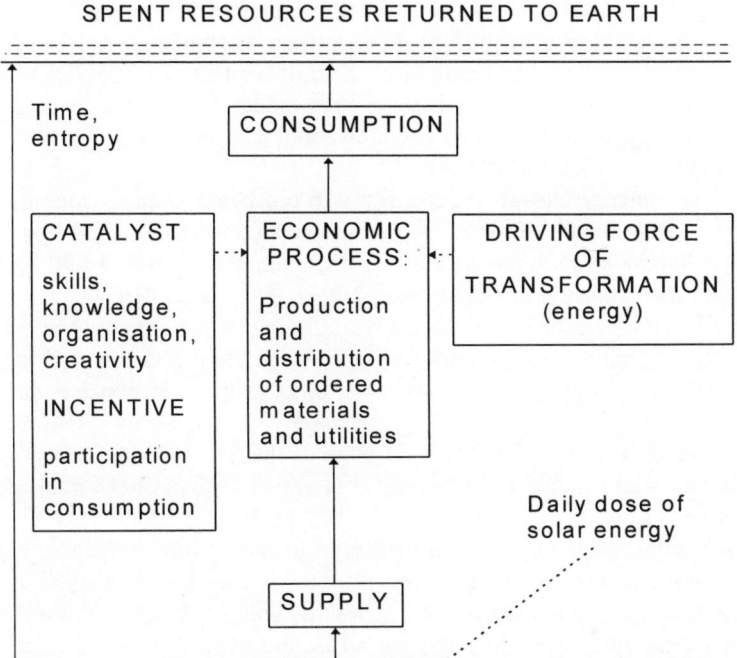

Figure 2.2 The Economic Process

Summarising the arguments which we have used, we arrive at the new classification in Table 2.1, which is rigorous, unambiguous and complete. To mention the earth, as the sun, is superfluous. There are no other sources on which economic activity can draw.

2.5 The Special Role of Energy

The introduction of energy as the driving force of conversion processes in effect makes it a new "factor of production" in economic parlance (2). However, energy is not a commodity to be bought and sold. No one has ever seen or touched any, even though the word is in common use. It is in fact a scientific concept. When change of any sort occurs in the physical world, it obeys fundamental rules which govern its direction and extent. The rules are independent of materials, and they do not change with time. The quantity of change is measured by the quantity of energy required to make it happen. This applies to all change, not simply that which is man-made; the economic process which is deliberate change brought about and controlled by man is subsumed within the total.

The energy change which occurs in a process is easily measured, but energy cannot be simply expressed as an absolute quantity. In this it is like height; a building may be fifty metres high, and we all know what that means, but fifty metres higher than what? Higher than the road outside or sea level? And if the building is in London, should the reference point be New York, or perhaps the moon? The answer is, of course, fifty metres higher than some point at the base which is easily identified.

So with energy the reference point is the energy state E in which the material is put into the process, but which does not have to be, and indeed cannot be, quantified. During the transformation process energy is in effect added to the input material to turn it into something else. This increment in energy content, which can be quantified, may conveniently be termed ΔE, the economic energy content. (Not the ΔE of thermodynamics). As energy is added to the product which is being made, so it must be supplied by or subtracted from the source which is driving the process. The energy content is therefore the energy required physically to transform the input materials plus the energy which is wasted during the process as waste material or heat.

Thus the economic energy content ΔE in this terminology is not an absolute, but depends on the efficiency of the process being used. As the product takes on its new order, so the total processing system must go from a higher to a lower energy state. Energy, like water, always flows downhill. The higher state is supplied by energy stored as fossil fuel and other primary stores. The sink into which it eventually flows is the ambient low grade heat which surrounds us; it just goes to warm the universe a little.

Table 2.1 Examples of the Elements of the Economic Process

PRODUCTS OF CONVERSION		FACILITATORS		DRIVING FORCE OF TRANSFORMATION
Ordered Materials (goods)	Utilities	Skills, Knowledge, Organisation, Creativity	Incentive System	Energy Sources
Bread Meat Wine Shoes Clothes Houses Cars TV Sets Roads	Electricity Heat Light Sound Motive power	Language Science Technology Industry Law and Order Medicine Politics Defence Planning Information systems Administration	Money Banking Insurance Stocks and shares Private ownership Public ownership Markets Land area	Sunlight Firewood combustion Oil and Gas combustion Coal combustion Combustion of spent products of the economic process (household and industrial waste) Nuclear

The Scale and Scope of Economics

For example, consider steel water pipes. The chain of production and consumption may be shown as follows:

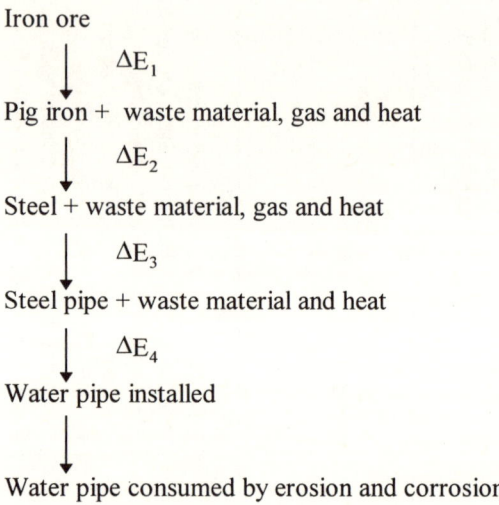

The pipe may be stated to have an economic energy content equal to the sum of all the ΔEs in its production and installation which will come from coke in the blast furnace, gas and electricity to make the steel pipe and so on. Consumption is equivalent to the waste of all that energy over its time in use. These changes may be illustrated as in diagram (Figure 2.3).

Similarly in agriculture the manufacture of bread may be expressed as in Figure 2.4. Eating the bread consumes all the economic energy needed to make it, but in this case the bread itself yields food energy to the eater. Though the economic ΔEs used in both examples are not absolute, minimum theoretical values can be calculated from thermodynamic data. These values are inflated in practice by the energy inefficiency of each step in the process i.e. waste, which is in effect immediate consumption.

The same calculations can be made to show man's energy contribution to the economic process. When man supplies energy to a conversion process in the form of manual labour, the natural state E should be the energy which he would normally use if he existed outside the economic process. The energy which he supplies to the economic process should then be the increment of energy ΔE over and above this level i.e. in simply living.

The most important feature of the conversion processes is that they are not reversible. They move only one way, which can be measured by time or entropy changes. If one wants to move from consumed iron in the form of eroded pipes back to iron ore or something similar, then additional energy must be expended to do it. All changes for better or worse require an input of energy.

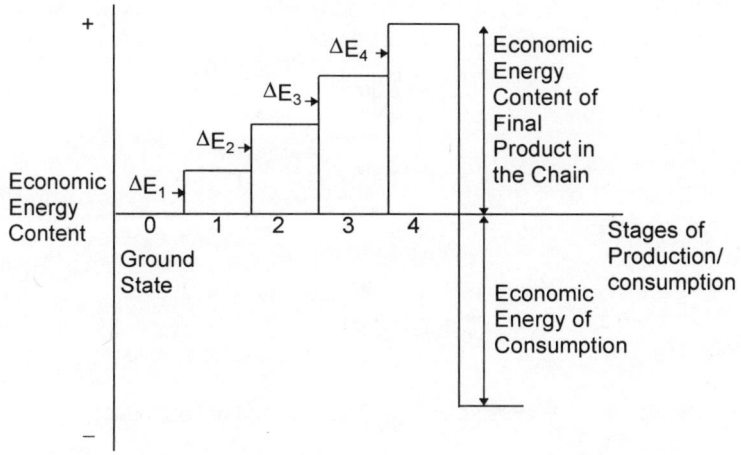

Figure 2.3 Increase of Economic Energy Content with Stages of Production and Installation

The result of this is that products which are close to the consumer have a higher energy content than the primary products further back in the chain from which they are made. Furthermore, when products are consumed, they are not annihilated. They are simply present in a different chemical form or in a different state of dispersion e.g. not as an iron ore body but as an iron-rich patch of soil in a rubbish dump. To transform the waste back into the ore would require the input of more energy. Consumption is the loss of the energy of conversion.

Lost energy may take the form of waste heat, but it may also take the form of stable chemical compounds such as oxides of carbon which escape into the atmosphere. On either score it would be irrecoverable without a great deal of energy being consumed, which would defeat the object of recovery.

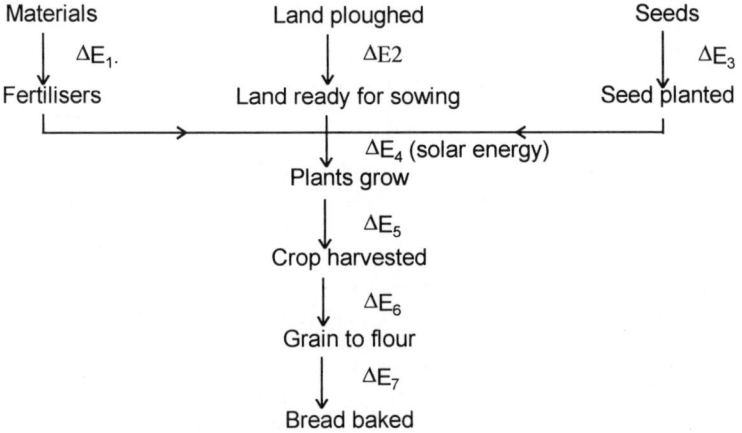

Figure 2.4 Economic Energy Content of a Loaf of Bread

Furthermore, it is implicit in the analysis that nothing can be lost in the economic process except energy. Everything which is produced is consumed either by man or by the ravages of time. What has been wrought out of the earth returns to it when spent. If conversion processes produce waste or products which are not required, they simply return to earth in the form of rubbish sooner rather than later.

All this is much clearer in the living world with which everyone is familiar. Life is a conversion process in which the material product, that is ourselves, and the energy which we need are provided by food. We know that we are physically what we eat less any waste material that we excrete and energy that we lose through body heat and so on.

The Economic Process

We too have an energy content in that sense, and we are all too aware that it is a one way process. That is just a microcosm of the changes which energy creates in the economic process.

Economic processes from the beginning of time have therefore been driven by the earth's stored energy resources, which were formed by energy from the sun over geological time, plus the current dose of energy from the sun etc. Economic development has been the use of increasingly more energy-efficient processes for making the products which man requires, thus enabling the economic process to be extended ever wider.

2.6 Time and Equilibrium

The one-way economic process through time may be depicted as in Figure 2.5. It cannot be reversible because of the energy loss. The term equilibrium implies reversibility, so that a point of equilibrium can be regained after a small displacement, like a ball rolling into a hollow.

The economic process cannot therefore be said to reach a physical equilibrium. The best it can do is reach a state which is approximately steady for a period of time before moving on downhill (3). Such a "steady" state may be reached when: either the available supply of energy remains roughly constant for a time, say with the discovery of a large hydrocarbon resource, because stored energy comes in packages; or because technological improvements in the efficiency of energy use reduce the energy required to make currently demanded products and utilities, which will last until demand increases again. However, any such "steady" state must be more apparent than real, because the economic system as a whole is a learning system, and new products and processes are generally an improvement on those that preceded them: the economy continuously evolves. Moreover in the long term unit for unit primary energy sources tend to become increasingly more expensive in energy terms to find and exploit. The most accessible sources tend to be consumed first.

How then can this be reconciled with the general equilibrium price/quantity relationship which economists believe would be the normal state of affairs, if markets could be made to work efficiently? The answer seems to be that their equilibrium is expressed in terms of supply and demand schedules which confound quantities from the conversion systems with prices from the incentive system. Incentives are a matter of common consent and, unlike energy, may take any value that man collectively ascribes to them. Thus in the very short term it is perfectly possible that people may be able to obtain a range of purchases which they cannot better by switching between markets, which may be considered a kind of equilibrium.

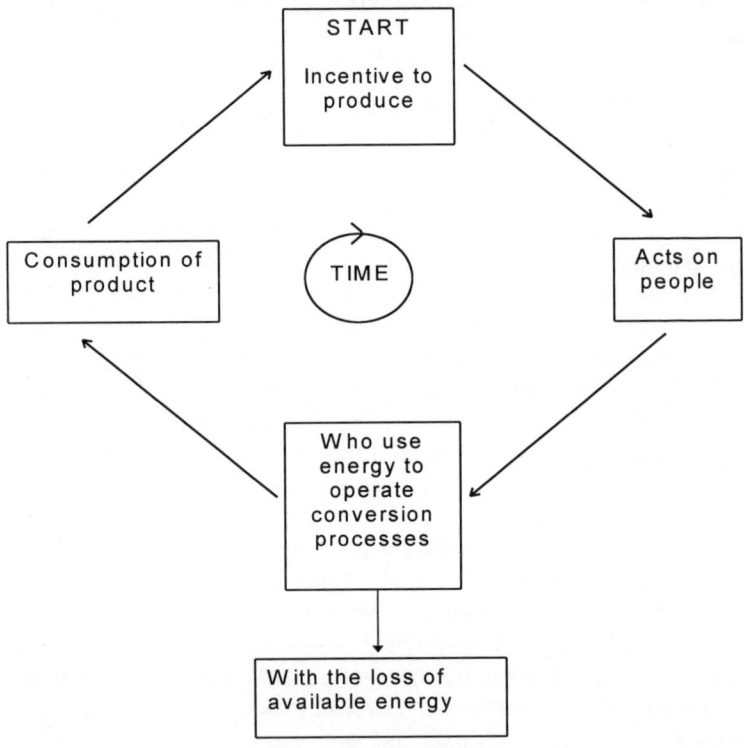

Figure 2.5 The Cycle of Production and Consumption

In the longer term, however, the effect of energy must show through, whether in energy supply costs or the efficiency with which it is used. Long run costs cannot be divorced from energy costs and so

The Economic Process

the balance must change, whatever people want. The supply/demand schedules can then be seen to have reached not an equilibrium but a temporary, apparently steady state on which fluctuations of smaller amplitude are superimposed. It is then like a slow, wide river seen from a distance. It scarcely seems to move apart from the ripples on its surface. Yet as the old adage tells us, one cannot step into the same river twice. Time reasserts itself inexorably in any system.

2.7 Rules of the Economic Process

The economic process is, therefore, seen to be governed by a number of simple rules:
1. The output of conversion processes cannot be changed except by a change in energy use, either quantity or quality or both.
2. Such changes in energy use can only be brought about by people. In the short term they manipulate conversion processes by pressing buttons, moulding materials and so on, but in the longer term they accumulate the skills and knowledge to develop new processes, which change energy use in economic chains.
3. Since in the long run no conversion process is carried out in a rational world except to make products or utilities which are more valuable than the inputs into the process, the economic value added by successive conversion stages must increase simultaneously with economic energy content, though it does not follow that there is a proportional relationship between the two.
4. Incentives have no energy content in themselves and so cannot influence conversion processes directly, unless one considers burning paper money in boilers. The incentive system can therefore act only on people, who may or may not have influence in the conversion system.
5. Similarly personal services i.e. those which use no incremental energy above what is needed for ordinary day to day living, are not conversion processes according to our definition. Their energy requirement is fixed; the number of people is given. Nor can they affect conversion processes

except by influencing people who are in a position to control these processes.
6. Those who work in the incentive and personal service systems i.e. the facilitation system must obtain their necessities of life from the conversion system by exchange of money for goods or utilities in markets. Exchanging incentives within the facilitation system itself simply redistributes incentives in favour of some at the expense of others. It cannot in itself affect the conversion system or its products until the incentives eventually re-enter the conversion system. For example, if a guitarist tells his bank to pay his lawyer to sue a television programme producer, the money flows from one player to another without producing any change at all in the products from the conversion system. That is, until the lawyer buys himself a car with the proceeds, which impinges on the maker of cars. If he simply keeps the money in the bank, that cannot affect the conversion system, until the bank lends it to a processor and so on. This is very similar to the classification of labour by the earliest of economists, though he described it in terms which are much harsher (4).

2.8. Incentives as a Feedback Loop

It will be apparent from the preceding analysis that the economic process may be considered as an evolving energy-consuming system which is regulated by incentives. Such a system may be represented diagrammatically as shown in Figure 2.6.

The conversion, distribution and consumption system may be analysed without consideration of the nature and efficiency of the incentive loop, provided the analysis includes the points at which feedback occurs. In quantitative terms the feedback may be considered as the money flowing around the system: for converters, the revenues they realise in markets, measured in relation to the expenditure which they are obliged to make to buy their materials and utilities in their input markets.

The Economic Process

In this way the response of the conversion/market system can be analysed for any set of incentives, and the interactions between the various parts of the economic system are laid bare.

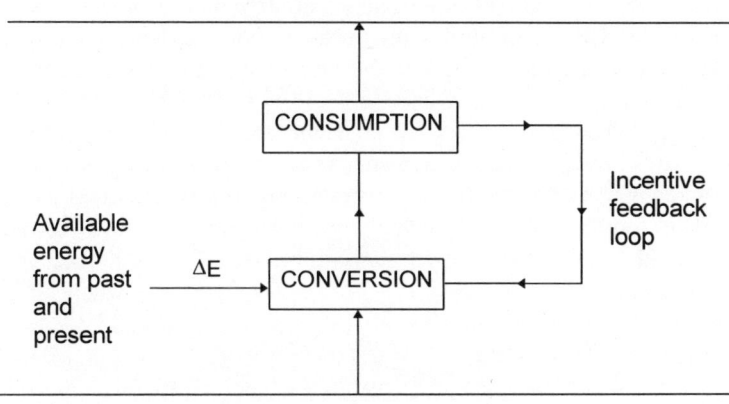

Figure 2.6 Economic Process with Incentive Feedback Loop

2.9 Use of Resources

The economic process is often described as the allocation of scarce resources, as if the product already existed and the only problem was to dispose of it. However, the preceding analysis suggests that it is more useful to consider it as the production and distribution to society of goods and utilities which require energy to produce. Energy and time really are scarce resources, and so economics is about the choice of what to produce: that is, the choice of how to allocate the available time and energy. Within these limits society can produce whatever it collectively chooses and has the skills and organisation to produce. The choices are by definition within the power of society to make. If the resources are misspent or misallocated, society has only itself to blame because of the choices which it has made or failed to make about production, the result of its decision-making mechanisms and perhaps a reflection on its values.

If, moreover, the economic process is not delivering the desired quantities of goods and utilities, the analysis suggests that there can be only three root causes: deficiencies in the available energy; inadequate skills, knowledge, organisation and creativity; or deficiencies in the incentive feedback loop. Problems of these sorts are particularly acute in the activities which represent the rate of change in the economic process: innovation and growth.

In the following chapters we consider one fundamental aspect of the incentive system, the mechanisms of exchange, or markets, and the pressures which these exert on conversion processes. After that we are in a position to analyse the behavioural catalysts for innovation and growth in the context of organisation. But first the exchange mechanisms.

Chapter Three

THE PERFECT MARKET AS A SYSTEM

The individual's study of his own advantage naturally, or rather necessarily, leads him to prefer that employment which is most advantageous to society.
Adam Smith, The Wealth of Nations, Book IV Chapter 2

Society was merely an aggregate of isolated individuals, who were wholly rational, wholly selfish and wholly free economically.
E.Halevy, A History of the English People in the 19th Century, Volume 1 579-583

Now it is characteristic of a system, as distinguished from a collection of heterogeneous and independent facts or propositions, that the number of its premisses, or in other words, the amount of variety in it, should be less than the number of its members.
J.M.Keynes A Treatise on Probability The Collected Writings of J.M.Keynes Volume 8 p279

Markets are the major mechanism in the economic process through which producers of goods and services exchange them with buyers. The mechanism is simplicity itself. Sellers take their wares along to market and set up their stalls. Buyers visit the market, examine what is on offer, haggle over prices and conclude their bargains. When all is done, the wares change hands in one direction and money in the other, and all go their different ways until next time.

Nevertheless, few apparently innocent ideas can have been the source of such bitter controversy between political ideologies, such is the power of the market mechanism. The source lies in the causal relationships which are thought to underlie the operation of the market. One school of economists, the neoclassical, believes that prices and quantities of wares in the market place are determined simultaneously, so that the mechanism cannot be influenced. For them, "market forces" produce the best possible outcome, and the only thing to do is to sit back and wait for them to do their job. This is in effect *laissez-faire*.

Another school, however, believes that markets only set the relative prices of the wares which have been produced as a result of other decision mechanisms, and so they can be legitimately influenced, for instance by planning or by government management of the economy. It is no academic question, for the consequences cut deep into ordinary people's lives.

The argument of the neoclassicals, a term derived from Keynes, who coined the name "classical" for those who followed the teachings of the early nineteenth century economist Ricardo, is based on the concept of the "perfect" market. The "perfect" market is a set of very specific hypothetical conditions, from which arguments are drawn to justify conclusions which are then extended uneasily to "imperfect" markets. The implications of the analysis are so far reaching that it is worth going back to first principles to get it clear.

We begin, therefore, with a consideration of the "perfect" market, and elaborate later on the nature of "imperfections" of which, unfortunately for the neoclassicals, the world is full. We further consider what the exchange mechanism can do and eventually, most important, what it cannot.

Since there is a host of assumptions buried in the economist's parameters of supply and demand and their interaction to give unique prices, we begin by developing time and energy based flow diagrams following on from those in the previous chapter, and as free from inherent prejudice as possible. They are not unlike what might be used by design engineers.

The Perfect Market as a System

In the interests of brevity we use the phrase goods and services to cover everything which is sold and therefore bought. We do not need to differentiate products from personal services at this stage.

3.1 Definition of a "Perfect" Market

A formal definition of the economist's term "market" might be: a point of interaction between all potential sellers and buyers of a particular commodity which permits exchange at a price determined by the matching of supply and demand (1, 2, 3).

The definition of a "perfect" market requires that it should satisfy three essential conditions. First, there must be complete freedom of access for all those who may want to buy or sell in it. Secondly, the commodity must be infinitely divisible, so that what is established is the commodity price, not the price of bulk lots, since this might vary with the quantity bought. Thirdly, the commodity must be entirely homogeneous, because heterogeneity would introduce considerations which are beyond the scope of a single market, so that the interactions between two or more markets would have to be taken into account. If any of these conditions is not met, the market cannot be said to be "perfect", and the conclusions of the neoclassicals do not hold.

Since buyers and sellers need to be able to relate to one another in order to carry out their transactions, practical markets too are often specific to one commodity or a closely related group of commodities in which participants have special expertise. Examples might be the corn market, the coal market or the tea market.

Each market is, however, a part of the total market system, and related to it by the market prices of the time, because goods sold in one market are manufactured from goods bought in others. The car market is related to the markets of all its component materials, which in turn are related to the markets of all their inputs, and so on. In principle, therefore, there is a network of market prices, all established by the matching of supply and demand "in the market place". Thus the total market network, which comprehends all the rest, eventually relates all sellers to all buyers, that is all the producers to all the consumers of marketed wares.

In business the term "market" is also used to denote the quantity of goods or services which is, or it is thought could be, sold through a market. One might say that the market for crude oil was about 45 million barrels a day, and the local markets of which it consists, such as Rotterdam, the Caribbean and so on, would handle a proportion. Or another example, the British market for new cars might be, say, 1.8 million cars a year.

3.2 Mechanisms of Operation of a Perfect Market

A "perfect" market may be represented diagrammatically as a node, as in Figure 3.1, where the arrows show the flow of a commodity from a population of sellers to a population of buyers. The flow of receipts is in the opposite direction. The number of parallel lines represents the number of sellers or buyers who want to deal in the market.

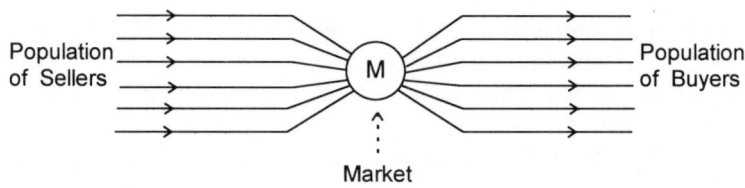

Figure 3.1 Representation Of A 'Perfect' Market

The importance of a market is that it is the focus of all the information which is necessary to the transactions, and without which the market cannot operate perfectly. On entering the market each seller must have a concept of the level at which to price his goods, based on his assessment of the circumstances of the other sellers, with whom he is competing, and of the needs of the buyers. If he prices his wares higher than his competitors, he will fail to sell. If he prices them lower, then he fails to make the best return on his sales, and will have less to invest in increasing production and improving the efficiency of his conversion process, which in the long run means poverty or extinction for that particular conversion operation in the face of competition. Or

The Perfect Market as a System

alternatively he has less to invest in other processes through the capital markets, which eventually brings the same result. Similarly buyers have a concept of what they should have to pay in competition with other buyers, based on their assessment of how plentiful the supply is likely to be.

The parallel lines in the diagram illustrate the idea that all sales move in the same direction, that is the provision of specific goods and services in the market, but they move independently. If there is any collusion among buyers or sellers, the market cannot arrive at the proper price. The number of separate lines on both the buyer and seller sides show that the goods and services for sale, and equally the receipts, must be divisible. They must also be of exactly the same quality, that is homogeneous, to form part of the same market.

The market place is where all this is played out. Sellers try to sell and buyers buy, and they eventually settle upon a common price which depends on the sum of their individual attempts to conclude transactions: that is, supply and demand.

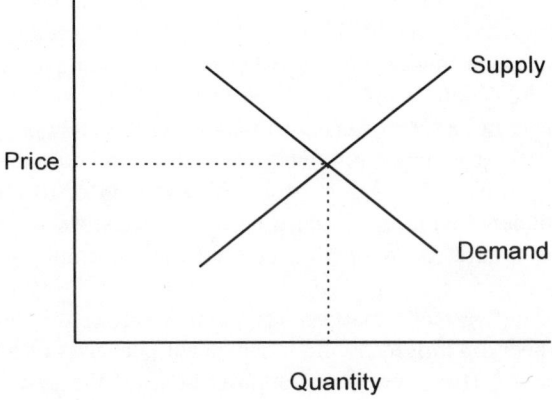

Figure 3.2 Supply and Demand Schedules

Thus in a "perfect" market there is by definition only one price at which supply and demand are matched. Figure 3.2 shows the conventional representation for goods of a type specific to a particular market. The lines marked Supply and Demand are called schedules. They represent the quantities of the goods which it is believed buyers and sellers would be prepared to buy or sell at different prices.

This is very difficult to put to the test, because a "perfect" market can only ever operate at one price by definition i.e. where the schedules cross, which is called the "equilibrium" price. There is no provision for departure from "equilibrium" on the diagram, because time is not included as a variable. Thus there is the danger of the illusion that it represents a timeless and hence permanent truth, though a moment's thought shows that this cannot be so; it must be specific to a time and place.

The process of reaching a price is facilitated if buyers and sellers are physically in the same place i.e. the market place. They can look one another in the eye and judge reactions. But provided the information flows take place, each participant may be in a different location. Some markets function entirely by telecommunication. Nevertheless visual and aural contact, even if only for part of the total market, is found to be useful in establishing prices rapidly and flexibly e.g. the New York Stock Exchange and the London Futures Exchange.

When they have bought or sold all they want, according to their circumstances, the market has been "cleared". Nothing is left in the market, by definition; supply has been exactly equal to demand. The price which is necessary to bring this about is the "market clearing" price, the price at which supply and demand are in "equilibrium" i.e. the schedules cross. There must be a sufficient number of buyers and sellers to render the market insensitive to the decisions of anyone of them, if the market is to operate perfectly in matching supply and demand.

When the "perfect" market has been cleared, the whole has apparently been optimised by the independent decisions of each seller and each buyer. However, such "optimisation" of the system should not be confused with the optimum outcome for the individuals involved; it is simply the best deal each of them can obtain. Some may find that their receipts do not even cover their costs, so that "optimisation" means minimisation of losses. Their losses may in fact drive them out of the market for good.

The Perfect Market as a System

The conventional representation of a market shows supply and demand as what are in effect vectors consisting of two components; quantity and price. These two components of the schedules are confounded; every quantity is inextricably bound up with a price and vice versa. This may be compared with the paradigm of the economic process presented in Chapter 2, in which the quantity of goods and utilities in a conversion process are a function of energy, and hence time. Whereas energy and time are certainly necessary to the conversion process, and may also be sufficient for it to operate, money may not be necessary and certainly cannot be sufficient for the conversion process to occur; price is part of the incentive system. Confounding price with quantity may lead to confusion, especially in forecasting, which is one of the main practical uses of a supply/demand diagram.

In our new paradigm the conversion process may operate independently of the incentive system. The two vary orthogonally, and it is the conversion axis which brings in time and irreversibility. The incentive system, however, does not postulate the passage of time and may be instantly reversible. It is only a change of mind.

During the period in which silver or gold were the medium of exchange such separation may not have been necessary, because they too were products of the conversion system, and so functions of time and energy. Silver and gold have energy contents like any other goods. It was like a system of barter in which exchange was facilitated by the universal acceptance of two of the goods being bartered, silver and gold. Hence the term "medium of exchange". But when the world moved of necessity into notional i.e. paper or computer money, this had no energy content. It was pure incentive and therefore reversible; it could be created or annihilated without effort, though not without momentous results.

3.3 The Role of Information

The "perfect market" model requires that each participant comes to market armed with perfect information about what is going on in the economic world around him (4). It further requires that he acts rationally on the basis of such information. But what he cannot know in advance is how all the other participants are going to behave. This is

The Scale and Scope of Economics

what will be determined in the bargaining process. If it could be known in advance, there would be no point in having a market. The market clearing price would already be known. There would in fact be universally agreed prices at which everything could be exchanged, and there would be no market system at all.

And so they come to market to settle the price/quantity relationship. But how can bargaining individuals who are acting in their own interests possibly arrive at a common relationship for price with respect to quantity? Why do they not arrive at a whole range of market prices? How does this whole system come to be "optimised" by the action of its parts, the buyers and sellers, optimising their own positions? For we know that this is theoretically impossible where there are interactions between the participants, and a market is by definition full of interactions.

The answer can only be that the participants need complete information not only about what can be known in advance of the market taking place, but also about the evolution of the price/quantity relationship during the bargaining. Since they are not supposed to collude, they must not be able to identify an individual's bargaining position before bargaining with him themselves. Moreover, they must not conclude bargains before talking directly to all the possible dealers i.e. all buyers must have the chance to talk to all sellers etc.

The solution to the problem of individual identification is to have a display of the aggregate state of evolution of the price/quantity relationship made available to everyone as the bargaining proceeds. This display we will call a blackboard. In the absence of such a display the result will be chaos, since the individuals will have no way of converging on a price as they act independently. They are free to go their own ways and simply keep doing so, failing to act as a system. With a blackboard, however, each individual is free to relate independently to the evolving market position as displayed on the board, and yet the system as a whole can converge on the market clearing price. The blackboard supplies the system with what may technically be called a degree of freedom, an exogenous reference point. The fact that it can be seen by everyone also supplies the system with the feedback which is necessary for control.

The Perfect Market as a System

The nineteenth century economist Walras postulated the same pair of functions being performed by an unseen "auctioneer", who presumably called out the prices and quantities bid.

This may be appreciated qualitatively as follows. Suppose we have a market consisting for simplicity of two sellers and two buyers. The first seller S_1 approaches the first buyer B_1 and they arrive at a possible price/quantity position for exchange with respect to each other. The second seller S_2 also approaches B_1 and then moves to the second buyer B_2, so that he has provisionally fixed his position with respect to both of them. But if these three positions are fixed, the positions of S_1 with respect to S_2 and B_1 with respect to B_2 are also fixed. The first would-be seller and the second would-be buyer find their positions already determined without their having communicated with each other. This may be represented schematically as in Figure 3.3.

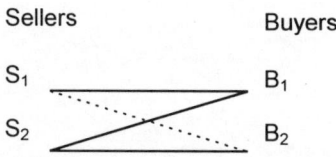

Figure 3.3 Progress of Bargaining between Two Independent Sellers and Two Independent Buyers

Between the four participants in the market as a system, there are only three degrees of freedom, or more directly, three independent bargaining positions. The dotted line S_1B_2 represents the other one which is missing. The first seller is not happy to conclude his bargain without having talked to all the potential buyers, and so he talks to B_2. As a result, they take up a new position S_1B_2, thus influencing the previous possible arrangements. In the light of the new information S_1 then goes back to B_1 to modify his stance S_1B_1, which causes B_1 to renegotiate with S_2, and so on. If they eventually reach a steady state in this way, it will be more by luck than judgment.

The same reasoning may be applied to a market in which the numbers of sellers and buyers are different. The layout of the position lines is simply more irregular. Figure 3.4 extends the previous diagram to any number of sellers x and buyers y, where x and y may be different.

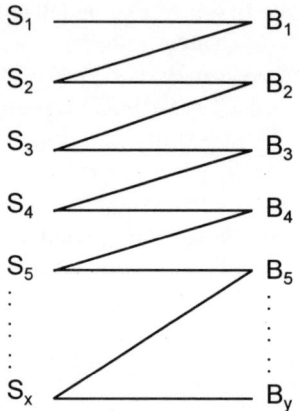

Figure 3.4 Progress of Bargaining between x Independent Sellers and y Independent Buyers

Even the first tangle of interactions for just two sellers and three buyers may be quite complicated to draw (Figure 3.5).

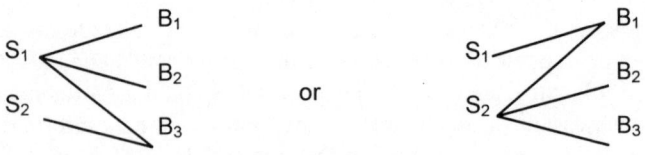

Figure 3.5 Alternative Interactions of Two Sellers with Three Buyers

The Perfect Market as a System

To generalise, if each line represents a bargaining position, or mathematically a degree of freedom in the system, then between x sellers and y buyers there are $(x + y - 1)$ degrees of freedom. But the market as a system requires $(x + y)$ degrees of freedom if it is going to be possible for all $(x + y)$ participants to act independently in their own interests, yet reach a common price/quantity "equilibrium".

It is in fact the blackboard which we have mentioned above that supplies the other degree of freedom or exogenous reference point for the system, by displaying the price/quantity information to all in the course of bargaining. Each may now take up a position which is independent of the aggregate of all their positions. The lines may now be drawn differently, as for two buyers and two sellers in Figure 3.6. There are then four position lines or four degrees of freedom for four participants. A ticker tape would serve the same purpose, as a guide to the progress of bargaining.

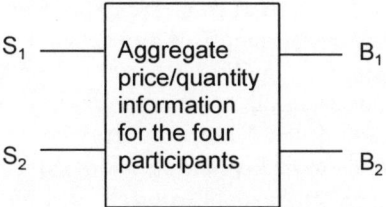

Figure 3.6 Blackboard Display of Bargaining between Two Sellers and Two Buyers

The same reasoning applies to any number of participants, say $(x + y)$ as before (Figure 3.7).

It might be thought that the missing degree of freedom in the system becomes less important as the number of participants in the market increases. What is one in relation to a very large number? However, it can be seen that this is not so by considering the information requirements of a market with large numbers of people involved.

The Scale and Scope of Economics

The theory is that they will arrive at a single price and quantity which reflect supply and demand. However, the number of interactions or pieces of information to be transmitted doubles with every new participant. Moreover every possible set of interactions must be tried because the aggregate price/quantity relationship reached at some intermediate stage of the process of bargaining will depend the particular interactions which have already taken place. Thus this intermediate price and quantity will be a function of the route by which it has been reached, and not an "equilibrium" pair of values at all.

However, the requirement for information is not limited to the particular market in question. All the buyers in the market have the option of spending their money in a range of markets which depends on their own particular preferences. They might, for instance, decide to buy gas instead of cheese, or perhaps more wool and less timber. All markets are therefore in competition with each other for the revenue which is available from buyers.

But the "perfect market" thesis is that the market for each commodity will reach a market clearing price/quantity relationship which depends only on the supply of and demand for that commodity. Markets which are in "equilibrium" with themselves must be in "equilibrium" with each other. In this case, if the markets have common participants in the form of buyers, they must have common information on which to make their decisions. Since one market needs one additional degree of freedom to reach "equilibrium" as a system, or as we have termed it, one blackboard on which all participants can read the progress of bargaining, so two markets will need two blackboards. Participants who are taking part in both markets must be able to see both blackboards simultaneously, if they are to be able to make their independent choices, and allow both markets to reach "equilibrium" with each other. For a whole "perfect market" system to reach "equilibrium", it is therefore necessary to have one large blackboard visible to everybody, displaying the progress of bargaining in all markets i.e. one large blackboard which is a collection of all the other individual blackboards.

This then brings us back to the fundamental contradiction in the "perfect market" hypothesis. As the number of participants increases, the influence of any one person is reduced in accordance with

The Perfect Market as a System

"perfect" market requirements, but the information needed to reach "equilibrium" increases exponentially, which vastly increases the time required for the transfer of the necessary information. However, the process of reaching "equilibrium" must be completed before people begin to change their minds as their circumstances change, or else a whole new series of interactions is set in motion. This puts a practical limit on the number of participants at any one time, of the order of, say for argument's sake, a hundred people, and that is for the simplest of interactions. With more people involved, bargaining is likely to break out in various parts of the market with the formation of submarkets, each with its own price/quantity relationship.

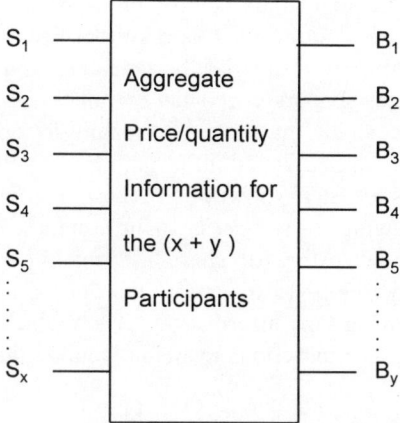

Figure 3.7 Blackboard Display of Bargaining between x Sellers and y Buyers

There is always, therefore, a compromise between the number of people needed to make a market more nearly "perfect" in the economic sense, and the quantity of information needed to allow it to arrive at a unique price/quantity relationship. "Perfection" is always unattainable.

This analysis relates to markets as behavioural systems, but the concept of degrees of freedom is widely used in different technological forms. In mechanical engineering, for example, it means the number of co-ordinates required to specify the position of all the elements in a mechanical system. If we know where one element in the reference grid is situated, then we know where the rest are located. Similar concepts are used in cybernetics. Except in fundamental analysis points of reference are normally taken for granted, but if we are not aware of the potential pitfalls our assumptions may lead us into irrational conclusions.

3.4 Examples of the Role of Information in Market Systems

Perhaps the nearest it is possible to get to a "perfect" market is the market for the stock of a very large, publicly quoted company. It fulfils the criteria of a homogeneous commodity and of many sellers and many buyers. It works quite well as a system because the prices are commonly available to potential participants, and they are even published in the newspapers every day for all to see. It is difficult to imagine how the stock market could begin to operate efficiently without this widely disseminated information. It is still some way short of "perfection" as a system, however, because there may be money to be made from having early access to information i.e. from market imperfections. Broadcasting of share information over the national television networks helps to overcome the delays, and nearer still to perfection is the ticker tape information system which makes quantity-responsive prices of transactions available nation-wide almost as they happen.

Many markets do in fact have real blackboards on which people with chalk in hand write up the latest prices. Others such as the London Metal Exchange use oral communication; the participants sit in a tight circle shouting prices at each other for all to hear, a kind of audible blackboard. Or they may sit in different offices around the world looking at the same prices on visual display units and shouting to one another down a battery of telephones. It should not be surprising that the financial sector leads the world in the use of information and telecommunication technology. Not only are the stakes high, but the markets cannot function efficiently without it; they need the extra degree of freedom which the global information provides.

The Perfect Market as a System

In the USA the New York Stock Exchange is actually nicknamed the Big Board, and the price of the last deal in a particular stock is relayed nation-wide from the floor of the exchange by electronic "ticker tape". Also in the USA the NASDAQ system is in effect an electronic stockmarket, which relays electronically the latest bid and offered prices, so that it in fact replaces the centralised bargaining of the stock exchange floor. The deals are then consummated by telephone. As early as 1983 NASDAQ had already attained 75% of the NYSE share volume and 25% of its dollar volume (5).

The role of information in markets is most graphically illustrated by changes in the London Stock Exchange. In 1986 it broke with its tradition of trading exclusively on the floor of the exchange, and introduced a new electronic system (SEAQ) after the style of NASDAQ. The system was screen-based, and enabled many more members in different cities and time zones to have access to current information on 3500 different stocks. Trading on the floor of the exchange under the new rules was to continue for those who wanted it. Within six months the floor was empty; the information was on the screens in offices elsewhere.

There are examples of systems lacking a degree of freedom from other spheres. For instance, there is the problem of public key encryption, where two users of codes are trying to exchange information by telecommunication. If they are using different codes, they cannot begin to communicate. But they cannot agree on a code without passing that information between them in an uncoded or common-coded form. This uncoded or common-coded message is the first lead to breaking the codes, if it is intercepted by a foreign party. So how do they communicate with each other while maintaining security? This is rather like two people trying to bargain in a market situation in which neither is allowed to make the first move. Another example was the delay to the first launch of the USA's space shuttle; it is said to have failed to start because its five separate computers could not agree on the time. Both systems lack a degree of freedom, the identity of the code in the one case, and a common time in the other.

3.5 Time in the "Perfect Market" System

The importance of time in the operation of a "perfect market" system is that it takes time for the transfer of information generated by the interactions of buyers and sellers to take place. These interactions must by definition be sequential in a bargaining process. But time is absent from the representation of supply and demand by conventional schedules.

A more fundamental representation might be as follows. A commodity passing through a "perfect" market is defined as homogeneous and infinitely divisible. The time-dependent process establishes the price. On leaving the market the commodity goes different ways, as the buyers take their purchases away for use. Figure 3.8 shows this in symbolic terms, where M is the market and the arrows indicate the direction of the flow of the commodity.

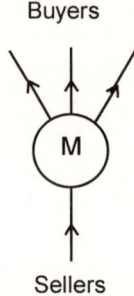

Figure 3.8 Flow of a Commodity through a Market

The state of the market in "equilibrium" is then characterised by the date and place where the market was held, the quantity of the commodity sold and the price, for example Figure 3.9.

The arrows imply that the process is one way, and indeed this is so. It may be physically possible to reverse the flow but this would take time and energy, so that it would be a different market. Moreover, reversibility would require that buyers became sellers and vice versa. Even if this were possible, there is no reason why their new needs should match the old, and so they would be most unlikely to arrive at the same price/quantity "equilibrium" values. The arrows represent time, which cannot be turned back. It is a form of entropy.

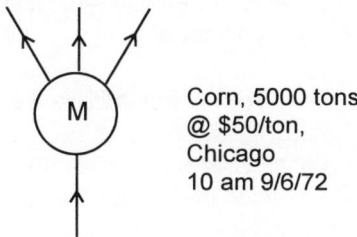

Figure 3.9 Example of the Flow of Corn through a Market

A similar symbol can be used for a conversion process. Since we have defined the economic process as production of products and utilities, the conversion process can be represented as the range of input materials and utilities needed to produce a homogeneous product for a market (Figure 3.10).

Different factories making the same product can be aggregated so that the symbol represents a particular industry.

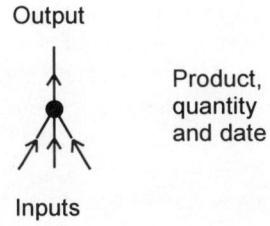

Figure 3.10 Flow of Materials through a Conversion Process

This process too is irreversible, as indicated by the arrows. Conversion incurs an energy loss in the form of waste materials and utilities consumed in making the product. In principle it is possible to take some products and turn them back into input materials, like recycling scrap, and generate some utilities. But however efficiently performed, this operation cannot be carried out without the expenditure of more energy and time; it is a new conversion process in its own right. This is entropy in action. Time and energy flow one way.

3.6 Model of Operation of the Economic Process

The economic process consists of conversion processes for making products and utilities from inputs bought in markets. The outputs are also sold in markets, until the last conversion process in the chain which is consumption, or conversion to waste. The symbols which we have devised may therefore be joined together in a chain representing both time and increasing energy use. Figure 3.11 illustrates a chain for the production and ultimate consumption of a single product, which is a small part of the network of production and consumption running throughout the whole economy.

There is one further factor which depends on time and energy, that completes the picture. Each of the conversion processes involves plant, equipment and buildings, since there is no other way of making use of energy. These must be subject to wear and tear with the passage of time, however carefully they are looked after.

This wear and tear could be treated in the diagram as a leak of materials to earth (Figure 3.12). Alternatively it may be considered as a form of consumption. Instead of what is normally defined as the consumers using the final product and consuming it, by which is meant converting it to waste, the conversion process itself consumes the plant, equipment and buildings, all of which were themselves bought in markets.

The conversion process is then the last node on the time and energy path to earth, in the same way as for any consumer product. If wear and tear are treated in this way, there is no need to adjust the diagram for "leaks", and a clear link is shown between the depreciating goods and the markets in which they were bought. Depreciation and obsolescence alike can be fitted into this mechanism.

The conversion/market network model thus contains all the possible energy-dependent elements. The result of setting them out in

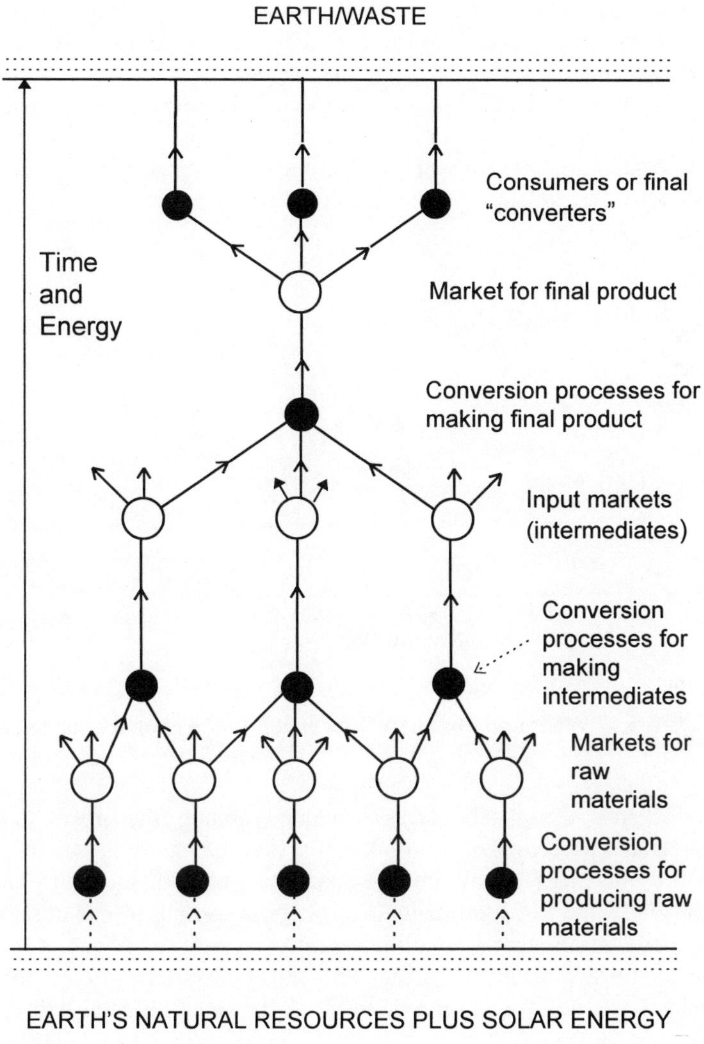

The Perfect Market as a System

EARTH/WASTE

Time and Energy

Consumers or final "converters"

Market for final product

Conversion processes for making final product

Input markets (intermediates)

Conversion processes for making intermediates

Markets for raw materials

Conversion processes for producing raw materials

EARTH'S NATURAL RESOURCES PLUS SOLAR ENERGY

Figure 3.11 Model of Operation of the Economic Process

The Scale and Scope of Economics

this way is that depreciation of the assets used in a conversion process appears separately from the process energy used during the process, so that each is related to its own path to earth. The problem of assigning ownership is thereby avoided and there is no double counting of materials and utilities.

The chains traced out in the model are all related to energy, whether directly as a utility such as electricity consumed in the conversion process, say in the form of heat or motive power, or indirectly as waste materials which are products of conversion processes.

Earth/Waste

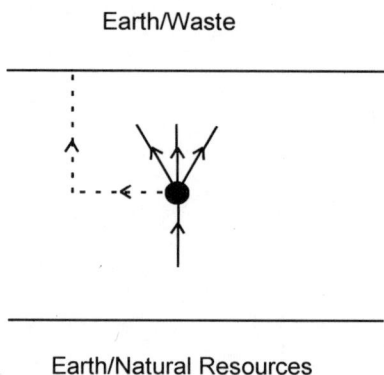

Earth/Natural Resources

Figure 3.12 Wear and Tear in a Conversion Process as a Leak to Earth

Whether labour should be included among the inputs into a conversion process is a philosophical matter. Certainly brute labour as a utility or energy source must be included, but skills are different in kind, being part of the facilitation system according to our definition. The facilitation system, like the incentive system or money, does not appear on the diagram. In the limit all conversion must be for the collective benefit of the providers of skills, since ultimately there are no other consumers.

What we have described is but one small fragment of the total network of conversion processes and markets across the world. The complexity of the whole network would be completely unmanageable

The Perfect Market as a System

on paper or even the most powerful computer. Each flowline results from a myriad of decisions on the part of those involved in markets and conversion processes, acting in their own best interests and bargaining to obtain the best possible terms.

In "perfect" market conditions everything which can be sold, will be sold, since price is considered to be the only determinant at the end of the day. It must be true that anything can be sold at a low enough price, because the supply and demand schedules are postulated to cross, and at a positive price to boot. This observation, which is really no more than a definition, is known in economics as Say's Law (6, 7).

Real markets show the same effect in the long run, because no one goes on indefinitely producing goods which cannot be sold. Common sense must bring the conversion process to a halt eventually, at least until conditions change. Such an economic process may be considered an efficient allocation of resources by those who obtain them.

3.7 Example of an Economic Chain

Let us suppose that the product in question is pencils. Consumers buy pencils and use them until they become waste i.e. return to earth. They buy their pencils in a market where price and quantity are determined by supply and demand. Pencils are sent to market by manufacturers who buy their inputs in the markets for intermediates, say sawn timber, glue, paint and pencil lead. These intermediate products are made by converters of raw materials such as logs, animal bones, resins and so on; back to the earth and the sun's radiation. Each conversion process will include inputs of one or more utilities to make conversion possible.

The equipment used by manufacturers to make pencils will be worn out to some extent in the process, and this forms an energy path straight to earth from the market in which the equipment was bought. Similarly wear and tear on the equipment used to make the intermediates and the raw materials will also form direct paths to earth from the markets in which they were bought. All these will appear as separate paths from those which mark the stages in the conversion of raw materials into pencils as such.

Finally all the products will be sold by definition at the market clearing price, settled on the basis of supply and demand.

3.8 The Incentive Feedback Loop

The market can be characterised by a parameter which is the change (Δq) in the quantity of a commodity passing through it in response to a change in price (Δp). The ratio $\Delta q/\Delta p$ or dq/dp describes the rate of change, which may not be symmetrical i.e. it may be different for price increases and price decreases. If these terms are put in proportion to the original values of p and q, then they resemble the elasticities of the two dimensional supply/ demand schedules i.e. $p/q.dq/dp$.

Price can be drawn more directly into the diagram as a feedback loop as in Figure 3.13. Prices might then be considered to regulate the throughput of the conversion process.

The feedback loop is more widely related to incentives in general, so that it would also include, say, the prospect of gain through barter or sharing in the product. Money is just the simplest expression of economic incentives. It is also vital for the response, and so the performance, of an economic system of any complexity, because of the problem of agreed "valuation" of one product against another in economic terms, whereas money is by definition independently quantifiable.

The rate at which output changes with time i.e. dq/dt, given a price change, tells something more fundamental about the system. There will be some inertia in a system, because changes of physical output involve obtaining and processing more energy and materials, which take time, not to mention the delay while the information from the market is interpreted by people who control the physical output.

The result will be that the system has a response time, the time taken to move to a new level of output, even with perfect feedback and information. Such a response time will depend largely on the inertia of the conversion process rather than the exchange system i.e. the market. Systems with similar response times may be grouped together to give categories similar to those of consumption and investment used in macroeconomics.

The most meaningful feedback parameter is not in fact the single figure of price, so beloved of economists, but the money flowing back to the conversion process from the market i.e. the revenue, or price

The Perfect Market as a System

multiplied by quantity at each instant. The response of the system then subsumes both price and quantity changes.

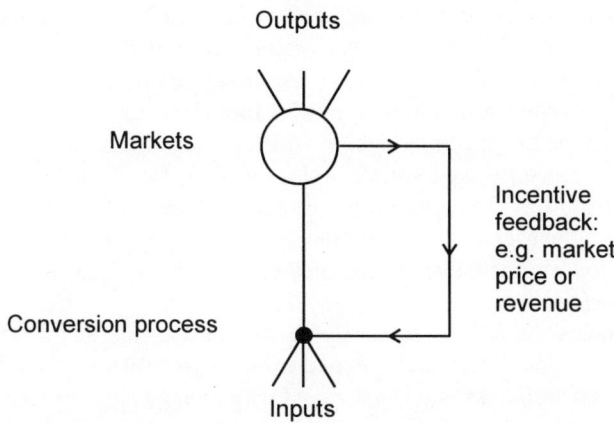

Figure 3.13 Feedback from Markets to Converters

A system which involves people and takes time to respond is unlikely to reach equilibrium of any sort. Equilibrium would require that it returned to its former state after a small displacement. But increased revenues would allow converters to make improvements to their processes which are unlikely to be lost on a return to previous levels of activity. These will not be simply physical improvements, but the learning which goes with the opportunity. Reduced revenues might lead to a similar result. It is all part of the response of a learning system.

3.9 Markets and Competition

In the theoretical "perfect market" system it seems that those controlling conversion processes need not know any more than input and output prices for their particular processes to optimise their use of resources. The market prices which they expect to pay for inputs and realise for products are, according to the theory, the summaries of all the external information which is needed to guide decisions concerning production.

This, however, is more apparent than real. Leave aside the obvious point that in planning future production they have to use not prices but price expectations i.e. forecasts of future prices with all their attendant uncertainties. Leave aside also that prices may not depend only on quantities supplied and demanded, as the theory requires. The illusion lies in the assumptions inherent in the formation of "equilibrium" prices across the range of markets, in which everyone has participated, even if only by considered withdrawal. If this has been achieved with the participation of the converters, watching all the blackboards and committing themselves to bargaining, then they have already performed their miracle by the time they come to make decisions about mere production.

Nevertheless it is not necessary to accept the "perfect market" theory to recognise that price expectations have always played an important part in the decision-making of converters, or if one includes the activities of trade and commerce, "entrepreneurs" generally. How else could they proceed?

For all economic activity is ultimately driven by the prospect of gain, betterment or enjoyment, whether for an individual or a society, and however measured for a particular system, in the same way that farming is driven by the prospect of a harvest which exceeds the quantity of seedcorn planted. The distribution of the harvest is a political decision, but a net yield is always necessary, because without it the activity is at best unrewarding and at worst a destruction of resources. No one sows in the expectation of reaping less.

With conversion processes the industrial harvest depends heavily on expectations of input and output prices. In the long run such prices reflect the positions of the various participants competing to supply inputs or outputs.

Thus expectations of prices, however formed, help to pull all goods and services through the economic chain. This is the "invisible hand" at which Adam Smith marvelled. Just how necessary a network of effective markets is, can be judged from the following consideration of the alternatives.

The Perfect Market as a System

3.9.1 In the Absence of Markets

Consider the economic supply chains illustrated above if there were no markets in which to buy or sell the individual inputs of materials and services. Every pencil manufacturer would have to plant the timber twenty years in advance, make the graphite, the glue from the bones of his own animals on his own farm, the paints from his own pigments from his own mines and from the resins from his own chemical plant using his own grown or found feedstock. In short manufacturing as simple an item as a pencil would entail an absurdly long chain of investments in supply activities.

Each of the individual investments would have much in common with the manufacture of many other goods, but without moving into the manufacture of these too it would be grossly uneconomic to service the total investment. But if one were to enter the manufacture of all the products on which the pencil economic chain impinged, it would all become totally unmanageable; indeed the prospect of all these costs alone would probably prevent a single manufacturer from entering the pencil business. Even if it were possible, how would he find sufficient buyers to utilise the investments fully, consume all his material inputs efficiently and so on? The whole process would scarcely be conceivable without buying or selling one of the intermediate materials or utilities, and that would have to take place in some form of market, however conditions of exchange came eventually to be fixed. This is undoubtedly why markets have existed since the earliest, even mesolithic, times.

It would be difficult indeed to start such a chain of economic activity moving. But suppose it did evolve in the course of time. How would one change it? Any change would initiate a set of permanent imbalances in the whole scheme which would take a very long time to settle down again because of its sheer complexity. No wonder there have always been mechanisms for exchange.

3.9.2 Coupling by Markets

Markets couple the individual conversion processes in economic chains to one another through the revenues flowing from them, and allow competition to reduce costs in each process, that is for each particular commodity individually. In principle anyone may enter the input markets, set up in manufacture and sell the product in the output markets, because the assumption is that the products in the same market are homogeneous i.e. there is no way of distinguishing the provenance, only the price. Competition thus encouraged hopefully ensures that only the most efficient manufacturers survive in the long run. Furthermore it allows innovation to take place in that process by reducing the cost of entry to manageable proportions; the innovator need enter only one link instead of the whole chain, in which his specific innovation may be relatively insignificant, so that it might otherwise not be adopted.

Each seller makes his production decisions on the basis of the net revenue R_n which he expects to be able to realise in the market, that is the revenue R which he expects to make from selling quantity q at price p, less the costs C which he expects to incur in doing so i.e.

$$R_n = R - C$$
$$= pq - C$$

Similarly buyers acting independently make their own decisions on the price they expect to pay and the revenue which they expect from their own conversion operations. Market price appears in the revenue of the sellers and the costs of the buyers. The result of breaking down the economic chain into links which are coupled by markets is that the gain from each individual conversion activity is obvious to all. If the gain is high, the converter will reinvest some of it in the process to increase output and gain still more. Others may be attracted by the prospect of gain, and so invest in the process. The result will be to increase supply and reduce price, so that converters whose costs are highest, the least efficient, will be forced to improve or close down. Thus the efficiency of conversion processes may be continually improved.

Furthermore there is the opportunity to by-pass one or more of the conversion stages between two markets, or indeed invent a new process to satisfy a new market. The market network is thus continually adjusting, expanding in one direction and contracting in another. Coupling by markets should then in this version of the economic system be a major aid to innovation.

The Perfect Market as a System

But there is another side to it. Problems of the "perfect market" assumptions will be addressed in the next chapter, but there are also difficulties with the network and revenue flows described above. First the network needs time to adjust to new processes, its response time, so that there is a limit to the rate and proportion of innovations which can be accommodated without undue adverse consequences for the whole system. The more complex and established the network, the more robust it is likely to be, but the longer it is likely to need to adapt. Greenfield sites are easiest in the short term.

Secondly the model defines the market nodes as the only points of interaction between the chains. These are very special links, because they permit only increases and decreases in the revenue flows between conversion processes. This almost what in other disciplines is called not "coupling" but "causal decoupling", operating side by side but not interacting. In practice there must be influences not only on the costs of inputs and outputs, but also on the underlying assets of conversion processes. Thus the basis of competition between them is constantly changing.

Thirdly if innovation focuses on one factor in an interacting network, such as one size of ball-bearing, microchip or car, not only may it replace the existing product or process, but by destroying the interaction, it may eventually destroy the other conversion processes too, a sort of deindustrialisation. A particular case is the attack on one link in an integrated industry; "optimising" one part may endanger the whole.

Fourthly the outcome depends on calculation of net revenue, which requires a figure for costs. But the only unambiguous costs are the total costs of a whole system over time; allocation of costs to specific parts of a system, whether a product or a process, is by convention. If competitors are using different conventions, even if they are playing by the same rules, the outcomes of competition may be distorted and unwarranted advantages gained.

Finally there is the question of learning and continuity. Conversion process are subject to continual improvement through learning and investment, which requires continuity of application by those involved. It is not sensible to treat them as if they can adjust instantly or totally. This is the meaning of response times. Rapid changes or excessive fragmentation are likely to be destructive. Everything in moderation !

3.10 "Equilibrium" and the Physical System Analogue

For the economic process we have shown that: all the inputs find their way to the output, since there is nowhere else for them to go; time and energy changes make the system irreversible; and conversion processes are coupled together by markets.

The whole process may be likened, therefore, to a network of pipes through which conversion processes pump goods and utilities, and the flow in any one line is regulated by the system of valves, which are the markets. The effect of markets is then to regulate the rate at which natural resources are converted into products and utilities over time e.g. the rate at which iron is turned into steel.

Economists use a static analogy with terms drawn from materials science, so that markets exert "forces", and supply and demand have "elasticity". Nevertheless the process must operate in a time dimension. How else could we take part in it? Moreover since markets are the couplings between conversion processes, they operate in the same timescale as conversion processes themselves (8). If this were not so, it would be like a vehicle in which the engine operated one day, but the power was transmitted to the wheels the next, stop/go with a vengeance. Such an arrangement would be exceedingly difficult to drive.

The throughput in this dynamic model is regulated by feedback from the market system in the form of revenue, expressed in terms of the medium of exchange, money, which must be universally and instantly available i.e. the monetary system should be effective and not itself cause additional constraints. Its power of regulation then depends on its distribution between conversion processes through the action of the markets. Furthermore if the conversion processes are to be regulated in this way, they need to operate in a common social framework, or here again additional constraints may be introduced and the coupling fail to operate in a stable manner.

The incentive feedback operates specifically on the people who control conversion processes. It encourages them to apply more or less energy to conversion, since only energy can physically achieve conversion. In an economic system which is working "perfectly" according to the definitions, output is therefore a function of available

The Perfect Market as a System

energy and the technological skills to apply it to conversion of inputs into materials and utilities.

Economists use the concept of the "equilibrium" of supply and demand which leads to unique price/quantity relationships in individual markets and hence in the whole network of markets. But we have shown that the network of conversion processes which markets couple together cannot reach a physical "equilibrium", because they are always consuming energy and so moving on down the energy gradient. It follows that the total network of markets and conversion processes combined in the economy as a whole cannot therefore reach equilibrium in this sense.

Moreover conversion processes take time to respond to economic changes depending on their individual characteristics, which complicates their contribution to the whole network, and they are continually being improved through learning and investment, neither of which features in traditional economic analysis. These alone are enough to negate the idea of "equilibrium"; the economic process always has a definite direction. Nor in that case can there be any automatic return to "equilibrium" after a disturbance to the system. If stability is to be restored, it has to be by some external agency. In a market economy, given the availability of inputs of energy and materials, and the necessary information, the only factor which can bring this about in the long term is a change in the energy efficiency of its conversion processes i.e. the energy consumed/unit of output for the same total production. This depends on the application of skills and design, that is technology, the factor which economics traditionally treats as exogenous.

The analysis of this chapter shows that information requirements alone would be enough to limit the extent to which any market could be said to operate in the "perfect" mode. Even if the requisite number of blackboards were in place, it would be difficult to encourage people, who after all must make all this happen, to scan all the information and become involved in the bargaining for each of the many products and utilities bought. There simply would not be time.

Not that the theory need concern ordinary people. They have dealt in markets since the beginning of civilisation, long before democracy began, it is thought, in the markets below the Acropolis. Markets appear in some form in all the world's economies, even those who

The Scale and Scope of Economics

profess to eschew them. It is scarcely possible to envisage the modern world without exchange. Effective markets can be shown to be not merely a useful adjunct, but a vital function of economic systems.

The problems arise when real markets are forced into the straitjacket of "perfect market" theory, and used to justify a *laissez-faire* approach to an economy. If unwarranted conclusions are drawn from dubious assumptions, and blindly applied to situations in which even the "perfect market" hypotheses do not hold good, let alone common sense, then the results can only be destructive, for the real world is quite different.

Chapter Four

THE MARKET SYSTEM IN THE REAL WORLD

> The Walrus and the Carpenter were walking hand in hand.
> They wept like anything to see such quantities of sand.
> "If this were only cleared away," they said, "it would be grand."
> "If seven maids with seven mops swept it for half a year,
> Do you suppose," the Walrus said, "that they could get it clear?"
> "I doubt it," said the Carpenter, and shed a bitter tear.
>
> *The Walrus and the Carpenter. Lewis Carroll.*

The market mechanism is much more complex than might be imagined. Information plays a crucial role, both before the market and during bargaining to reach a stable price. Time must elapse as the market finds a stable price/quantity relationship. Stability, if it is reached, is better described as a steady state rather than an "equilibrium", because of the flows of time and energy which are embedded in the economic process. Even "steady state" is a dubious description of a system which is always learning and developing.

Such theoretical considerations need have no special practical influence for most people. Markets in the real world have always sent very powerful messages, and market economies of one sort or another have taken turns in leading the world in economic growth in the past 200 years.

Nevertheless "perfect market" theory, and the "equilibrium" into which the economic process is supposed automatically to fall, is at the heart of a particular school of economics. If the reality of the process does not conform to their views, then their reaction is not to recognise the limitations of their theory, but to sweep away the perceived obstacles to "perfection". Not that economists themselves are unaware of the limitations of the concept (1,2), but there is still a persistent feeling that if only markets were more nearly "perfect", the world's problems would disappear.

In the real world "imperfections" of particular markets may or may not be a problem. Each has to be considered on its own merits, though there is no doubt that restrictions often suit vested interests. So, of course, do any changes to the rules of exchange, which is why they are the subject of such intense international negotiation. But being incompatible with the theoretical "perfect market" is not of itself enough to damn any system of exchange. Many theoretical difficulties stem from the fact that markets are full of people, with all their limitations and unpredictability as economic agents. Not surprisingly many others result from their governments' trying to protect them. Perhaps common sense and negotiation are a more useful brooms.

The divergences of real from "perfect" markets fall under five general headings: flaws in the basic thesis of "perfect" markets, flaws in the operation of the mechanism, distortions imposed from outside, problems of interpretation of price signals and the problem of markets for common goods. Quite a shoreline!

4.1 Flaws in the Basic Thesis

4.1.1 Limited Number of Effective Buyers or Sellers

People being what they are, it is unlikely that they will act entirely independently if they can avoid it; it may be advantageous to stick with the crowd, and perhaps much safer. What "perfect market" theory

The Market System in the Real World

regards as collusion may therefore occur, even if it only takes the form of looking over someone's shoulder during bargaining.

Moreover in some markets there may in fact be only one seller or one buyer, or at least very few of either. Such arrangements may be simply represented using the same notation as above (Figure 4.1). Such deviations from "perfect" market requirements undoubtedly affect the mechanism by which a price/quantity relationship is reached.

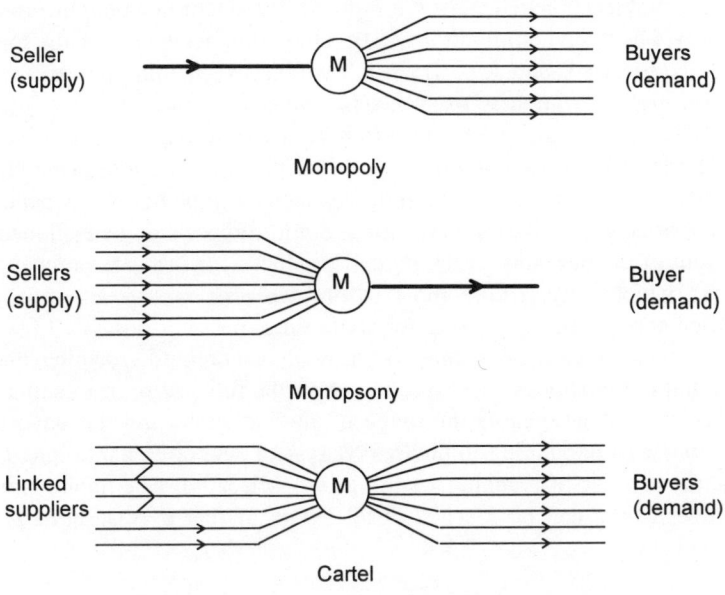

Figure 4.1 Some Deviations from the 'Perfect' Market

In fact they must simplify it considerably by reducing the number of effective participants in the market. Furthermore, the market will not respond to perturbations in the same way as a "perfect" market would. The price/quantity relationship will therefore be affected, but it does not necessarily follow that prices will be higher or quantities different in the long run, even though those who enter into collusions sometimes have exactly that in mind, as Adam Smith was well aware (3). It is often

The Scale and Scope of Economics

simply a change of mechanism rather than an "imperfection" in the derogatory sense.

4.1.2 Divisibility of the Commodity

The requirement that the commodity should be homogeneous and infinitely divisible simplifies the information flows during the bargaining process. Infinite divisibility allows every possible participant to hold at least some of every commodity in a continuous distribution, and so the decisions concern the ratios of the quantities bought in each market. For three commodities A, B, and C, the decisions for the buyer are the ratios A/B and A/C which fall within his spending power, where A may vary continuously from zero to a lot.

When commodities are not infinitely divisible but come in discrete units, the choices become much more complex because there is a whole range of alternative sets of commodities which can be bought, depending on the price settled during bargaining. Some choices may be excluded as a result of the bargains struck on unit products, for instance purchase of a car, which may require most of the available money and rule out participation in other markets for some time. It is not possible to settle for 80% of a car. Or it may occur with a commodity which has a threshold of usefulness, like a drug, where the full course of treatment is necessary. In these cases the range of alternatives facing the buyers in the course of bargaining in the market system generally is multiplied, so that the process of reaching "equilibrium" prices must be much slower, if indeed they can be reached at all. None of that ever stopped a car being sold.

4.1.3 Definition of the Commodity

A clearly defined product is necessary if all participants in a market are to be able to relate during bargaining. Complex products from different sources may not be identical, except superficially, so that it is not possible to describe them as homogeneous as required by "perfect market" theory. To be certain of homogeneity, each might have to be described as belonging to its own market, with its own blackboard, which is not very helpful to the bargaining process.

When people were buying corn, they probably understood what it was they were bargaining for in the market, so that there was a common

The Market System in the Real World

basis of understanding. The same would have been true of a scythe. But this is much less likely to be true when the commodity is technologically complex like a computer, an aircraft or even a refrigerator. One is buying not just the piece of equipment but also its specification, because few people would understand the parts of the machine, let alone be able to judge their quality.

Furthermore one is also buying the future performance of the machine in operation, its fuel consumption, reliability, service costs, length of life, resistance to obsolescence etc. Probably the only guarantee that any information obtained on these points is valid is the reputation of the manufacturer. Purchasers estimate his chances of surviving the guarantee period. Brand names are a way of simplifying information flows. Such problems of defining the commodity, and so handling the information necessary to arrive at a stable price, are magnified a thousandfold when counterfeit goods, such as are flooding onto the market at present, find their way into markets for genuine products. Buyers will be unable to distinguish unless they are experts, and sometimes that may need chemical analysis or destructive testing; there is no way of knowing, until it is too late. But this is a recent phenomenon in an industrial context.

Services pose particular problems of product definition. Services are always bought forward, because they cannot be kept in stock. If they have already been performed, the market exchange has taken place. Payment is then a legal matter between buyer and seller. Bargaining must, therefore, always relate to the promise to provide a service in the future. Even if identical promises are on offer, and it is very difficult to specify future obligations exactly, the buyer must take into account the chances that the contract will be fulfilled when the time comes, especially if it relates to some time in the distant future. Hence the use of standard, enforceable contracts, reputable firms of long standing etc, as in the financial services industry.

No less problematic in the "perfect market" sense are definitions of health products (money back guarantees, if you do not survive the operation?) and education (certificate first, examination afterwards, to simplify information flows for the purchaser?). The problems of definition here concern not just products but people, with all their fallibility and unpredictability.

Labour as a product sold in markets follows the same pattern. Labour for economists is a catch-all term to describe the work contribution of people to the economy in terms such as "unit labour costs", which are thought to be all important in competition. They consider a labour market to be just another facet of the "perfect" market for goods and services, and draw the conclusion that all labour can be sold at a low enough price, so that unemployment must be voluntary.

There are a number of reasons for treating the idea of a labour market with extreme caution, let alone a "perfect" version. Not the least of these is that the economic process is devised by man for his benefit, as both producer and consumer. It is a social invention, an outcome of a political process. Labour as an undifferentiated commodity went out with serfdom.

People are differentiated by skills, language, intelligence, families, homes and all the things that make life worth living. Each person is then a market of one, if the requirement of a homogeneous commodity is taken literally; each will provide his or her own service. What is being bought is not in fact an absolutely defined product but a contribution of so much time and effort, the outcome of which depends on the unique quality of the person involved in relation to the task in hand. Far from the price/quantity relationship and homogeneous product of the "perfect" market! Far from the conclusions which depend on it for intellectual validity.

The problem is that the idea of labour markets originated when most labour was simple agricultural manual toil in the context of what seemed to be the natural order of things, with labourers, landowners etc. But things have fortunately change a good deal in the past two hundred years. Little wonder that so-called labour markets turn out not to respond as "perfect" markets, if even the classifications are open to question.

People feature in the economic process first of all as consumers; that is its raison d'être. But it has to be made to work i.e. resources from the earth and the sun have to be transformed into goods and utilities that people want. The contributions that people make can, therefore, be classified by reference to the diagrams of the economic process as follows:

1. Manual work, literally manpower, in effect the provision of an elementary utility for consumption in a conversion process. Since this cannot sensibly be heat, light or usually

The Market System in the Real World

sound, it almost certainly means motive power: pushing, lifting or carrying, a source of energy, part of the driving force of transformation. The competitive supply of such power is another source of utilities, such as electricity, fuel for internal combustion engines, coal for steam engines etc. There is no reason why man power should necessarily be cheaper than those, especially in advanced economies. Man needs food, shelter and transport to be able to supply man power. Other sources of power may be free from at least some of these overheads. If this is so, then the same will happen to man power as to any other commodity, whether or not it is a source of energy; it remains unused until the economic conditions favour it, like coal or copper buried under ground. The difference is that people have to live even if they are not providing man power; they become unemployed. Unemployment is not simply leaving a resource untapped at a particular time, to be picked up later; it is an injustice and a burden on the very society which economics is supposed to help. Moreover the unemployed cannot spend the money they do not earn, and so buyers are removed from the economic process. So much for "perfect market" theory.

2. The catalytic skills, knowledge, organisation and creativity applied to the conversion processes which turn raw materials into products and utilities for consumption. Catalysts have two major characteristics. First they must have a process to catalyse; if there is no process, say because it has been discontinued, the catalyst cannot function. Secondly they vary enormously and are very specific. In this case they are as varied as the individuals that make up mankind, their accumulated knowledge, their capability of organising themselves to achieve their ends and not least their creativity, the ability to generate entirely new catalytic effects. These after all are the elements of civilisation as we know it. If catalytic skills are not being used, it can only be because the processes of conversion are insufficient in total to occupy them.

3. The incentive, which is the prospect of participating in consumption of the products of the economic process. The

incentive system is money for current or future exchange for goods and utilities. The incentive system must be within the control of the social system of which it is a part i.e. it is endogenous to society and can only be addressed by society as the whole system. For the individual and the firm too the incentive must by definition come from outside i.e. it is exogenous, so that it also depends on the rest of society. The prospect of participating with others cannot be generated without the help and agreement of those others. Employment, and so unemployment, is everybody's concern sooner or later.

4.1.4 Links between Markets

The "perfect market" model of the economy in effect treats all markets as if they were in competition for the same money which buyers have to spend. However, setting out the economic process in the form of chains of production as in Figure 3.11 shows that they are distinguished by their relative positions in the chains which link them. Thus there is already a time-dependence built into the process, and decisions made in markets at one level will interact with the others linked to it.

However there are products which are linked in a different way, by associated use. For instance anyone who buys a vehicle must also be prepared to buy its fuel, lubricants, tyres etc. A decision to buy the vehicle therefore automatically generates subsequent expenditure in the other markets. These markets are not so much competitors for buyers' money as complementary to each other. Sales in one must lead to sales in the other, whether there is any bargaining or not.

A different sort of linkage occurs in shops such as supermarkets when shoppers are usually looking for a range of goods, not just one. The geographical distribution of markets forms a link between them, because transport costs can be spread over a range of purchases, so that minor price differences are averaged out. Furthermore not every shopper is willing to shop around, and sales may then depend on habit and convenience rather than price competition. This is a form of geographical differentiation.

Much the same occurs in industry. A company may feel that it is wise to buy related pieces of equipment from the same manufacturer, especially if they have to be connected in some way, whatever the price, within reason. Unforeseen problems of compatibility or delivery may occur, or servicing may prove difficult if suppliers feel they should have taken the whole order instead part of it.

In all these cases the price cannot be expected simply to respond to the quantity of the commodity demanded. Price and quantity are not the only considerations..

4.2 Flaws in the Mechanism of Operation

4.2.1 Timing of Information

The analysis has shown that two sorts of information are essential if the market is to reach "equilibrium" values of price and quantity: information about the economic environment surrounding the market, which participants can obtain before the market opens; and information about the progress of bargaining displayed to all on a "blackboard", which can only be made available as the bargaining proceeds.

In some markets where the deals are called out in open forum, everyone can follow the progress of bargaining, and it remains simply for participants to be alert to the proceedings. But in most markets the only information available is on deals which have already been struck, and then just the price. Buyers and sellers have to judge whether the last deal is any guide to what should happen next. If it acts as a reference point, it can only be a historical one. The result is likely to be a good deal of oscillation of prices, rather than convergence on a single price.

This is particularly so where markets operate continuously. There is always a lapse between the conclusion of deals and their display, so that new deals are always being struck in the absence of the most recent data, if dealing is busy. Participants may have to find other ways of keeping abreast of the situation, and rumour may play a destabilising part.

4.2.2 The Quantity of Information

In the discussion of "perfect" markets we saw that the quantity of information which had to be passed during bargaining in order to converge on a unique price/ quantity relationship increased rapidly with the number of participants, because of the need to allow everyone of them to interact with all the others. It effectively doubled with every new participant.

It follows therefore, that as the number of participants becomes very large, the necessary information flows become much larger still and the time needed to allow this to take place increases greatly, even with a common reference point or "blackboard". As the numbers tend to infinity, so the information flows also tend to infinity, though even faster, and the time taken to reach "equilibrium" increases accordingly. In a literal interpretation of the conditions of the "perfect" market, therefore, "equilibrium" is never reached, and certainly the participants would have changed their minds or gone home before proceedings could draw to a close.

But there is a further multiplier of information in the multiplicity of markets in which each buyer must deal to acquire all that he wishes to purchase. Since all these markets are in principle in competition for his money, "equilibrium" in the whole market system requires "equilibrium" to be reached in each one individually and in the interactions between them. Information from all markets must therefore be available to everyone who might want to buy i.e. one large blackboard, and so the quantity of information is multiplied yet again by a factor which is at least equal to the number of markets.

Furthermore it is most unlikely that two manufacturers will make identical goods or provide identical services, unless they are commodities or utilities e.g. copper or electricity. Rather they will regard differentiation or scope, which is a change in quality to confer distinction, as a way of attracting buyers away from other purchases. The supply and demand decisions depend, therefore, not only on price but also on quality. Thus the car market, the washing machine market and the fast-food market are all subdivided into homogeneous but related markets which compete with each other for buyers i.e. car submarket with car submarket etc.

Product differentiation was no news to sellers of wines or cheeses, even in the old days when the main commodity of trade was corn, and it is described by Marshall at the turn of the century in his Principles of Economics. But amalgamating the total supplies and total demands into non-homogeneous aggregates leads to confusion over the nature of competition and decision-making.

A treatment more rigorously in keeping with the tenets of the "perfect" market is to consider each new variant as a homogeneous market in its own right. If for example a manufacturer introduces a brand B which competes with an existing brand A, it will attract buyers away from the market for A. The original market then splits into two markets which, although closely linked, still compete with each other in the same way as all markets compete for the same revenue (Figure 4.2).

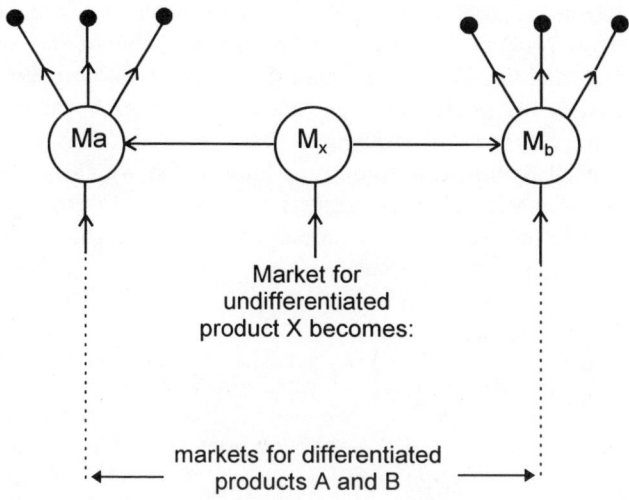

Figure 4.2 Product Differentiation

Differentiation, therefore, brings a new requirement for information on the nature of the differentiated products, and on the course of bargaining in the separate markets for all the variants i.e. M_a, M_b etc.

Seen in this light the markets for differentiated products dissolve into a multitude of more nearly "perfect" markets, all competing for the same revenue. But this is the essence of the market economy: on this narrow definition of market, the market for Fords competes with the market for Datsuns, just as when there was only one cheap production car, the market for it competed for revenue with markets for cheese and bicycles. It simply makes the total market and the information required for it to reach "equilibrium" an order of magnitude more complex still. The price/quantity relationship is even more tenuous than before.

As a result, people sometimes resort to phrases which are ill-defined (for these analytical purposes) such as moving a product "up market" or "down market", which really means into a different market. The result of such differentiation may be to attract buyers away from the established market to the new one. It may generate new buyers for the generic product i.e. people who had not bought the original product. It may however simply split the buyers, their revenue and so production to the point where general diseconomies begin to occur, which is to everyone's disadvantage.

The result of this vast amount of information which needs to be processed is that breakaway markets with their own prices tend to form. If the effect of distance is added as a barrier to communication, this is more than likely to occur.

4.2.3. The Effect of Stocks

Stocks of materials and partly finished goods are an integral part of any conversion process. They represent a degree of "inefficiency" in the system, materials and their energy content tied up because the practical operation cannot function without them. One of the major trends in manufacturing today is the progressive reduction of such stocks. This is a matter of judgment, because stocks also provide a buffer which facilitates continuity of output. In uncertain times this also has a value.

Stocks of finished goods may come into the same category, for example while awaiting despatch to customers, but some of the stocks represent a temporary withholding of goods in the hope that conditions will be more favourable later. (In the commodity business large stocks of silver were accumulated in an attempt to push up the price.)

Stocks may be represented in our notation as a hold-up in the conversion stage of the economic process (Figure 4.3).

The Market System in the Real World

Whatever the reason for their existence, stocks represent an inability or a decision not to compete as fully in the market at any instant as resources would permit. The withholding of quantity must also increase price above the level which it would otherwise attain.

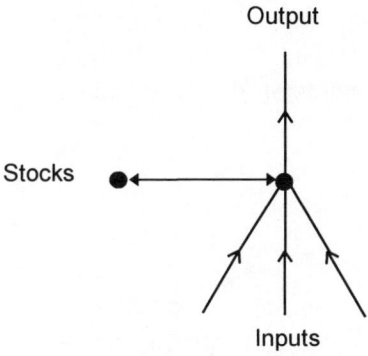

Figure 4.3 Representation of Stocks in the Conversion Process

This is perfectly reasonable. Not even "perfect market" theory insists that everything has to be put into the market at once; you are allowed to take your pigs home again. It is in fact essential for market stability; it would be foolish to pour out everything into the market at once, with no contingency reserves etc. But it does mean that, if the outcome of the bargaining is not acceptable, you withdraw and the process has to start all over again. The number of participants in the market may change while it is in progress. Back to time!

4.2.4 Trading

Trading is buying commodities in one place and selling them in another at a higher price so that a "turn" can be made on the transaction. In this sense it depends for success on "imperfections" in the market, because with perfect information there would be a single unique price for all places and the price differential on which trading

The Scale and Scope of Economics

relies would disappear. Using our notation, trading may be represented as in Figure 4.4.

Arbitrage is a similar activity which depends on spotting the price anomalies which may arise in markets, and making use of prices before they "equilibrate".

Trading increases prices in the market in which the commodity was first sold by removing quantity from it, and reduces prices in the other market into which it is then sold. Thus the differential or market "imperfection" tends to disappear. In this sense trading is a form of negative feedback.

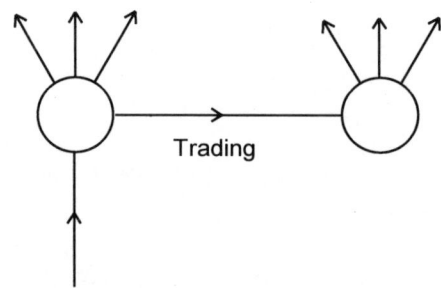

Figure 4.4 Diagrammatic Representation of Trading

4.2.5 Speculation

Speculation is buying commodities in the expectation of selling them later in the same market at a higher price. It represents a hold-up in the flow of commodities through markets, and may be represented as in Figure 4.5

Successful speculation on a small scale may also smooth price fluctuations, but under some circumstances it may act as positive feedback, which tends to exaggerate price rises and falls. Particular danger arises if the market is "imperfect" enough and the speculator large enough for his own purchases and sales to affect market prices significantly. Successful speculation is then in effect manipulation of

The Market System in the Real World

the market price at the expense of other participants. In this case the positive feedback soon becomes sufficient to shake the system apart.

Speculation must be a source of confusion to the participants in a market and indeed the rest of the economic process in reading price signals. If it has a useful feature, it seems to be that it may elicit information essential to the operation of a very "imperfect" market which would not otherwise be generally available, because of the small number of deals.

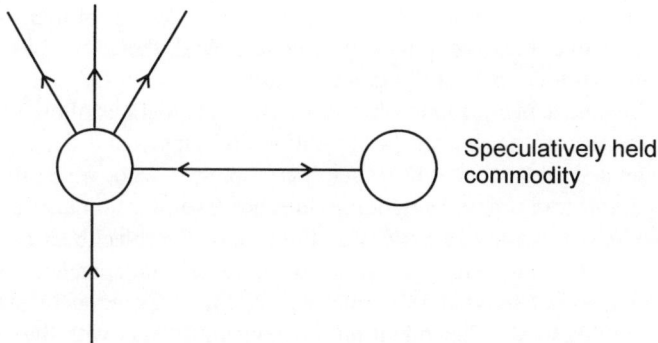

Figure 4.5 Diagrammatic Representation of Speculation

4.2.6 Psychological Constraints

The "perfect market" system, since it takes no account of time, requires that buyers and sellers should have total information, but act as if they had no memories. Buyers and sellers must be anonymous, or else they might form alliances. But in practice they often know each other very well, and in particular they will remember not simply the former price/quantity relationships, which is part of their universal knowledge, but also how they were arrived at.

Moreover, when buyers have to choose between commodities, and hence markets according to the definitions, they will remember factors such as the relative volatility of prices in the respective markets, since transactions commit them not simply in the present but possibly for some way into the future.

On both sides of the market, therefore, there is frequently a tendency to refrain from driving the hardest possible, as opposed to a good, bargain for fear of reprisal on another occasion. As a consequence, pricing may be to some extent linked to other prospective decisions, perhaps even in other markets. Such psychological factors influence the attitudes of buyers and sellers in addition to the quantities currently available and required. Continuity of relationships with suppliers may be important. Driving suppliers or buyers out of business is an action with repercussions well beyond the present market day. Some large customers even go out of their way to help improve their suppliers' businesses. And there is always the thought that there but for the grace of God....

A related aspect of man's behaviour is his tendency follow fashion. His response to any particular conditions of supply and demand may be dictated by what the other participants, who are often his competitors, are doing. Bargaining does not take place on a strictly one to one basis, with everyone watching only the blackboard, as the "perfect" market requires when it specifies independent action. Everyone watches what everyone else is doing. Survival in the long term may be totally dependent on the decision to stay with the herd or leave it, and this consideration may also weigh on the minds of the individuals who take the risks in the bargaining process. If it becomes the dominant consideration, it may result in panic buying and selling.

4.3 Exogenous Distortions of Markets

The market network often fails to give the results society wants or governments need, and so the outcome is influenced by controls or subsidies. After all, markets are supposed to be for the benefit of society, not vice versa. The problem is where to stop. And if such "distortions" are removed, who benefits from change? How to ensure that the benefits are shared fairly, particularly by those whose livelihoods may be damaged? Otherwise it is no more than the imposition of dogma.

The Market System in the Real World

4.3.1 Subsidies

Subsidies are paid to producers to allow them to make more net income than their costs would otherwise permit. Subsidies do not directly affect the bargaining mechanism , and so it is still possible in principle to reach a unique price/quantity relationship, but they allow producers who may be less efficient to stay in the business instead of being forced to withdraw. The overall effect is to keep the quantity supplied above the "equilibrium" level, and reduce prices.

Subsidies played an essential part in the rise of economic powers such as Britain, the USA and Japan. Most countries, including these, still pay subsidies of one sort or another to protect some parts of their industries, or particular ways of life, or their countrysides etc. They may be vital in maintaining the social fabric on which the economic process depends, and which it is supposed to serve. The political pressures are too great to resist, and in any case they are a useful way of moderating the rate of change of the economic system.

Not all subsidies take the form of money. They may be hidden as part of defence expenditure, for instance, which trickles down through research contracts into commercial activities and helps realign a country's technological base. Or they may take the form of subsidised water for agriculture.

4.3.2 Tariffs

Tariffs are a charge on goods imported into a market from foreign parts, in effect a negative subsidy on imports. The result is the same as for subsidies. The market mechanism can still function in the sense of reaching a stable price/quantity relationship, but higher cost producers in the importing country are protected from the full force of competition, and may stay in business longer than they otherwise would.

Much of world trade is subject to tariff barriers.

4.3.3 Quotas

Quotas are a larger distortion of the market mechanism because they act directly on the quantity part of the price/quantity relationship. Producers who are permitted to supply only a limited quantity to the market have nothing to gain by competitive pricing. They are content to accept the market price which emerges because this will be higher than if they competed.

Low cost producers such as the Asian countries sometimes find themselves limited in their export markets by quotas, or agreements on "self-restraint" or orderly marketing, which amount to the same thing. However they themselves had little concept of reciprocal trade when they set up their conversion operations; they expected traffic to be one way, not in "equilibrium".

4.3.4. Price Guarantees

Interference with prices affects the other part of the price/quantity relationship. Price guarantees are one method which governments use to protect home producers of a product. However, if the price is guaranteed, there is no competition to be the most efficient producer, because there is no reward for being so. The greatest rewards in fact go to those who produce most, and so every bit of commodity which can be produced is produced, provided the production costs are less than the guaranteed price. What is more, any producer, however inefficient, is given the incentive to produce goods which he might otherwise have foregone.

The net results, therefore, may be a total quantity of the product surplus to the requirements of the community, profits for the larger and more efficient producer exceeding those which the free market would have brought him and a population of marginal producers brought into the market by the guaranteed price, but still scarcely making a living. Thus, in the absence of additional counteracting measures, price guarantees may prolong the very situation which they were intended to remedy.

Agriculture provides some particularly striking examples of these effects. Free markets are often a less than ideal way of rewarding farmers, and many have suffered bitterly from their annual vagaries in the past. In good years abundant harvests bring low prices, and in bad years poor harvests may bring extreme cuts in quantities produced and hence income. There is therefore an inherent instability in this kind of economic activity, and ways need to be found of securing the food supply and giving a decent compensation to the agricultural industry generally as a vital part of the conversion system.

The Market System in the Real World

However, if prices are supported without constraints on the quantities produced, the predictable consequences are surplus mountains of wheat and butter, and lakes of wine, which are costly not only to produce but also to maintain, since they cannot easily be disposed of. Farmers on rich soils have abundant crops and make very large profits, because their unit costs of production are low. Marginal producers, who by definition produce less and have high unit costs, remain poor. In fact they would be better served by a direct subsidy to their cost of living out of general taxation instead of producing what the community does not want, if this turns out to be the case.

But such a policy also encourages measures which are extremely dubious, such as uprooting hedges and draining fens which are centuries old, and moreover brings into use land which is increasingly unsuitable for agricultural use. Some of this land is of outstanding beauty and environmental importance, and by any standards should be maintained as a public asset. The overall result, therefore, may be the payment of public money to alter some parts of the environment which society as a whole would prefer to leave untouched.

4.3.5. Barter

Reaching a unique price/quantity relationship in the "perfect" market depends on the medium of exchange, although this is normally taken for granted in the analysis. Certainly any general "equilibrium" of a range of "perfect" markets would have to depend on a free flow of infinitely divisible incentives of agreed value, i.e. money, if the incentive feedback is to function rapidly and effectively.

The force of the argument can best be illustrated by considering exchange in the absence of money, that is barter. Consider, for example, a simple country market for cows, pigs and sheep, ignoring for the sake of illustration the requirement that commodities should be infinitely divisible.

With money available as the medium of exchange, the market system allows the price to be established by matching of supply and demand, provided all potential participants know the quantity and price of cows, and have the time to complete all the bargaining. The price/quantity data supply an extra degree of freedom, or a blackboard as we described it earlier, which allows the system to work according the rules. The system requires all participants independently to strike for themselves the best bargains that they can. What is established in this way is market price of cows i.e. the cow/sterling ratio, if they are dealing in sterling.

If buyers are not sure whether they want to buy cows or pigs, there are in fact two markets which they can attend, one for cows and the other for pigs. There is no particular problem in doing this, provided there is total information about the prices and quantities of cows and pigs i.e. they can see both blackboards on which the progress of bargaining is displayed. Buyers and sellers will assess the total information for the two markets and allocate their money between them accordingly. Prices and quantities will then be settled in each market separately by the normal mechanisms.

The outcome is a market price per cow and a market price per pig i.e. a cow/sterling ratio and a pig/sterling ratio, which can be compared. If there were three commodities, there would be three ratios and hence three choices, and so on. Choices arise from the facility to take money from one market and use it in another, perhaps at another time i.e. use it as a medium of exchange.

But suppose there were no medium of exchange. First of all there could be no cow market; one would have to establish the ratio of cows to something else, say pigs. Even if total information were available, the best that could be established would be a cow/pig ratio. The exchange rates for cows and pigs could not be independently determined, since each commodity could be expressed only in terms of the other. The only choice would be to take the cow/pig ratio or leave it.

If other participants wanted to exchange either commodity for something else, they would have to make other arrangements and arrive at other ratios in other markets, but this could lead to insuperable problems. For instance, if sheep were introduced into the system, it would be impossible for buyers and sellers of sheep to act independently of the cow and pig markets. These would establish a cow/pig ratio and a pig/sheep ratio, but by so doing they establish the cow/sheep ratio without the dealers in cows and sheep market even talking to one another. There are three commodities but only two independent ratios, and between these there is only one choice i.e. only one degree of freedom, which is one less than is necessary to allow the markets to operate as "perfect" markets within the same market system. Even with as few as three commodities it is no longer possible for the market to reach "equilibrium" values of exchange. Many will find their bargains settled for them in advance, and since they will not be happy with this, they will start the whole process over again. Furthermore the complexity of the system is likely to increase with at least the square of the number of commodities, and so it would become completely unwieldy.

The upshot is a range of exchange ratios with oscillations between them as the process continues, until individual bargains are settled out of sheer exasperation. This is not what the "perfect" market had in mind at all. On the other hand it is exactly what countries which engage in international barter are trying to achieve; adjusting the normal market mechanism in their favour, because it is not working for them. The only situation in which barter is satisfactory is not a market at all, but when two parties happen to have a double coincidence of wants (4) and no other opportunities to satisfy them.

What the medium of exchange does is to provide the system with a degree of freedom. Units of currency are agreed to be arithmetical in quantity and undifferentiated in quality i.e. every pound sterling is identical to every other, and equally acceptable everywhere and at all times. This agreement has been reached outside the market i.e. exogenously, and is reinforced by government guarantee. It is not open to dispute in the course of bargaining; it is complicated enough establishing a price when one part of the ratio of goods to money is differentiated, without the other varying too with some pounds being more valuable than others. This understanding is absolutely vital if anything like unique market prices are to be reached even locally, let alone in the context of a putative "equilibrium".

Of course it is always possible for one of the commodities to be used as the medium of exchange, for example exchange values have been measured in hides or playing cards, but then by definition its value too could not be established independently of the other commodities. It is simply an expression of their relative values. Money has no intrinsic value.

4.3.6 Bilateral Trade

Bilateral trade is an agreement between countries to trade with each other up to a given level of expenditure. The agreement involves the medium of exchange and may cover a whole range of commodities, say £100 million of ships, machinery and food on one side for £100 million of shoes, handbags, coal and strawberry jam on the other.

It is not as restrictive therefore as barter, but it does in effect reduce the number of participants in each market to two, one buyer and one seller, which is far from the rules of the "perfect" market. The two parties may of course take prices from the other markets as proxies e.g. the world market prices for each commodity, but they have influenced those prices by abstaining from competition in them. The agreement in effect restricts entry of other possibly more efficient suppliers into the market in question.

4.4 The Interpretation of Price Signals from Markets

The value for producers of markets as a mechanism of exchange lies in the information about market clearing prices and quantities of throughput, which allows them to make decisions about future production. The price "signals" direct them towards goods and utilities which people want to buy, and competition between them ensures that only the most efficient survive. In principle therefore the totality of products and utilities becomes progressively more desirable and more efficiently produced, which benefits all purchasers.

In systems terms price/quantity information from the market, specifically market revenue, which is calculated from them, provides the feedback from markets to converters which is the incentive to produce and controls the economic process as we have defined it. This information relates not only to outputs from conversion processes i.e. revenue received from the markets for goods sold, but also to costs i.e. what has to be paid out to others in markets who supplied the inputs. The feedback is then the difference between a converter's income and costs, which is the net revenue. Interpretation of price signals is therefore of the utmost importance to the progress of the market system.

As we have seen, the "perfect market" of the economist is timeless; it slips from "equilibrium" to "equilibrium" as fast as an electron between shells, because any time spent in transition would be an "imperfection". But as soon as time is taken into account in the system, it is clear that market quantities and therefore prices at any time will be changing in response to a whole series of actions taken by producers in the past, however recent, to adjust the quantity of product which they are making. The time which elapses between an action and its effect on revenue from the market is the response time.

4.4.1 Categories of Market Price Response Time

Four different categories of response time can be defined, two relating to the conversion process as it exists and two to changes in the conversion process itself in response to market expectations.

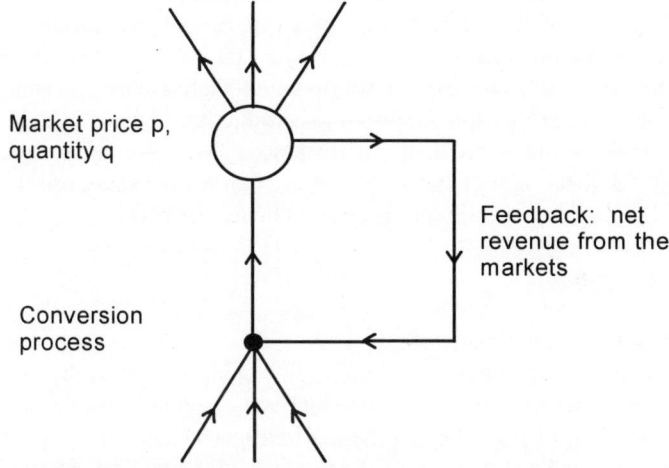

Figure 4.6 Net Revenue as Feedback

Each may refer either to sellers in their capacity as converters or to buyers, who are also converters, even if they are the last in the conversion chain i.e. consumers. It is necessary to distinguish between the two because they may each act independently according to their

The Scale and Scope of Economics

own circumstances in the short term. Over a long period, however, their actions must match each other's, since everything which is produced will be sold, or in a rational world production will cease. This must be true in the conventional representation of markets too, because the supply/demand schedules always cross at a positive price. The actual response time in the market will be the combined effect of the four separate contributions.

1. Immediate Response

This comes nearest to the classical concept of a market where instantaneous demand is matched by instantaneous supply, and a price is immediately agreed which just sells all the goods, so that the market is cleared. This may be represented in our notation as in Figure 4.6.

Response of the conversion process cannot be instantaneous because it is a physical system which must take time to change, but it may be quite fast. However it follows that such a change cannot be very large in proportion to previous production. This might be the baker making one more loaf, for instance. The consequence of this type of feedback in a physical system is often a very small oscillation, in this case of the quantity produced and hence the revenue.

2. Stock-linked

More sophisticated participants may take a different view of the market, especially where the commodity being sold may be cheaply stored, whether by seller or buyer. Each may decide to take a position in the holding of stock before the market opens such that he need not compete to the limit if the market price does not suit. The seller leaves some of his product in stock in the hope of achieving a better price at a later date. The buyer may also hold off buying until a later date because he thinks the price will fall, particularly if he has had the foresight to lay in some cheaper stocks beforehand. Or alternatively, either or both may decide or be forced to run down their stocks because of costs, which has been a widespread practice over recent years. In addition there is also the stock built up or unloaded by speculators who are trying to anticipate price moves to their advantage. This may be summarised as in Figure 4.7.

The Market System in the Real World

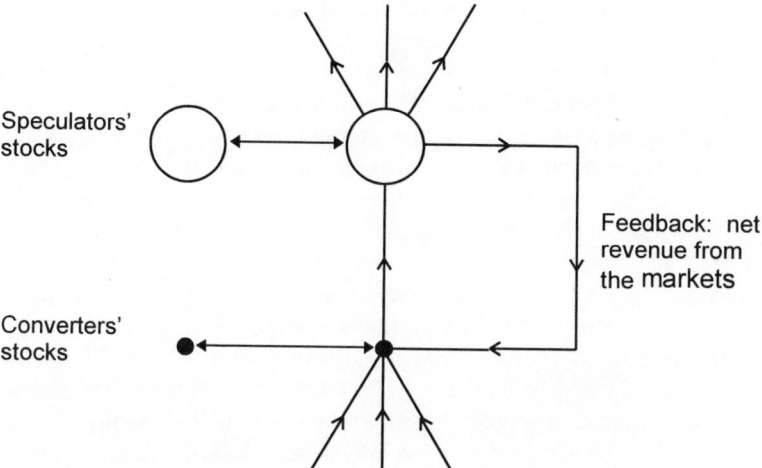

Figure 4.7 Effect of Stocks on Feedback System

The price which emerges in the market as a result depends not only on the rate of production by the conversion process, but also on the rate of inflow into or outflow from the converters and speculators' stocks. The effect on price will depend on the phasing of the flow back into the conversion/market system. It may have the effect of smoothing out variations of price over time, which is the usual justification given for the practice. It may equally well have a destabilising effect if it reinforces or even causes the swings and roundabouts of the markets, even if operator's try to do otherwise, because their anticipation goes collectively wrong. Since these are longer term decisions, the response time of the market price will be longer, and the number of separate influences will make it more difficult to interpret.

3. Organisation-linked

If demand changes and the increase cannot be met out of immediately available production or stocks, the converters may decide to manufacture more, and accept the higher costs and risk of oversupply. Thus they may operate their equipment for longer periods by working additional shifts or overtime, or even operate the equipment more intensively, if that is possible, by speeding it up etc.

Such a response requires a change in the internal functioning of the supply organisation, and it is the rate at which this occurs which determines the time taken to respond to the market. This change may take the form of more intense activity, with more room for mistakes or waste, or longer hours of work, more co-operation between individuals, groups and departments, more risk taking etc. Furthermore it almost certainly requires a similar response from suppliers of raw materials, products and services all the way back up the supply chain. In this case the response time must be longer than for the instantaneous or stock related responses; organisations of any size do not readily respond to external stimuli, especially where there is room for doubt about the meaning of market signals and different attitudes to risk.

4. Investment-linked

The longest response time will occur when investment is required to meet the expected needs of the markets. Equipment has to be bought and commissioned, raw materials and other supply chains set up to feed it, stocks established to smooth the increase of output, extra people employed and trained, and above all an effective organisation established to handle it. The planned increase or output depends on all these investments, each of which is necessary but not sufficient.

All investments are undertaken with an expectation of reward in the future, which may not accrue in the event. All require the commitment of resources, the cost of which may be irrecoverable, if the products remain unsold or the price falls. The costs and risks are therefore much higher than for other categories of response. It depends not only on the marshalling of resources, but the estimation of likely prices over the minimum lifetime of the investment, the decision-making mechanisms within the organisation concerned, its attitude to collective and personal risk, its evaluation of competitor's actions, the possibility of technological change etc.

Such a process must result in much longer response times than the previous three categories. It may take up to 5 years to build and commission a chemical plant and 10-15 years for a power station, only to find that the product is not required in the expected quantities at the end of that time.

5. The Combined Effect

Clearly the model of the "perfect" market is far from the reality of the system. At any particular time there will be a market price for a product as it changes hands, but it will depend on quantities which for the most part have been decided in advance. Decisions to stock or release stocks need to be taken before market day in order not to cause too much adverse change in the market price. Organisational response is a more complex phenomenon which is to some extent a function of the history of the organisation, including its previous investments, and its environment, since people's collective habits and relationships seldom change fast. Some even think that the response of an organisation and certainly its attitudes depend on the character of its founder, often long since dead, though that may be stretching a point. Investment-led response adds yet another dimension of uncertainty and commitment over a long timescale, sometimes many years. The intervention of governments with subsidies and tariffs and doubt about their future actions compound the problem of interpretation even more.

A market response time is subject to the same principles as those which govern the response of any system, for a market is a system if it is more than a collection of random responses. The elements of the response are:
- detection of the present state of the system i.e. price/quantity information,
- decide what response to make to it from an assessment of both one's own position and the total economic environment i.e. sell, make, invest or not,
- implement what has been decided.

If the system operates efficiently, the result will then be an overshoot in the direction in which price is moving, followed by an undershoot as a result of overcorrection, and then settling down at the new price, as in Figure 4.8.

If there is any delay in detecting the present state of the system i.e. information does not get through, then the oscillations may be exaggerated by precipitate and concerted responses, and there will be noise in the price signal.

With four difference response times there will be four simultaneous movements with different time periods to combine: four overshoots, undershoots and estimates of the new price level which the system will eventually reach. There will be no way of separating the effects in the absence of universal and perfect knowledge both of the present state and the future. The best outcome is a damped oscillation. The worst is perpetual oscillation as people rush from side to side of the boat in response to rumour.

A market price thus reflects the present result of four time trends originating at various times, from the most recent to the long since past. As a signal for the future it is a confused summary of all four. Moreover each market will have its own characteristic response times, linked through conversion operators to give a network of responding elements. It is not surprising therefore that the usual position is not rapid fluctuation of market prices but stability; the inertia is too great. In the normal course of events prices in the shops do not change by the minute. There are so many forces acting in different directions that the total result is little movement in any direction, a sort of Brownian motion. Equally, once the system begins to drift it is difficult to stop. There is no question of moving the whole network in a desired direction by acting on particular markets. There must be measures which act on them all.

The argument has been developed by analysing the position of the seller, but there is an exactly parallel situation for the buyer. He too may respond immediately or slowly, depending on his stock position etc. His organisation will need to be geared up at some cost and risk to take more of the product on sale. He too will have similar problems of additional investment to be able to process his purchases. Much easier to stay where he is in a stable state, even if it might mean competing slightly less efficiently than he might in principle be able to do.

The Market System in the Real World

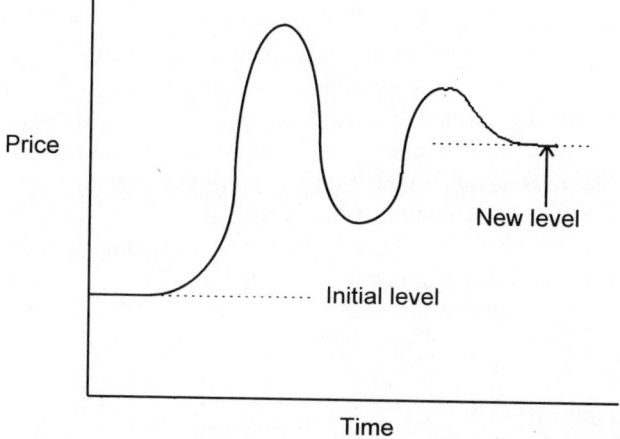

Figure 4.8 Market Response to Change of Conditions

4.4.2 Examples of Market Response Time

In such a complex situation clear examples of response times are difficult to find, but occasionally situations arise where a market price is given a push from outside which induces change. The effect of the exogenous stimulus can then be followed, rather like a pendulum given an extra push. Two examples come to mind. One is launching a new share on the stock market, which can only demonstrate the first two categories of response, since organisational changes and fixed investments are not part of the share itself. The other is the price of a commodity, oil, which was given a push to a new higher level over the period of a few months.

The Scale and Scope of Economics

1. British Telecom

Half of the stock of Telecom, which was a publicly owned company, was sold to the private sector on the 28th November 1984 at a price of 130p a share, of which the initial instalment to be paid was 50p. The price was expected to be below the market clearing price, because it was required to be certain of selling the whole issue, and the exact market clearing price was impossible to guess. When the shares were traded in the market, they immediately rose to 98p, and then fell back as some buyers had second thoughts and sold their allocation of shares. The price behaviour during the first four days of trading is shown in Figure 4.9, which is what might be expected of a fairly well damped system.

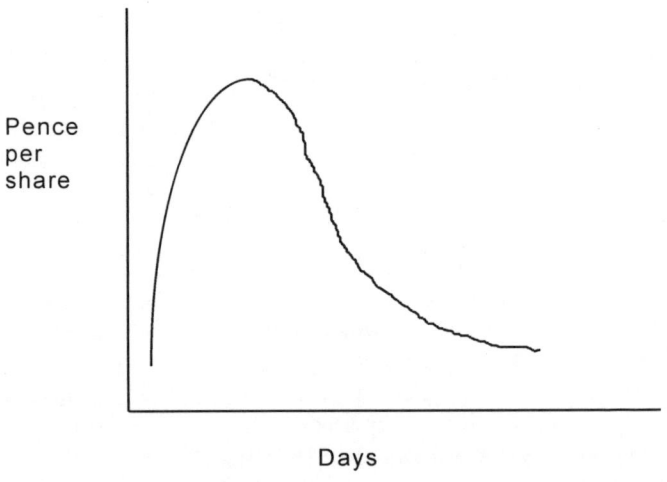

Figure 4.9 Price Response on Launch of British Telecom Shares

At this point the entitlements to share allocations and the attitude of owners became clearer, and new buyers and sellers came into the market. The price then increased to 102p during the next ten days and settled down to about 100p for a few days until circumstances prompted yet another change, after the manner of the stockmarket, and so on.

2. *The Price of Crude Oil*

In 1973 circumstances conspired to cause the sellers of crude oil to raise its price from $3 to $11 a barrel in the space of a few months, and to allow the price rise to hold. Buyers had little choice but to pay higher prices for their oil products, and make arrangements to reduce their purchases to compensate. The shape of the response of oil product prices during the two years from mid 1972 is shown in Figure 4.10.

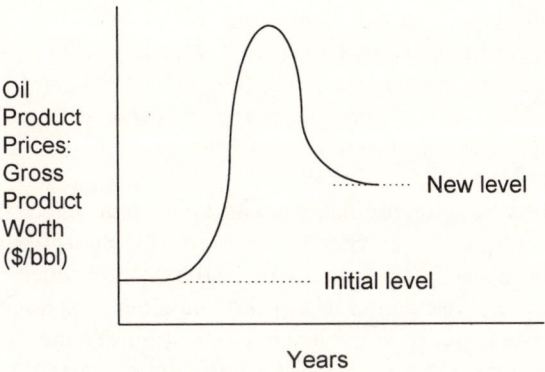

Figure 4.10 Response of Oil Product Market Prices to the Oil Price Shock of 1973

This was in effect an organisational response during which users adjusted their habits in order to reduce consumption after the initial shock. The response time was 1 - 2 years.

The investment-linked response was much slower, with a response time of 5 - 10 years on the producing side, which is equivalent to conversion in our nomenclature. It required new suppliers to come into the market, which meant finding and producing oil, a 5 - 7 year process even after permission has been granted. For their part buyers, that is users, improved the efficiency of their cars, machines, boilers etc and insulated their houses, which took a similarly long time to introduce and take effect.

The subsequent trend is obscured by a further price rise in 1979 which seems to have arisen from panic on the part of buyers in the market, but after about four years it had drifted back to its pre-1979 level in real terms in spite of drastic reduction in production by the original suppliers, again a 3 - 4 year response time.

Compared with this case and the share issue, the foreign exchange markets can adjust world-wide in a matter of minutes because only the first type of response really applies to them.

4.4.3 Business Cycles

It is well known that business activity is cyclical. The short cycles of 4 - 5 years are best established, but people believe they can discern longer term and even very long term cycles of activity with periods of up to 50 years. Yet there is no room for cyclical behaviour in the "perfect" market, where preferences are expressed and met instantaneously, and the market network is by definition in "equilibrium".

Cyclical behaviour, or oscillations, can only occur where there is an imperfect response to change, because of either imperfect information or an inherent structural inertia effect which causes overshoot. A general oscillation of this sort could not be caused by the response time behaviour of individual markets. It reflects the collective behaviour of the market network, the conversion processes that feed them and the general set of interactions between them.

Such interactions can take place only through some common element, that is the incentive system, effectively expressed through the medium of exchange. Whatever the nature of the link, it is clearly the case that the price/quantity relationship in individual markets is varying independently of the factors which might normally be expected to affect it in isolated systems.

The problem of relating the dynamics of real markets to the static representation of conventional supply/demand schedules has given rise to discussion of "dynamic cobweb" behaviour (5, 6), if that is not a contradiction in terms.

The Market System in the Real World

Cyclical phenomena in business are strong evidence of the market/conversion process network behaving as a system.

4.5 The Problem of Common Goods

4.5.1. Networks

Networks derive their value from their utility to a range of people who are geographically widespread. It is seldom useful to build more than one network covering precisely the same territory, because costs of installation are much less than proportional to capacity. Builders of networks must usually allow enough capacity to cover all potential requirements, which renders a new installation uncompetitive.

The outcome therefore is that there is usually only one network, in a monopolistic position, serving a whole population of buyers, none of whom is large enough to strike a bargain independently of the others. Because of this disparity of market strength, network owners are always subject to regulation of the services they must supply and the changes they can impose. Any competition must come not from within the market for the network itself but in a competitive product, frequently a different sort of network.

For example the network might be the national road network. There is no way of relating the "price" of roads directly to the use by particular users. The system must be seen as a whole, because the value of a network is that the parts are linked together. An alternative to the road network might well be rail or even telephone networks. But there is a certain proportion of traffic which is tied to a network, and so competition from other products or networks is limited to the margin.

However that may be, networks must remain "imperfect" in market terms by their very nature, and pricing of their services will remain a matter of dispute. They are a product where the interests of the whole community must be considered together rather than the "perfect" market concept of each optimising his own position separately.

4.5.2 Common Goods

There are other goods not included in the conversion system which are indeterminate in value because they depend on a collective response

The Scale and Scope of Economics

over a period of time. The price of such social goods is therefore impossible for an individual to determine.

For instance there is the problem of selling the services of fire stations on the open market. Buyers who enter such a market could call on the services of the fireman if their house caught fire. But it might be their neighbours' houses which caught fire, and if their neighbours had chosen not to buy the service, not only would their houses burn down but they would also set fire to those of the more prudent citizens. It would be no consolation to these that the fireman then came to damp down the flames; prevention would have been a thousand times more valuable than the treatment. So what would they have bought? One might think of this as the Pudding Lane effect.

Similar situations occur with car insurance. It is not a complete consolation to car owners who are themselves insured, if they are the injured party in an accident when the other party has no insurance against which claims may be made. Nor on a different track is it effective for a small proportion of a population to be vaccinated against, say smallpox, because there is threshold level below which the disease still spreads. Purchasers of the vaccinations may still not be able to insulate themselves entirely from all the effects of the disease, if it spreads through the rest of the population, though they might avoid the worst.

A similar case can be made where the common goods relate not to prevention but to opportunity. An example of this might be education. The economic return on the education of an individual may depend very much on the general level of the community in which he or she lives and works.

In each case the buyers are paying for an opportunity of achievement or the chance of avoiding something unpleasant, but the chance or degree of success depends on others' taking up the offer in large proportions. If they do not, then the value of the purchase is much reduced, whatever the price paid.

Since these are all useful things to do, the way to make the systems work is to introduce a legislative requirement or else persuade large proportions of the population to take up the "commodity". Everyone pays for the fire service, all car owners are obliged to be insured, and large proportions of populations have been persuaded to be vaccinated, so that smallpox can be eradicated. In education the state has the responsibility, and educates all children up to a minimum level and beyond, in the interests of the whole community. The market mechanism is irrelevant. The economic problem lies in the best use of the resources which the community dedicates to education. Such difficulties are much less likely to arise with tangible goods and current services, since they are here and now, and the consequences of expenditure can more easily be discerned.

4.5.3 The Medium of Exchange

Money is to be classed not so much among common goods as among common agreements. When it is treated like goods whose price can be determined in the market, the results can be quite surprising. For instance the preceding analysis of the barter mechanism has a parallel in the markets for foreign exchange. In a market system where currencies can be freely bought and sold, the value of any currency will be determined by the sellers and buyers of that currency. But the currency is exchanged not for goods, since that would be an ordinary commodity market such as analysed above, but for other currencies.

Thus the situation arises where sterling has a dollar and a mark (DM) exchange value i.e. the £/$ and £/DM ratios are fixed. But in fixing the £/$ and £/DM ratios the exchangers must also have fixed the $/DM ratio. Just as we showed in the discussion on the bartering of cows, pigs and sheep, that there was only one choice or one degree of freedom, so it is with three currencies. Given a £/$ exchange rate, you can choose the alternative of a £/DM exchange rate, if that is more attractive, but that automatically settles the $/DM exchange rate too. Or to generalise, in foreign exchange between n currencies there are n-2 degrees of freedom. One might conclude therefore from such an analysis of the system, that it is not possible to reach stable "equilibrium" exchange values of all currencies simultaneously under individual bargaining conditions, even with total information about prices and quantities (and modern information technology makes total information very nearly achievable for currency transactions).

It might, of course, be objected that prevailing currency values are supposed to be related to the underlying economic situation of countries, in which case these would supply the necessary reference points. That was one of the basic assumptions behind exchange rates. But over 80% of currency transactions are now said to be speculation, that is buying and selling currencies as commodities in their own right, with a view to exchanging them for other currencies later and with no intention of exchanging them for products or services. In any case the rapid changes which occur in relative values show that they cannot possibly be linked to physical factors, because no physical aggregate could change that fast and remain reversible; such physical changes tend to be explosive and final.

Foreign exchanges do of course take place, and in very large volumes, and so the mechanism obviously works. What is misleading, however, is to assume that the exchange is in accordance with the principles of the "perfect" market.

4.5.4 Facilitators

There is a further class of social activity which cannot by definition be subject to exchange in a market place. This includes the facilitators which were part of the main classification of the economic process.

Law and order, for instance, cannot be open to the highest bidder, nor should government be. Scientific knowledge, creativity, local customs and language are independent of the "market place", though not independent of the economic process, as nothing to do with man and his economic well-being can be. Health, education, fire services and public service broadcasting are national concerns which are vital to every citizen, not just those who can afford them in a "market place". And what about defence, security and national and local administration? Should these be settled on the basis of some price/quantity relationship, assuming that a definition of the "commodity" could be found? That would be obvious nonsense. Yet they are all essential parts of the economic process.

There are perfectly good, commonsense ways of dealing with these without invoking the "market", still less the "perfect" market.

4.6 Conclusions

Markets are a mechanism for exchanging goods and services. By coupling the elements of economic chains together they allow modern industrial economies to function with all their complexity. They are essential to change, and they permit innovation. Markets are not well represented by the conventional supply/demand schedules, in

The Market System in the Real World

particular because these cannot include the effects of time as an explicit variable. It is much clearer to represent them as systems in the form of flow diagrams showing the movement of products from conversion processes through markets to consumption. Revenue from the market then supplies feedback to converters, and the whole system responds at different rates to different levels of feedback. An effective medium of exchange is necessary for proper responses to be made. The system may reach a stable state, but not a position of "equilibrium", because that is not possible with such flows. This failure to reach "equilibrium" applies not only to individual markets but also to the whole market network, not least because by far the greater part of international currency flows, the international media of exchange, no longer even relates to the exchange of products.

The complexity of the modern world is such that the conditions for the economic theoretician's "perfect" markets, where price and quantity in the market are all, cannot exist. Price signals are often confused by the profusion of products, imperfect or incomprehensible information and the various effects of time, and in any case quantities to be supplied to the market have to be decided well in advance of market day.

The whole trend in modern industrial economies is towards product differentiation, where manufacturers deliberately move away from the condition of homogeneity of products, which the "perfect" market requires, in order to tempt customers away from neighbouring markets. There is nothing wrong in this; it is simply an attempt to give people what they prefer. Services too cannot be fitted into price/quantity schedules because it is impossible to define the product. Particularly foolish is the categorisation of people as "labour", having a price/quantity relationship, when they are clearly far from "homogeneous products"; each is an individual learning system, changing every day of his or her life, and changing the economic process accordingly. Under such conditions it is doubtful whether the economic process can ever be said to reach even a steady state, as the changing fortunes of countries relative to each other bear witness.

"Perfection" is still further removed by the actions of governments, cartels, monopolies, monopsonies and all kinds of individuals, which must necessarily be accepted as a feature of modern life, as people seek to protect themselves in a greatly enlarged economic environment. Indeed by limiting the rate of change such actions may in no small measure be a condition of stability for the people in an economy. Markets are weighted towards those in an economy who have most with which to participate, that is the better off. Exchange is not about fairness, but society and democracy are, and any conflicts between the results of markets and the values of democratic society will also damage the economic process itself to the detriment of all.

The structure of the State, government, defence and the law, are outside the mechanism of the market, and other social goods require collective provision. If it were left to the action of individuals alone, the results for society at large would be as bad as eighteenth century roads.

None of this is to deny the advantage, even necessity, for many goods and services of balancing supply and requirements through an exchange mechanism i.e. matching populations of buyers and sellers. That is what markets have always done; the economic process could not function without them. Nor is it to deny that improvements may be made to achieve better and fairer operation of economic systems. It is merely that sweeping away obstacles to "perfection" as a pursuit for its own sake seems a fruitless task, particularly as the "perfect" market could not work even if it the obstacles were removed; there simply would not be time. If changes are made, it must be to achieve positive benefits, or it will be no more than an implementation of ideology for its own sake. Such benefits should be shared equitably or they will just evaporate.

It is a question of understanding the mechanisms involved and making a balanced social choice of what is appropriate. In the real world commonsense and negotiation are much better guides to progress. There are situations in which the exercise of individual preference has its advantages, and others in which the optimum result for the whole requires collective rather than individual arrangements. The analysis shows that whatever theoretical interest the "perfect" market may have, real markets are not like that. People do not collide in them like billiard balls. Markets are systems in which the subsystems, whether people or firms, interact, if it is necessary to say it at all. The consequences rebound through the whole of society.

Chapter Five

THE COST BASIS OF ECONOMIC

ACTIVITY

The revenue which returns to the operators of conversion processes provides the feedback which allows them to decide how to respond. Implementation of their decisions gives rise to the response times described in the previous chapter. Conversion processes produce what may be considered as an economic harvest. The aim is to obtain as good a yield of "corn" as possible, and at least as much as the seedcorn which was planted. Otherwise it would have been better to eat the seedcorn instead of burying it. No one sows in the expectation of reaping less. Indeed, because of the risk of drought and pestilence, one is probably expecting to reap a good deal more to compensate for the bad years, which will always occur.

So it is with the economic harvest yielded by a conversion process, except that in economics the harvest comes from the market i.e. not the yield of corn but what it fetches when sold. Suppose a quantity of product q is sold at market price p. The harvest, which is the total revenue received R, is then pq, or
$$R = pq$$

But in growing the corn it was necessary to incur the cost of the seedcorn, or in the case of a conversion process, the cost C of its inputs. The real harvest of the conversion process is then equivalent to the net harvest i.e. the yield of corn less the seedcorn etc from which it was grown. In the case of a conversion process this is the total revenue less costs, the net revenue, which we call R_N. The harvest is then:

$$R_N = R - C$$
$$= pq - C$$

The aim of conversion is to maximise R_N, especially over the long term, because the outcome in any year is almost as uncertain as the harvest, and we plan to survive more than one year.

The obvious response is to grow a more valuable crop, say change from wheat to sunflowers, if the prices are expected to be higher. The converters' equivalent is product differentiation, making products with better design and more facilities, which people are hopefully prepared to pay for. Alternatively one might improve the process of manufacture, even if the product is the same. Both of these responses are changes of scope, as described in the analysis of the next chapter; they involve changing the character of the product and/or process over time.

This chapter sets out what determines cost, the other factor in the equation for net revenue, if we assume that we can change only the scale of operation, and not the scope. This is the usual hypothesis of conventional economic analysis, even if it is not normally stated. More precisely we can describe it as the analysis of factors which affect the instantaneous input costs into revenue-seeking conversion subsystems of the economy i.e. firms, corporations etc. It is an unreal analysis, because it permits of no change in the structure of assets, as noted above, nor of any progress or learning in the human assets, because it does not include time. It is the effect of scale on costs, "other things being equal", the phrase so beloved of economists, although of course they never are.

Nevertheless it is useful to consider the economies and diseconomies of scale, and there can be a certain logic in it, not only for simple goods, but also in the long term for more sophisticated products. Once you have moved as far "up market" as it is possible to go, and a number of competing products are equally sophisticated without possibility of further improvement, then the maximum net revenue will accrue to the converter who can achieve this at lowest cost. In a world of technological innovation this state of affairs is reached much less frequently than might be imagined. Just when it appears that everything has reached a position of near stagnation, along comes something new. But there is also a fundamental limitation of scale built into any conversion process, which requires great ingenuity and skill to overcome, after the plant has been built. We can examine the basis of these limitations, provided we understand that they are not immutable.

The analogy with a harvest may be taken one step further. Crop production depletes the soil of some of its capacity to produce, and so it is necessary to replenish it with fertilisers and water, and generally use good agricultural practices. All too often it is assumed that this will happen automatically i.e. it is costless, because the replenishment is from the sun's rays and the rain which falls every day afresh, at least in more fortunate countries. Moreover the instantaneous costs of production may take no account of damage to the soil itself, which may lead to disastrous soil erosion after a few apparently good harvests.

In conversion processes there is always some wear and tear of the fixed assets, the equipment, buildings etc, which reduce their capacity to produce in future, and so any projected cost of conversion needs to include an allowance for what has been lost in this way. Of course after the money has been spent on the plant it is no longer a cost of operating, because the capital has been sunk whether the process operates or not. The object of maximising net revenue then is to recover it as soon as possible. This is not technological obsolescence which results from development of better ways of meeting market needs i.e. changes of scope, or depreciation which appears in the accounts. It relates to the energy content of the fixed assets which are slowly being consumed as conversion proceeds; this is inevitable entropic degradation, and in the long term it cannot be hypothesised out.

There is a further point relating to hypothetical instantaneous costs. Low price bargains may lead to repercussions later, by influencing a supplier's ability or willingness to supply. Thus what seems to be advantageous now may adversely affect the assets of the firm at some time in the future, when circumstances will have changed, and so increase the costs of conversion then. By ignoring time, conventional analysis rules out the possibility of this kind of interaction, though it undoubtedly exists. Other "off balance sheet" costs are similarly ruled out though they may make themselves felt with a vengeance later, as the deluge sweeps the soil/assets away.

Even if they are off the balance sheet of the firm, and do not directly affect its costs, they may not be off the balance sheet of the society in which it operates; in effect they may transfer costs to society . Such costs may be difficult to quantify, such as the cost of air, water, dirt, noise and inconvenience to others. These are treated as "external" to this particular type of reckoning, even though society at large may have to pay for scrubbing buildings, widening roads etc.

Costs and revenues in the economic process are measured in terms of money, not quantities of products, because it is the medium of exchange. Money can normally be exchanged for the necessities of life, whereas more imponderable values are less tradeable, especially in times of need. But it should be remembered that in estimating economic values in monetary terms we are valuing apples against pears, a concept which may not make much sense outside economics.

The exchange value of a product in economics is not what a producer thinks it should be, based on costs or sentiment, or what its purchaser would like to pay, but the compromise which all involved are prepared to reach, given the pressures and constraints on them individually. The exchange value or price thus arrived at may not satisfy everyone. It may even offend against the sensibilities of society generally if it places ephemeral luxuries for a few above the dire necessities for many, but they are still the best economic values which can be determined by the collective judgment of all those involved in buying and selling that particular commodity at that particular time under the prevailing values.

Nevertheless it is worth remembering that the economic process is only one facet of society, and that it is for the benefit of man. The arithmetic of exchange may not always express its wider values. If it produces particular results which are unacceptable to society, such as starvation or unemployment, the remedy lies outside the economic process itself in some form of common consent other than money; not exchange but some kind of political solution. The economic process is

The Cost Basis of Economic Activity

necessary to man's existence, but there is no reason to accept that it is sufficient or immutable.

This chapter considers the factors which affect costs according to the conventional treatment, ignoring wider factors, especially time. Costs are treated as if they depend solely on the scale of the conversion process (1, 2). The argument then moves forward into discussion of the problems of responding to feedback from the market, not costs which have already been incurred but those which might be incurred, as well as any revenues which might flow in, as the result of what response it is decided to make.

5.1 Scale-related Costs

The scale-related costs of a conversion process are those which are directly related to the scale of production, that is the quantity of goods or utilities produced by the process. The term is most simply illustrated by reference to agriculture.

5.1.1 Agriculture

Suppose a farmer plants his land with seedcorn and harvests it at the end of the season. This may be represented diagrammatically as in Figure 5.1.

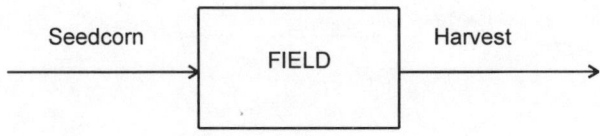

Figure 5.1 The Harvest

In this simplest of systems if the harvest fetches revenue R, which is the quantity of corn multiplied by the market price per ton, and the total cost of seedcorn was C, then the net harvest R_N can be expressed as:

$$R_N = R-C$$

The net harvest is the reason for planting. If the farmer reaped only the equivalent of the seedcorn which he had planted i.e. $R_N = 0$, then he would have produced nothing of value, and at some risk.

Some of the costs which a farmer incurs vary directly with the area under cultivation. For instance if he uses fertiliser or employs someone to plough and weed, these costs will be directly proportional to the area of land cultivated. All such costs which vary with the area of land cultivated are called variable. The cost and revenue relationships which apply under the conditions postulated here are illustrated in Figure 5.2.

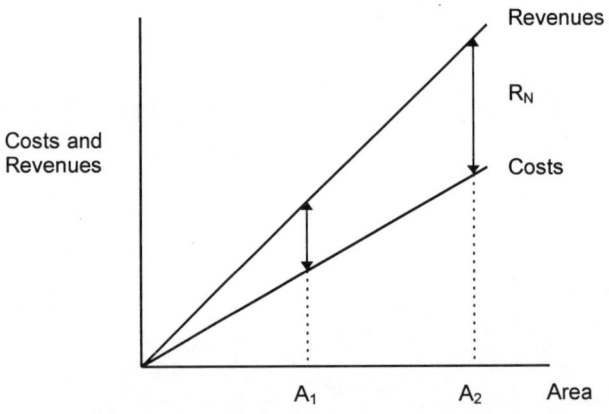

Figure 5.2 Increase of Market Revenues and Costs with Area Cultivated

Hopefully for the farmer the revenue from the sale of the corn will exceed the cost of producing it, so that R will be greater than C. If he cultivates twice the area, an increase from A_1 to A_2, then his costs double and so does his revenue, so that his net harvest also doubles. He may use the best available seed, fertiliser and cultivation methods, but

The Cost Basis of Economic Activity

other things being equal, he has no other way of increasing his harvest except cultivating a larger area. If he cannot do this, since his land is limited, he cannot increase his net revenue and will remain at the same income level for ever, subject to market prices and the effects of weather. If he still wishes to increase R_N, the only solutions are to find a way of realising more than the market price, which penalises buyers, or to obtain a subsidy of his costs, which passes some of the burden to society at large.

5.1.2 Industry

A similar model can be used for a factory, where the fixed assets are not simply land but also buildings and machinery (Figure 5.3).

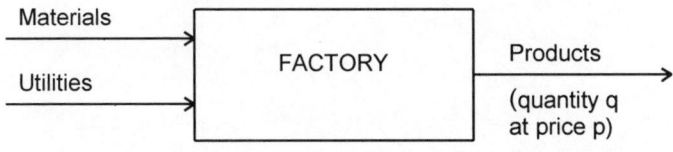

Figure 5.3 Model of a Factory

This is different from the agricultural example, because the size of a factory, and indeed the land which it occupies, cannot readily be adjusted after it has been built in the same way that the area of land cultivated by a farmer can in principle be adjusted continuously at least between harvests, say by buying or selling some. Apart from the buildings, which are constructed to a size appropriate for the total operation, it may include pieces of equipment which are essential to the conversion process, whatever the level of production, and cannot be sold off or added to incrementally. Furthermore such buildings and equipment need maintenance whether they are used or not, and standing charges for utilities such as electricity may be payable whether they are used or not. Such operating costs are therefore independent of the level of production q during the lifetime of the factory.

On the other hand raw materials and the quantity of utilities bought in, such as electricity, are likely to be proportional to the production q. But revenue from the market increases in direct proportion to the quantity produced and sold q, assuming that any quantity may be sold at the market price p. The resulting cost/quantity curve is shown in Figure 5.4.

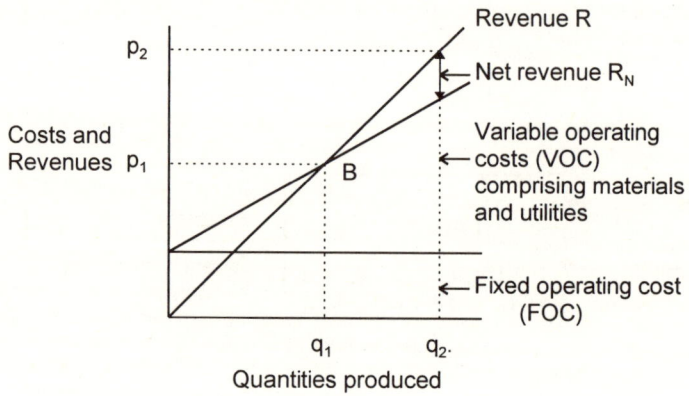

Figure 5.4 Simple Production Curve for a Conversion Process with Fixed Costs

A certain level of revenue is required to pay the fixed costs, and so a break-even point B exists at production level q_1 at which revenue earned $p_1 \, q_1$ just covers the fixed costs and the variable cost of production. At any point q_2 above this level of production the industrial harvest or net revenue R_N can be seen from the graph. It may also be expressed as:

$$R_N = R - C$$
$$= R - (FOC + VOC)$$

The Cost Basis of Economic Activity

5.1.3 The General Production Cost Curve

Conversion processes, such as those described above, are in general intended to operate at a given scale of output. Thus a factory might be scaled to produce ten million units of this commodity or 2000 tons/year of that. If the actual scale of operation differs much from that planned, then the variable costs of each increment of production tend to be different from what the straight lines in the previous graph suggest. Revenue from the market, however, still increases linearly with quantity sold, because every unit of a commodity sold has the same price. The cost/revenue curve, drawn to exaggerate the features, may look more like Figure 5.5.

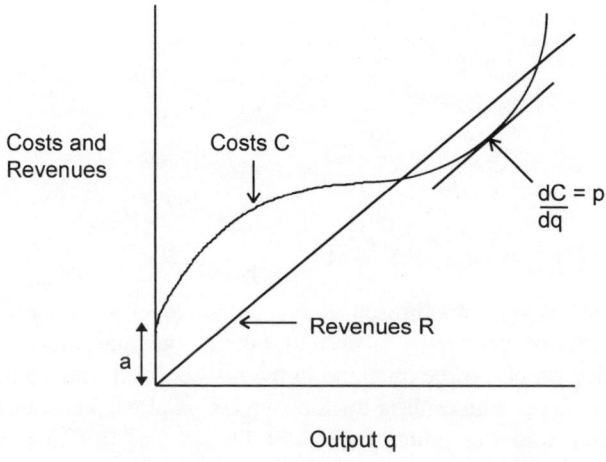

Figure 5.5 General Cost/Revenue Curve for a Conversion Process

If the quantity produced is q, and it is sold at the market price p, then revenue:

$$R = pq$$

as before. Cost has the two components which we identified above: those which tend to be fixed, or independent of the quantity produced,

which are designated collectively as the constant a; and those which vary with the quantity produced, the variable costs, designated f(q). Then:
$$C = a + f(q)$$
The industrial harvest or net revenue of the operation is therefore:
$$R_N = R - C$$
which by substitution gives:
$$R_N = R - (a + f(q))$$
$$= pq - f(q) - a$$

The most efficient use of the resources invested in the operation is achieved when the maximum net revenue is obtained for a given market price p. By calculus it can be shown that this occurs when:
$$\frac{dR_N}{dq} = 0$$

which gives:
$$\frac{dR_N}{dq} = \frac{d(pq)}{dq} - f'(q) = 0$$

or
$$p = f'(q)$$

Net revenue is thus maximised at the output level at which the incremental cost of producing a unit of output, the marginal cost, equals the price which can be obtained in the market for it. Indeed this is embedded in the design criteria for the conversion plant. This output level corresponds to the point marked in Figure 5.5. Running the operation at a higher or lower level of output produces a lower net revenue; the resources embodied in the investment and its operation are producing a poorer industrial harvest than they ought, a less useful activity for the producer and for society than it should be, provided the initial investment itself was a wise one socially.

For the sake of simplicity in this analysis the cost of transporting goods to and from market has been ignored, but geographical location must have an effect. Since not all producers and all buyers can be in the same place, the costs of each of them are increased by the cost of transport, which in effect becomes simply another component of the variable costs of the conversion process.

5.1.4 Efficiency of Production

If at any time one producer has higher costs of operating than the others, he makes less net revenue, because he can only obtain the same market price as everyone else, the market price. He is therefore making less efficient use of his economic resources; his "harvest" is poorer than the others'. The other producers will be better able to withstand a hard winter of low prices and will have more to reinvest in conversion facilities. As a result the least efficient producer, if he does not succeed in improving his use of resources and reduce costs to the level of his competitors', is eventually forced out of business. Thus within the limits of the conventional scale-based analysis the efficiency of producers is continually improved and the most effective use of the resources available to the community is made according to the criteria of economic values. In short the crops should come to be planted where they grow best.

The under-utilised resources locked up in the inefficient operation are not necessarily entirely lost. The producer may learn in time to use them better, so that he can eventually compete on more equal terms, or he may give way to another who knows how to manage the resources more efficiently. If however the inefficiency has a deep-rooted cause which cannot be remedied, or even a producer who is capable of improvement but refuses to act, then the resources run down to extinction faster than ordinary wear and tear would cause them to. They are lost to society for ever, because very little can be salvaged from the ruins which is of use in other productive processes. It is the breaker's yard.

In a "perfect market" situation this loss is only a small part of the total productive capacity, since the postulate is that no producer has sufficient weight to influence the market, but simply joins the general competition to supply. By definition, therefore, the loss is minuscule compared with the benefit to society from the efficiency of the surviving producers, maintained by the constant incentive which is afforded by the threat of extinction. It may seem much less minuscule to those who are forced to adapt in this way. In addition there is the tacit assumption that the process is in some way reversible i.e. that others will automatically fill the gap caused by the loss of a conversion process when the need arises again. This is not necessarily so for a business of any size and complexity, as we show in the next chapter; it may be all loss for society as a whole.

5.1.5 Economies of Scale

For some conversion processes the costs of producing a unit of output may be reduced by increasing the scale of the production operation. Total costs increase with the scale of output, but by less than the revenue obtained in the market place. The conversion operation has economies of scale. In agriculture, for example, it was said that the only way for a farmer to increase his net revenue significantly, once he was farming as efficiently as possible, was to increase the area of land under cultivation. But there might be a case for increasing the area under cultivation in order to make better use of a piece of equipment, such as a tractor, and so spread its cost over more production.

For a specific type of conversion process, costs which are relatively independent of output provide the opportunity for economies of scale, because they do not increase in proportion to the designed scale of operation. For example, it may be possible to build more than one floor in a factory with consequent doubling, trebling and so on of floor space on which to work. In addition utilities such as electricity or gas have a fixed connection and operation charge over a wide range of energy units actually used. Once the connections have been made, it is quite likely that the fixed charges will not vary over a wide range of use. Thus building a larger factory and using more electricity will reduce the cost of the fixed charges per unit of output, if all goes according to plan.

But the major economies of scale have a simple geometric origin, which is virtually calculable. In a building which is the shape of a cube, the wall area will be four times the square of the height of the building. If the length of the base and sides is doubled, so that the building retains the shape of a cube, the wall area will increase four times, but its volume will increase eight times. Assuming for the sake of simplicity that the cost of walls is proportional to their area, then the wall cost of the larger building per unit of volume is only half of the smaller building. Moreover other costs which depend on wall area, say

The Cost Basis of Economic Activity

heat losses through the walls or the insulation to reduce them, are also halved.

Of course there will be offsetting factors such as the cost of foundations, which may need strengthening to take heavier walls, which in turn may need to be thicker to prevent buckling etc. But most materials are a great deal stronger than necessary to do their job; the ordinary building brick has far more compressive strength than its load-bearing normally requires because weight, rigidity, dimension and appearance are the major requirements. Thus the offsetting costs, although not negligible, may be much less than supposed.

However, the effect of geometric scale is most marked in the processing industries. Much of their equipment is in the form of variations on the simple pipe or sphere. The sphere shows precisely the same sort of advantages as a building. The volume increases in proportion to the cube of its radius, but the area in proportion to its square. Doubling the radius of a sphere thus increases the volume eightfold but the area only fourfold. Within wide limits the larger sphere needs only half the material to build it and half the paint to maintain it for each litre stored.

Pipes have other advantages associated with scale too. Their volume increases with the square of the diameter, so that a pipe with twice the diameter has four times the capacity. But their surface area is proportional to their diameter, and when they are used to convey fluids, which tend to move more slowly near the walls because they stick, the further away from a wall the easier the fluid is to pump. As a result a larger pipe can carry the fluid more than proportionately easily, with resultant cost savings in the power and equipment needed to pump at a given rate. Pumps themselves behave in the same way; a pump with twice the capacity does not cost twice as much to make, just as a car engine with twice the capacity does not necessarily cost twice as much, and so on.

The simplest illustration of such geometric economies of scale is in the cost of chemical plants. As a rule of thumb, a chemical plant with twice the capacity will cost only 30-40% more (a factor of $2^{0.6}$). Crude oil tankers show similar effects. Both increased in scale tenfold in the 1970s and 1980s.

No wonder then that there has been a tendency everywhere for manufacturing plants to grow in capacity. And not just manufacturing, because a similar theoretical case can be made for other changes such as bringing dispersed offices together under one roof, centralising services, or local government and many other familiar themes. It can always be calculated that it is cheaper to concentrate and build big. However this is a paper exercise because, quite apart from the damage that such changes of scope might cause to the effectiveness of their functions, which is the reason for their existence, there is another side to the argument, even within the artificial restrictions of scalar analysis.

5.1.6 Diseconomies of Scale

An operation becomes uneconomic for the producer when his production costs are greater than the price which can be obtained for the product in the market. This may be the result of the normal forces of competition inherent in the concept of the "perfect" market, in which case the high cost producers will go out of business and the system will adjust itself to a lower cost level. But there is a special situation which makes production uneconomic that is worth analysis because it is uncomfortably close to reality, not only in a world of imperfect markets, but also in some markets which could in principle be considered fairly close to "perfect" operation, if only human beings did not intervene.

We have already seen how a reduction in revenue would make a production operation uneconomic. As the slope of the revenue line decreases, because price has fallen owing to the balance of supply and demand in a "perfect" market, so the net revenue of the producer must decrease until it barely covers his costs. If different producers have different cost curves, some producers will reach their break-even point sooner than others, and so the weakest go to the wall. The mechanism therefore relies on a significant degree of differentiation between producers.

But what if they all have nearly identical cost curves? This is theoretically possible if all producers invested at about the same time in identical operations of equal efficiency, say as a result of their all perceiving some global opportunity. Such a position is much more likely to be approached if variable costs, especially raw materials available to all in the open market, are a large component of total costs. If producers are similarly resolute to boot, and refuse to give

The Cost Basis of Economic Activity

way (and the concept of the "perfect" market does not require that they should), then they may be forced to operate for long periods under conditions where revenue does not cover costs; they all lose money together. At the very least they will produce less revenue or a smaller "harvest" than originally planned, and the resources available to society have been used in a way which is less than optimum.

Clearly such a loss-making situation cannot last, but the response generated by the market may be very slow. If the producers continue to produce, and also to act rationally, they continue to operate at a level at which they lose least revenue, namely the design output at which marginal cost most closely approaches price. They are particularly likely to maintain production if conversion depends on a stage which cannot easily be scaled down, say one large furnace or one vessel which must be run near to capacity for efficient operation. They also try to reduce prices in the input markets to their operation, and to increase the price of the product. But in a "perfect" market that is what they have been trying to do all along. Nor is there any obvious or prior reason why input costs should be more sensitive to pressure than output prices, particularly if the industries' purchases from raw material markets are only a small fraction of what passes through those markets. Yet there is no "rational" basis on which to shut down entirely. They are caught in an all or nothing situation.

The simplest example of this might be in agriculture where small farmers producing the same crop would find their income oscillating wildly from year to year as they all responded to last year's market prices, and the weather, which presumably affects everyone equally, would exaggerate the effect. They cannot easily scale down their operation between harvests. Another might be in the processing industries, such as petrochemicals or oil, where many new producers with the latest equipment appear on the scene at the same time in response to the same global threats and opportunities.

A neat solution to the problem is a concerted reduction of output in which some producers agree to annihilate productive capacity provided they are compensated by those who do not. This is a collective recognition of a collective mistake under some form of central agreement. It seems to have been the Japanese approach to overcapacity in petrochemicals, and at least it has meant that the market can be allowed to operate once the surgery has been completed.

Other solutions, applied particularly but not exclusively to agriculture, require continuous regulation of inputs or outputs of the markets in order to influence prices, with all the economic distortion that brings. Such regulation normally requires the intervention of an external agency, since producers themselves are forbidden to collude. The "surgical" solution in agriculture is for production to be restricted by agreement to land which is best suited to it, but others to be compensated for what they have foregone. What often happens in practice is the exact opposite; more and more unsuitable land is being brought into cultivation, leading to diseconomies for society at large, sometimes with disastrous results in both developing and developed countries.

5.2 Opportunity Costs

All the costs discussed so far are costs actually incurred, money paid out to someone else in return for products or utilities. Such costs are both sunk in the past and exogenous. They are incurred as input costs when products or utilities move in the direction of time and energy in the economic process.

There is a different concept, which is that the best use should be made of resources in the future. If one opportunity for using the resources is selected, then another potential use will be foregone. The value of the opportunity which will be foregone is termed the opportunity cost (3). Opportunity costs are therefore distinguished from input costs by time. To be meaningful the concept must include the implications of all opportunities. The great majority of them will be irrelevant, since they are clearly less valuable to those concerned than the opportunity selected, but the choice becomes important when the value of opportunities is open to doubt, and/or the decision is likely to affect the disposition of resources well into the future.

The term "opportunity cost" gives the misleading impression that it is some kind of liability which has already been incurred, and so it might be better to consider it as looking forward to see what potential opportunities can be identified. Each opportunity will then have a potential opportunity value, which may or may not be realised, and the associated costs, which may vary from opportunity to opportunity. The difference between each value and its associated costs may be

The Cost Basis of Economic Activity

considered as the net value, the net potential benefit. The potential value of the benefit foregone by choosing one opportunity rather than another is the difference in net opportunity values. This difference may then be termed the opportunity cost of making that particular choice. If the definitions seem laboured, there are many who seem too petrified to take any of the opportunities which present themselves for fear of being sunk by mounting opportunity costs, fear of abject poverty in the face of an embarrassment of potential riches.

Opportunities may be evaluated from two different viewpoints, that of society and that of a business enterprise.

It is wasteful for a society to sell its output to others at a lower price than it could otherwise obtain. Similarly it is wasteful for it to incur higher costs than it need when making purchases from others. The best opportunities are those which maximise prices and minimise costs, if the transactions are with outside agencies i.e. exogenous. However when the transactions take place entirely within a society i.e. they are endogenous, the case is not so clear, because one man's costs are another man's revenues. The transaction is thus a reallocation within society rather than a net benefit to it.

For a firm opportunities are considered to arise in the market i.e. they are always exogenous. The potential cost of not taking the best opportunity is failure to maximise the harvest R_N in future. This may leave the firm at the mercy of competitors who succeed in taking the best opportunity. However an opportunity missed does not actually deplete the firm's resources, and other opportunities may present themselves in the course of time.

One method which is widely used to evaluate opportunities of potential projects is discounted cash flow (4). Probable revenues that would result from making the investment required to take the opportunity are matched against costs year by year of the expected lifetime of the projects. These give estimates of the probable harvest R_N which is likely to be obtained in each year following the decision to spend money. These are then discounted, or compared with the money return which could be obtained by leaving the money in the bank. The comparison is not quite as easy as that because even if the prospective reward from the project is greater than that from the bank, the revenues which the project will bring in future are not certain, and so it is usual to scale them down by estimated probability factors. The technique fits readily onto computers and can reach considerable sophistication. The intention is to take account of the value of money over time.

However the philosophy of the calculation is the comparison of the economic processes of conversion and distribution through markets with the incentive feedback system in the form of money, the medium of exchange. Money is homogeneous through time by definition; it has only one dimension, quantity. Conversion processes on the other hand are certainly not homogeneous through time, nor are people, and hence organisations. The commitment of resources and the application of skills have incalculable effects on costs and revenues, both for better and for worse. Markets are not the only source of variability by any means. Costs may change in unforeseen ways, say through legislation or technology. The environment may change in such a way as to open up new opportunities which can be taken only if the skills are available and the organisation is aware. Such opportunities may be far from the narrow view taken of necessity in an evaluation of probabilities and costs. The analysis also needs to take account of the opportunity to get out of a project half way through, and so limit losses should they arise, and of the other unforeseen opportunities which participation in a project may open up in future. In short the weighing of opportunities needs to be complete, and should take into account not only those elements which can be quantified in advance such as revenues and costs but also those which are unquantifiable. In the long run these may be at least as important.

For an ongoing business which must make investments to be able to match its competitors, there is a further opportunity cost. If the business fails to invest because its discounted cash flow evaluation suggests that the return would not reach its hurdle rate, this might or might not be the right decision; it may simply be biding its time until a better opportunity comes along. If however such analysis prevents it from investing over the long term, but its competitors succeed in improving their positions by well judged investment, it may well find itself at such a disadvantage that it is eventually forced out of business altogether. It will have settled for a safe return of money from the bank, but gone out of business probably for ever, since recovery from this position is almost impossible if competitors continue to exercise their judgment well. The opportunity cost will then have been the survival of the business itself with all the future stream of earnings and

The Cost Basis of Economic Activity

other opportunities for participation and creativity which it would have offered. Compound arithmetic is an aid to strategic management, not a substitute for it.

The notional value of money over time may turn out to be largely a diversion except in the field of financial transactions, where it began The compound arithmetic inherent in the concept sets the evaluations of opportunities on tramlines, and anything which is further than a few years away is so heavily discounted that it vanishes from the calculation.

But we neglect the long term at our peril, whether it be in the improvement of our products and processes on the one hand, or in avoiding soil erosion, industrial waste or urban blight on the other. Our children's futures and our own are in the long term. What is missing from the evaluation at the most fundamental level is time as a variable, specifically the non-homogeneity of real assets through time, and the opportunities which that affords. That is the subject of the next chapter.

CHAPTER Six

ECONOMIES OF SCOPE

Economics is a science of thinking in terms of models joined to the art of choosing models which are relevant to the contemporary world. It is compelled to be this because unlike the typical natural sciences, the material to which it is applied is, in too many respects, not homogeneous through time.

J.M.Keynes

It is a great fault of symbolic pseudo-mathematical methods of formalising a system of economic analysis ....that they expressly assume independence between the factors involved ....whereas in ordinary discourse we can keep "at the back of our heads" the necessary reserves and qualification ....Too large a proportion of recent "mathematical" economics are merely concoctions, as imprecise as the initial assumptions they rest on, which allow the author to lose sight of the complexities and interdependencies of the real world in a maze of pretentious and unhelpful symbols.

J.M.Keynes
(The General Theory of Employment, Interest and Money, Chapter 21, Section III)

Conversion processes run up and down the scale of production in response to the market revenue flowing back to them from the sale of their products. In neoclassical economics the quantity of output is the only change permitted; product and process remain exactly the same,

Economies of Scope

and so the optimum production level can be chosen and related theoretically to the unique price for the precisely defined product in a "perfect" market. Since nothing changes but quantity, there is no way of distinguishing quantity from the passage of time; a timeless process, a contradiction in terms. Nevertheless this is the basis of much economic analysis, though in recognition that the real world might be a little more complicated it is usually qualified by the catch-all hypothesis of "other things being equal".

Other things are never equal. Economic systems are populated by people, who are always learning and adapting, and trying to make better products and processes. They try to achieve higher market prices by giving their products some distinguishing feature which they hope will attract buyers away from other products and/or generate new buyers, what marketers call "product differentiation". In effect they try to move their product into a new market, perhaps thought of as "up market" or a "market niche", but certainly a separate market for analytical purposes, if we adhere to the "perfect" market requirement of a homogeneous product. Even if they cannot do this, which is unusual in these days of increasing technological innovation and communication, operators continually try to improve their processes in order to reduce costs. This may be only commonsense, but it virtually nullifies scalar analysis; the economic process is not homogeneous through time.

All these changes we describe as the scope of the economic process to distinguish it from the scale. If we return to our flowline representation of conversion processes, with products flowing down an energy path to markets and hence to the consumer, and with net revenue from the market providing feedback, then changes in scope take the form of changes in the nature of the conversion processes as they are being continually improved, and changes in the nature of the products as they seek out new buyers. If changes of scope produce favourable results, these are economies of scope. If however the results are adverse, they are diseconomies of scope.

The term scope is not new in economics, though it is certainly not in widespread use. By making the role of time explicit in this analysis, we treat changes of scope as synonymous with the concept of "differentiation" used by Marshall as a parallel of evolution as long as ago as 1890 (1). Either term will suffice, but "differentiation" may have unnecessary and possibly misleading biological connotations, and its adoption by marketers has diffused its original meaning. It is also used in mathematics in differential calculus. "Scope" has the advantage of being a more neutral term.

Whatever the description, the principle is absolutely fundamental, and it may be stated more succinctly by the fundamental rule of systems behaviour that: "an open system orders and differentiates itself in response to its environment". Such ordering and differentiation is change of scope. It consists of adaptation of the system's assets in response to feedback, with consequent effect on its inputs and outputs.

Conversion processes are production systems, and indeed we have analysed the whole economic process in terms of systems. The term "economy of scope" thus implies change in the pattern of assets, and hence in the pattern of use of inputs into the economic process, especially energy i.e. new subsystems and new interactions to form a new, optimum system. It always requires the investment of new resources, even when these are only needed to link the old subsystems together differently. By contrast "slimming down" a conversion operation is not a change of scope. Nor is increasing output by scaling up the process plant.

Time runs implicitly through the concept of scope as through all systems changes. In the real world it is not possible to differentiate products or processes except in time. Changes of scope are driven by the ingenuity and creativity of man for his benefit. The overall result is to move the process in the direction of economic improvements, in effect the behaviour of the economic system as a learning system. Time introduces all the risks and opportunities which present themselves to the processor.

In the analysis which follows we classify and illustrate the various aspects of economies of scope under the traditional economic headings of labour, capital, and land. Energy and information are considered too, because they are fundamental to all systems and processes. The classes cannot be completely distinct from each other because they are all facets of the same changes in what is after all one system.

6.1 The Scope of Labour

6.1.1 Specialisation

The best known example of an economy of scope in this category is the division of labour. This is the splitting of complex processes into stages in which a worker can specialise, thus allowing him or her to perform that particular task more efficiently i.e. at lower cost per unit of effective output than if he had to undertake the whole process. Such an improvement in efficiency results from the more effective learning, greater development of skills and more intensive application over a period of time which becomes possible when a task is easily within the capacity of one person.

This is the phenomenon which Adam Smith described with his example of the pinmakers, who by specialisation were able to produce many more pins a day (2). It is easily confused with advances in technology, capital investment or scale of operation. Division of a complex process into stages may subsequently allow the development of specialised technologies for the individual stages, and this may result in specialised equipment, and hence capital investment. Similarly, if the process is carried out with less labour and/or lower raw material costs for each unit of output, those concerned may in principle decide either to produce more output or to produce the same output with less input. Thus the eventual outcome may be an increase of scale, but the causes are essentially different; it is the change of scope which makes possible the change of scale.

The negative aspect of the same phenomenon is diseconomy of scope through excessive specialisation. Improvements in efficiency may result from the division of complex tasks into manageable stages, but if they are divided too much, the result may be such fragmentation that the individual is confined to a trivial aspect of the process, such as tightening a nut a hundred times an hour, every hour, on an assembly line. The consequence may be boredom and lack of interest in the wider aspects of the job as a contribution to the whole. People cannot be motivated by such a restricted view of the process of which they are a part, and the co-operative framework may then suffer. Specialisation without co-operation is useless. The scope has then been limited to the point that diseconomies occur, and the solution must be to enlarge the scope again by some means.

Specialisation has many different manifestations. For instance shops are sometimes arranged such that one must queue twice to buy anything; once to choose and a second time to pay. Specialisation of the staff promotes hygiene., if it separates money from food. But the cost is the diseconomy of queuing imposed on the purchasers. On the other hand if they are allowed to choose their goods and then pay, this becomes self-service, which has revolutionised shopping.

6.1.2 Technology

Specialisation relates to personal skills, strength, fleetness of foot and so on. But there is a different sense, in which the scope of labour has been increased by enabling people to reach out well beyond their own personal experience: the accumulation over time of an accessible body of technological knowledge.

Skills and knowledge once used to be developed by individual people through their daily lives, with help and encouragement from family, friends or tribe. Writing extended the range of useful sources to those beyond immediate acquaintance, including past generations. In the course of time the development and recording of improved technological methods built up a body of knowledge on which anyone could draw, so that the cost of achieving a particular result in a conversion process was universally reduced; each could build on what had been done before, instead of starting from scratch. The result today is a vast accretion of technological information without which the modern way of life, as opposed to the medieval, would be totally unsustainable. The cost would be too great. Technological progress stems primarily from changes in the scope of the processes in which man invests. Link that to geographical changes of scope, and we have the remarkable growth phenomenon in many of the developing countries.

There is a sense, however, in which new technology imposes a diseconomy on the old; it supersedes it. Factories using old technology are at a cost disadvantage and must adapt or eventually disappear under free competition. But obsolescence as a scope effect is not confined to technology; growth and decay are the stuff of life. Just as this is the source of vigour and change in life, so new technology is the source of growth and adaptation in economics.

6.1.3 Creativity

Specialisation relates to tasks, and technology draws on experience. But there is another dimension of man which transcends both; creativity, perception, inventiveness, call it what you will.

Man is the only animal which can imagine the underlying patterns of change around him. The whole body of scientific knowledge is an accumulation of imaginative perceptions, tried, tested and recorded for others to build upon elsewhere. The result is a coherent interpretation of the framework of physical processes, from the genesis of the solar system to the secrets of reproductive molecules. It enlarges man's perception of the universe and his place in it. It is a discontinuous extension of his being, a quantum leap. Such leaps have led to unimaginable changes in man's manipulation of the biosphere, as the perceptions become assimilated into the technology. Through them the scope of man's influence has increased a thousandfold. His progress is the story of changes in the scope of the resources available to him.

There are no limits to creativity; it is a continuously changing scene. Nor is it confined to the intellect, but it includes all artefacts, all paintings, all sculptures, all buildings and so on which are the result of new perceptions of the world around him. Anything man-made which breaks fresh ground by definition increases his scope. One may think of works of art as of little relevance to economics, but the drive which produces them also produces innovation and growth, and the phenomenon of product differentiation in which the producer rings the changes on his products to make them distinct from his competitors', whether motor vehicles or haute couture. Creativity washes uncomfortably around economics, and while it may produce great changes for the better, its misapplication may produce similar diseconomies.

6.1.4 The Group

Creativity has been used above in an individual sense, but it is also expressed collectively as social organisation. Groups often generate a degree of creativity which exceeds that of any, or indeed all, of the individuals of which they are composed. The scope of all involved is increased. This is the simplest meaning of the word "synergy", which is literally working together.

The scope of people is much wider than implied by the terms economies or diseconomies, or productivity of labour. This is a fact of life that is sadly neglected in the pursuit of the simpler scalar economic effects. People almost always constitute themselves into learning systems, given the chance. They exchange skills and knowledge by being and working together in a complementary way, and so increase their cost-effectiveness over time.

The result may be a ferment which unaccountably gives rise to a host of new scientific discoveries or the high technology complexes of a Silicon Valley. In traditional economics such co-operative effort is usually taken for granted, and simply built into the fixed or variable cost profile, so that each person is treated as a unit of homogeneous labour. The result is a theory of marginal productivity, "laws" of diminishing return etc, which may have been all very well for agricultural labour in the eighteenth century, but scarcely bear scrutiny today. What if the marginal labourer happens to be the pilot of the aircraft or the goal kicker of the football team? Their groups could hardly perform their functions without them; in a world of specialisation the team is the unit which produces. The value of the individual is the value of his contribution to the team, and each one's contribution may enhance the others'. Teams improve after working together after a period of time. Malthus might have seen things in a somewhat different light if he had viewed the world from a less privileged point. He knew about the captain of the ship, but the labour which he described was the apparently homogeneous mass on the lower deck. These days captains are not so readily distinguishable; they too are specialists of a sort. It is the marginal productivity of the group which counts, and that depends on a different set of factors entirely.

The time relationship of people in groups, which may be called "organisation", is so fundamental to the economic process and so neglected in the conventional treatment that we have separated it out for discussion in a later chapter.

6.1.5 The Producer as Consumer

Treatment of labour ignores man's basic diseconomy of scope; he must eat and drink to live, and on a fairly regular basis too. Whereas commodities may be stockpiled to smooth out fluctuations in demand at the opportunity cost of the capital tied up in them, living creatures, once produced, need food and water to survive, whether or not they are taking part in the economic process at the time. Man needs a certain minimum sustenance, which in a civilised society is a basic cost the community must bear. The quantity of people "produced" is not open to short term control by economics. Even if it were, the cost would not be unambiguously controlled; man is the consumer as well as the producer in the economic process, and so the scale and scope of production cannot be manipulated independently of consumption. The economic process is for the benefit of man and not vice versa. This is the difference between a whole economy and its subsystems, such as firms.

6.1.6 Extension of Time

Work occupies only part of most people's day. Thus one of the options open to those in some jobs is simply to phase their work or spread it over a longer time period without necessarily doing more of it, unless the passage of time itself is considered to be work. The small shopowner extends his opening hours in the hope of picking up extra customers who make use of the convenience of late shopping. His unit costs may then be reduced by a greater turnover at the sacrifice of the opportunity cost of his own time. This cost structure is thus linked to the neighbourhood in which the shop is located, and the customs of the people.

If however all the shops open late, no one gains more trade and everyone's cost structures remain comparable. Publicans in Britain have this sort of problem with licensing hours. If all their hours were unlimited, it is claimed that they would all keep the same volume of trade but over a work period which is three times as long, with commensurate inconvenience.

The solutions to a diseconomy of scope lies in a change of scope, for example in this case different establishments operating at different times, and perhaps with different prices.

6.1.7 Language

Language changes the scope of relations between people and allows them to achieve their joint results at a lower cost than would otherwise be the case. Yet there are many situations where people feel that it is a waste of money to learn the language of those with whom they must co-operate. They emphasise doing, not learning. Hence the term "talking shop" for Parliament, as if communication were a waste of time.

But the diseconomies of scope caused by differences of language are incalculable. Wars have been fought over them in the past, and today some small measure is given by the budget of the European Union, a substantial part of which is devoted simply to translating the same material into a dozen or more different languages at a very real cost. A less tangible but nevertheless enormous economy of scope, one which is rapidly declining, was conferred on the USA by its adoption of English as its common language. If it had been divided in its formative period by as many languages and their associated cultures as Europe, its economic progress might have been more chequered.

Nevertheless times change. Translation is becoming easier, both as the familiarity of peoples with their counterparts improves through education and information technology, and as the mechanics of translation lends itself to computerisation. Translation in the central directorates of the EU is not now a problem, and the benefits will outweigh the costs by an increasingly bigger margin.

6.2 The Scope of Capital Investment

The capital assets of conversion processes may often be arranged in new configurations which give lower processing costs without reducing their design output. Similarly products which are the embodiment of capital invested in processes may, if they are differentiated, be improved to give longer life and better use, which in effect reduces their cost in use. Such re-arrangements bring economies of scope. Different types of capital-related economies of scope can be distinguished as follows.

6.2.1 Design

Continuing advances in technology allow processes to be designed in such a way that they deliver the same output with ever decreasing inputs of materials, labour or energy. Thus waste is minimised by planning and the conservation of process energy, and maintenance is reduced by change of design or the use of new materials. It may often be worth spending more on equipment initially to reduce these time-dependent costs. This sort of efficiency is the most obvious effect of scope rather than scale.

However such economies are not confined to processes. Consider the type of passenger trains that need extra labour because they have hinged doors all along each side, any of which may be left open by a passenger and must be shut before the train can depart. More economical trains have electrically operated sliding doors, which can be safely operated by the driver alone, and may also cost less to maintain since they are not slammed. The old trains were designed in an age when labour costs mattered less.

The same is true of offices and commercial buildings where the materials and finishes can affect maintenance costs, and the arrangement of rooms or facilities can help or hinder the processes taking place in them, simply at the whim of the designer. English stately homes, built to grand designs in the days when labour was indeed cheap, have such large diseconomies of scope that their owners sometimes turn them over to the nation to maintain. Features which drew the attention and now delight the eye, the great number of windows with painted frames, the pediments and scrolled columns, the lead gutters, the stuccoed walls, the high corniced ceilings, the grand fireplaces and so on, all add up to such costs that the owners can no longer afford to keep them or bring them up to modern standards of comfort. Elaborate gardens have the same problem. Many redesign their own small acres as they grow older, in order reduce the labour of weeding and mowing.

Even the colour and shapes of products may help to lower the cost of use by reducing the chance of mistakes or damage, and such features often cost very little to incorporate at the design stage. An example of this is the colour coding of electricity cables or process plant pipes. Another is the treads on tires which have been redesigned to give better adhesion to wet surfaces, and now less road noise too. This cuts the cost of motoring as they reduce the risk of accident.

Maintenance of integrity over time is where economies resulting from good design often show up during a product's lifetime. Radial tyres last much longer than cross-ply. Buildings are less likely to burn down and equipment lasts longer with better design. The additional cost for good design may often be trivial in the context of the product's lifetime. What a mistake to absolve designers and architects from the results of their work over the whole of its working life, and short-sighted clients too! Nevertheless it is quite a common practice to make false economies, usually because expenditures are on different budgets: building on the capital and maintenance on the revenue budget. The early builders of British railways even made their separate systems incompatible deliberately by choice of different designs. The resulting diseconomies of scope are still in evidence today.

6.2.2 Shared Assets

Design in the sense used above relates to the permanent arrangement of either assets in a conversion process or features in a product. However there are situations where the use of assets may be continuously adjusted to changing needs provided they are designed to be used in that way. For instance a process plant may be designed to make either Product A or Product B, for which the markets vary independently, so that the best use of capital equipment may be made by switching from one to the other when prices are favourable. This gives them a potential economy of scope. An example might be a factory for making either one type of thermoplastic of another by a simple switch of catalysts. Another example is the manufacture of petrol, a mixture of liquid components from different refining processes with different and varying costs; the proportions can be adjusted to give the cheapest blend which meets the specification at a particular time. Such economies of scope must be measured against the diseconomies which arise from having the additional capital equipment to achieve such flexibility.

An example from new technology is the development of flexible manufacturing systems (FMS). These are automated, computerised and robotised systems which make components as they are required, either individually or in small lots. The instructions programmed into the

Economies of Scope

system switch it from one function to the next in a way which would confuse and tire a human operator. In the extreme example even cars of different types and finishes may be made to the customers' orders on the same production line. The initial cost of such systems is likely to be in excess of simple machinery for making a single product, but when the full cost of the flexible system is discounted over time it may well be much cheaper. Not only is the combined demand from independent markets almost certainly greater and statistically more stable, but starting as it does far back in the manufacturing process, the flexible system also makes or calls on components as it needs them, so that the stocks can be very low. The normal level for car manufacturers used to be components sufficient for, say, six months production. That is, half of the annual output of cars was lying around in stores at any one time.

For the flexible manufacturing system developed initially by the Japanese it may only be a matter of a few days of stocks. The costs of stocks fall in proportion. Moreover a system with such flexibility is amenable to continuous learning and improvement, because the barriers which form a diseconomy of scope in the simple process have been removed. Indeed even without full FMS Japanese manufacturers were thought to have been able in the mid 1980s to make and deliver a vehicle to the USA for $1000 less than their American competitors, not through cheap labour or economies of scale, but largely through economies of scope (3). The proof of this is that they were said to have achieved this result with less capital investment per man. Their competitors responded and it has been quoted that major capital investment for each new model has now been almost eliminated. Whereas each model used to take 8-10 years to introduce, this has now been reduced to five or less.

But not all high technology leads in the direction of such flexibility to reduce costs. A petrochemical complex, for instance, consists of an assemblage of very sophisticated conversion processes which are intricately linked. "Upstream" processes are carefully balanced to produce just the right combination of products to form inputs for the rest, so that the whole becomes integrated in the most complicated network.

The fixed costs of such complexes account for a large proportion of total costs. When the price of crude oil rose dramatically in 1973-4,

The Scale and Scope of Economics

feedstock costs also increased considerably and the balance between fixed and variable costs changed. The break-even point of petrochemical complexes thus fell from about 90% to about 60% of design throughput, which was just as well because in the ensuing recession demand also fell to about that level. This was the scale effect.

The problem was that to pick itself up and become profitable again, the industry not only had to reduce scale but also to change scope by making more of what was in demand and less of what was in oversupply. But the problems of adaptation of such interlinked processes, not only technical and commercial but social, were so great that many complexes remained frozen in their current configurations. In Europe some prompted by governments preferred the very costly solution of waiting until demand picked up, thus incurring enormous losses. Even this was only a temporary measure until the next threat came along. The integrated nature of the complexes, which had wasted no part of the inputs of raw materials in an effort to gain economies, led inevitably to commensurate diseconomies when times changed, and in particular the price of oil increased. The size of these diseconomies could be counted in hundreds of millions of pounds.

In a different context entirely there is an imaginative extension of the idea of sharing capital in the form of using assets during a period in which they would otherwise be idle. A neighbourhood social care scheme arranges to provide those in need with transport in cars which would normally be left in the garage or at a commuter station. The vehicles depreciate and need servicing whether or not they are used for a few extra miles. They may be used to transport the elderly and needy for short journeys at apparently no more than the marginal cost of fuel plus extra insurance and of course the time of the driver, which is gladly given. The capital invested in the cars is thus worked harder with no loss to anyone and considerable benefit to many.

Another example is the car boot sale. People fill their car boots with what they wish to sell and drive to a meeting place which acts as the market place. For no additional capital cost to them, and probably no additional revenue cost either, they can use their cars for a purpose quite different from transportation. This may lead to diseconomies for others if some of the goods sold turn out to be not quite as wholesome as the example suggests.

6.2.3 Experience Curves

There is a well established empirical relationship that in some industries the unit costs of production decreases by 25-30% with every doubling of cumulative output over time (4). As the factories continue to produce, adjustments and adaptations are made to the equipment and its layout and operation in a continual drive to reduce costs, spurred on by competition, and each new phase of investment incorporates the resulting economies of scope.

This phenomenon is not necessarily generated by scale in spite of the linking of experience with quantity produced. The cost reduction stems from the learning experience of the people involved in the conversion process. As one might expect, they learn to produce more easily and cheaply with experience. Those who do not learn, do not survive to appear in the industry statistics.

Some Japanese companies are said to be particularly adept at this; they expect not 25-30% but 35-40% reduction of costs for each doubling of cumulative output, which soon builds up a formidable cost advantage. The secret is to learn how to learn.

6.2.4 Extending Capital

There is a growing tendency to view the cost of developing products in the perspective of a potential series of developments. In this way the costs incurred in the first product may be high, but provided there is foresight, the results may benefit not only the current product but the next one and the next. The capital invested in the first has in effect been stretched over the second and third too. Thus modern aircraft are often "stretched" versions of previous models, with consequent economies in development. Similarly new vehicles from car manufacturers are now sharing designs and parts with other vehicles in different ranges. Contrast this with the short sighted strategy of developing each product as completely independent of what went before and might come afterwards!

6.2.5 Deterioration and Obsolescence

Wear and tear are the changes which occur in artefacts as they are used i.e. deterioration, or changes in quality or scope with time. These are not simply time effects because they depend both on the original design and on the conditions of use, such as maintenance skills and even simple care and attention. But however good these are, the artefacts eventually deteriorate; bearings wear, materials stretch, alignments shift.

The rate at which this happens may be very different from depreciation, which is the rate at which the money invested is notionally consumed. The rate of depreciation is in effect a considered accounting opinion or an agreement with the tax authorities; it operates entirely within the financial incentive system. By contrast wear and tear are firmly in the world of conversion and energy consumption. They are losses in the battle against entropy. The rates of change of the two systems coincide only by chance.

Obsolescence, on the other hand, relates to the battle in the market place. The network of markets brings all goods and therefore all conversion processes into competition for the same revenues. Old products fade away because they become harder to sell. Conversion processes also fade away, whether or not they make products which can be sold in the market place, if their costs are higher in the long term than those of their competitors. Eventually their shrinking net revenues, the difference between these costs and what they receive at the market price which they share with everyone else, undermine such operations to the extent that even their variable costs may exceed the total costs of their competitors. The result is extinction under the pressure of competition. That is after all how the "cleansing" action of the market system is supposed to work in principle.

Obsolescence, therefore, depends not only on time but also on competition. Industries may become vulnerable to competition from far off parts in the same line of business; Europe struggles to keep up with the USA and Japan in the production of the latest integrated circuit technology and so on. But obsolescence also depends on the differential response of competitors to price changes of some commodities for which the world economy moves towards a global market. In the USA for instance a considerable amount of fixed capital investment, calculated to be as much as 20%, effectively disappeared overnight when the price of crude oil rose in 1973, because brand new plant had been designed for cheap energy regimes. This effect was by no means confined to the USA, but in countries with different energy regimes the effect must have been different. Thus in the international competition some competitors might be said to have suffered from diseconomies which resulted from inevitable changes of scope.

A similar problem arises when public standards or expectations change. Buildings and even nuclear reactors on the San Andreas fault have to be reinforced to withstand earthquakes because new standards of safety are now required as knowledge increases. The cost of reinforcements is a direct measure of the diseconomies of scope. Other diseconomies are appearing in nuclear installations in other parts of the world, because of changes in the political and social environment.

6.3 The Scope of Land

Land gives scope for economies both as an element in the conversion process i.e. agriculture, and in a geographical sense as area or distance. (Land as a source of minerals has in effect been treated under capital because of the assets required for production). Closely related to land are the new developments in the distribution of products. These separate elements are considered below.

6.3.1 In the Conversion Process

Consider first the nature of agriculture. As we defined it above, in agriculture the area of land brought into cultivation is clearly a scale related factor. The more land, the more product, though this must eventually reach a limit, because of the limited cultivable area of the earth's surface.

But much of the increase in global agricultural production has in fact resulted from changes in scope rather than scale. Selection of seeds and the act of sowing are changes in scope from their natural distribution. Methods of cultivation are also changes in scope; the medieval field system in which a man owned a couple of strips in one field and more in others, led to serious diseconomies of scope. Even the open nature of the fields themselves led to diseconomies. Rationalisation of cultivation methods to give larger, dedicated fields brought economies of scope for the same total area, and hence increased yield. The whole English landscape was man-made in this way, subject to the limitation of course that man cultivates only at the surface and can do little to influence the scope of the underlying terrain.

Crop rotation is a scope effect. The twice-yearly corn harvests of Ohio are scope effects. Many of the problems which beset the poor and hungry nations result from the diseconomies which are the inverse side; overgrazing by custom, entrenched differences of culture and religious taboos are scope effects. Cultivation of cash crops, where only vegetation for indigenous consumption grew before, is a scope effect. In the course of time, just after the end of the five year period which is all that discounted cash flows really consider, the scope may deteriorate dramatically through, say, drought, as is happening in parts of Africa and elsewhere. The result is irreversible soil erosion, loss of fertility and eventually disaster for the people who must go on living beyond the end of the discount period. This is a diseconomy indeed, especially when the prices commanded by cash crops themselves are low in the international markets.

For developed countries, once all the available land is under cultivation and the economies of scope have been brought into play, the limit is reached. The advances in agricultural technology which have taken place in the world are largely the result of the increased application of energy, both to plough and reap and in the form of fertiliser. Pesticides also change the scope.

But the absolute limit is the photosynthetic efficiency of the crops planted. Neither this nor the quantity of sunlight falling on the earth is likely to increase in the foreseeable future. Thus, though there is no global shortage of food at present nor one on the horizon, eventually there may be well defined limits to economies of both scale and scope in agriculture, which all the subsidies in the world cannot vanquish. The problem must then eventually become not simply the quantity of food but also its quality and distribution, as well of course the "quantity" of people.

6.3.2 Surface Area

The surface of the earth is certainly limited, but any view from an aircraft's window shows that the distribution of habitation is extremely uneven. It is not simply the scale but also the scope of the earth's

Economies of Scope

surface which is important to man. The island of Manhattan is packed to overflowing with people, while a few miles away there is plenty of open space.

Man has devoted enormous ingenuity to making more of the earth's surface than might appear to be available to him. He builds skyscrapers and apartment blocks to increase the effective area of land in a particular locality. He gathers increasingly in great conurbations such as New York, Tokyo or London. While most Englishmen dream of their little cottage in the country, they actually live by choice in or within easy reach of a town or city. Why? The reason is that, in spite of protestations to the contrary, the cost of meeting their needs and expectations is lower in an aggregation of people than in a sparsely inhabited region. Thus the combined costs of shelter, transport, work, food, drink, entertainment, health and security are lower than they would be if the same number of people were evenly distributed. In a small country like England there would be no question of an even distribution of the population because it is much greater than the land and the other resources could sustain. The pattern of segregation into more and less dense regions allows the whole to survive, which is an economy of scope not entirely dissimilar to the multiphase systems which are the lowest energy configuration in alloys and other materials.

That is not to claim that the present scope is optimum, or that everyone is better served in a town than he might be in a country cottage, but on the whole it is probably true that the cost of attaining what people want is less than it would be otherwise. But if that is an economy, there may be equally significant diseconomies. If the structure of a community begins to crumble, it is not simply a scale effect which can be cured by the allocation of more resources, though this is necessary. The cost of the adverse scope may well outweigh what a scalar increase in the quantity of resources could achieve, and so the deterioration continues. The scope of the problem must also be addressed.

There are considerable benefits to be derived from economies of scope. Financial institutions do not cluster together in the City of London because they like commuting from the suburbs or because they like the scenery, which is no better than Wall Street, though image may play a part. Rather it is that being in close proximity to one

The Scale and Scope of Economics

another speeds information and action, and hence reduces the cost of achieving the same result in the market. Indeed participation in some markets such as the Eurobond market in London with its syndicates and its common language, English, may in practice depend on it. The value of a particular area, therefore, is not intrinsic; it is conferred largely by the arrangement of the rest of the community, and if that changes, the value changes too.

All over central London old office blocks have been gutted and then rebuilt within the old shell, so that there is not likely to be much of a change of scale of total floor area. The developers expected that the change of scope which resulted from the redesign, and the rents which tenants were therefore prepared to pay, would outweigh the costs of refurbishment.

But there are diseconomies too. Every day commuters bring their cars into the cities and cause congestion by parking in the streets. This is no more than a change of scope, because most of the cars were almost certainly parked in the streets in the suburbs. It is collecting them in the same limited area which causes the problem, like clogging of the arteries. The result is a cost to everyone who travels by these roads, and a bigger cost still to those who live in the congested areas, suffer the concentration of pollution and cannot pass freely outside their own homes. These are not notional costs, however difficult they are to calculate. They turn up eventually as health charges, maintenance bills, insurance premiums etc. The counterpart of this in the country is those who cannot move for lack of rural transport.

In the UK a decision was made to change the scope of dwellings for a great number of people. They were moved from their old, small back-to-back houses with poor facilities to new blocks of high rise flats. The new blocks housed about the same number of people as the old houses when the spacious grounds in which they were set were taken into account, and so there was little change of scale. The need for investment was taken as an opportunity to shift people from an area on the ground to an area in a tower block.

One of the driving forces behind the change apart from the whim of architects and politicians was the opportunity for economies of scale by using prefabricated building systems. But the new systems did not withstand the effects of time, and damp and corrosion began to damage the structures. The arrangement of the flats was such that

Economies of Scope

frustrated youth soon disfigured the environment and vandalised the lifts, thus isolating people at the top of the blocks. Moreover, few of the people who were put into them were consulted about the change and many were unhappy. The increased costs of maintaining the buildings more than outweighed the economies of scale, and it was expected that many would eventually have to be pulled down and replaced. Such were the diseconomies of scope. The cost to ordinary people's lives was much greater.

There is one further aspect of area which is a source of cost. It is well known in agriculture that the quality of land affects its output, but a similar effect occurs when there is a need to maintain a balance of resources between areas. For instance, if one has three factories in different areas, and they can sell only two thirds of their total production capability, it may not be possible to solve the problem by simply shutting down one factory. That factory may be a vital part of the conversion processes which take place in the other two i.e. the assets, which may not be removable, are in the wrong place for the conditions of the time. Any adjustment will require a change of scope as well as scale. Investment of resources will be required to bring it about.

In a similar vein there is a problem of falling rolls in English schools over the next few years, and the question arises whether there is money to be saved. If it were simply a problem of scale, it would be possible to solve it by shutting down a commensurate proportion of schools as the number of children fell. But it is also a question of scope. Cuts in scale would leave the right number of school places wrongly distributed by area and facilities. It is in fact a diseconomy not of scale but of scope. Problems of scope can be solved only by a change of scope, and that requires investment not surgery.

6.3.3 Distance

The other aspect of land which affects the scope of the economic process is the distance between centres of activity. Transport of products from factory to factory, and factory to consumer is a direct cost component. but new ideas and new technology may influence the total cost, and even turn distance into an advantage by changing the scope of the whole process.

The Scale and Scope of Economics

For example the best site for an electricity generating power station may be close to the users of electricity because of the loss of energy along the transmission grid system. At the same time it will use large quantities of cooling water and must therefore be sited near a river. These are technical factors related to distance which impose certain requirements for a given technological process. In the course of time however a number of changes may occur in the environment in which the station must operate that affect costs in unforeseen ways. Changes in public attitudes may give rise to legislation on toxic gas emissions which necessitates cleaning of the gases before they are vented into the atmosphere, if they are within a certain distance of population centres. An increase in population density or even in the use of cars in the vicinity may cause congestion which increases the cost of transportation or the cost to the community in terms of by-passes or other special arrangements. A change in government policy might require the station to burn locally mined coal, in which case it might be better sited in a coalfield. Or it might allow it to burn cheap imported coal, so that it would be better sited on the coast. All these changes which might occur during the power station's lifetime would affect one of its fundamental costs, that of transporting coal, even though none of the distances changed at all.

Another change which reflects the changes that have occurred in society is the growth of garden centres. Nurserymen used to grow their plants, send out beautifully illustrated catalogues for their customers to make their selection and then dispatch their produce by rail or road at the appropriate times of the year for planting. Spring bulbs had to be ordered in mid-summer for planting in the autumn, and some happy days were spent around Christmas trying to imagine what various shrubs looked like from the descriptions and pictures in the catalogues so that they could be delivered for spring planting. The whole process needed a good deal of planning and co-ordination at both ends: for the nurseryman to grow the plants, and the gardener to prepare the soil. As always the weather was a major uncertainty.

Times have changed with the advent of widespread personal transport. A selection of shrubs is always available within their season in garden centres which are located for convenience of access of the customer. When the weather is right and the soil prepared, he can get into his car and go along and buy what he wants. He can see what the

Economies of Scope

plants look like, judge whether they are healthy and read the description to ensure that they will fit the space and produce the required display. What is more, the plants are likely to survive the move, since they have had the minimum of disturbance on the journey. Plants and packaging are chosen for minimum risk of damage. The scale of distance is probably no more on average than it was. It has simply been allocated more profitably by interposing garden centres, with a consequent redistribution of total costs, making use of the personal transport facility afforded by changing social conditions.

Supermarkets and hypermarkets use the same effect. Customers avoid congestion by shopping out of town by car. They manage their households in such a way that they buy a larger quantity and a wider range of goods than they would from their local stores which have only sufficient space for a limited range. Bulk purchases lead to lower costs and so on. Personal transport has transformed the scope of living and the scope of the economic process for great numbers of people.

An example from industry might be a process for making metal strip for a particular type of industrial customer. Suppose a process has a different cost structure from the traditional technology, as a consequence of which it is able to reach its optimum economy at a smaller scale of operation i.e. use five factories to do just as economically what four did before, a difference of scope. Even if the production cost per unit of output was the same for both processes, the new process would have an advantage because it could change the scale of operation by building or closing a small plant, instead of throttling back one large one to unworkable levels. But there could be a further advantage related to scope if the customer industries began to disperse to make use of more favourable conditions for manufacturing, as for instance has happened in the USA with the move to the South. Factories using the old technology would have to stay where they could distribute to a wide range of customers because of the size of their output, and so they would incur increased transport charges. Smaller factories, however, could be located alongside their main customer, especially if their outputs matched their customer's requirements, and so reap the economy of scope.

Networks of all sorts offer economies of scope by definition. In the electricity industry the linking of England with Scotland and with France promises economies because of different hours of peak use. By

The Scale and Scope of Economics

transmitting electricity from two of the countries to the third at its time of greatest load, the optimum use may be made of the generating capacity in each. Economies of scope, of course, are conditional on the arrangement being reciprocal i.e. transmission both ways through each of the links. The USSR derived a similar advantage because it was so long from east to west that it crossed many time zones, and so somewhere was almost always operating at peak load, whereas most generating systems run below capacity for long periods.

The effect of distance on economies of scope can be seen in the emergence of industries which make full use of global facilities. In the personal computer business, for example, components are flown around the world to have successive stages in their manufacture carried out. This makes best use of the low costs of specialist factories. In process industries, separations of all kinds, such as the refining of crude oil, are a change in scope with products going to different corners of the globe. Transport must be cheaper before separation of materials than after, because of the cost of handling each component separately, but if market prices are different in different places, there may be an overall gain of revenue. In the financial community it has been claimed that London will always have the edge over its rivals because it is the only financial centre in the world where you can call both Tokyo and the United States during normal business hours before going home for the day at a civilised time.

The other side of the coin, as always, is the diseconomies which may result from changing scope. The new supermarkets, hypermarkets and garden centres do nothing for those who cannot reach them, having no personal transport. Moreover the loss of trade may even increase prices in the traditional area where they have to shop, a diseconomy of scope which may bear on the poor, to say nothing of the destruction of town centres around which the whole community revolves.

An industry which felt the effect of changing scope was the British breweries. They changed the scope of the industry by buying up local breweries and centralising the brewing process to obtain economies of scale. But the change of crude oil prices in the 1970s raised the cost of transporting the beer to the customers, who were back in the localities from which the breweries had been withdrawn. What is more customers did not always like the centrally produced beer either, preferring the local brews to which they were accustomed. Thus two diseconomies of scope appeared after they had embarked on their cost-cutting centralisation.

There are numerous other examples of the sort of diseconomies which distance may bring over time. When design faults appear in newly launched vehicles, it is much cheaper to rectify them before the vehicles have been distributed than to re-call them for modification. The same is true of dangerous toys and appliances being imported into a country. It is much cheaper and more effective to stop illegal drugs at frontiers than to try to trace them after they have been dispersed through the networks of dealers. These are really just further examples of physical separation processes.

When the early railway lines were laid in England, the first in the world, the owners imposed a very strange diseconomy on travellers. Even though their various lines linked to form a network, they refused to allow passengers to book tickets for complete journeys where these involved changing from one line to another. Passengers had to leave one train and then buy a ticket for the next, which could be a great inconvenience, especially if time was short. This needless diseconomy of scope for travellers was eventually solved by setting up the Railways Clearing House, which re-allocated the fares between the various owners of lines and probably reduced their costs too.

In the USA the era of cheap oil, and hence private transport, encouraged the development of a style of living in widely distributed housing connected by long highways i.e. having wide scope. As a consequence public transport, which is by definition narrower in scope, all but disappeared. When the price of oil rose tenfold, the society was left with geographical diseconomy of scope which had to be paid for until either the scope of technology or the distributed investment in houses or highways changed, or the price of oil fell again. Technology did in fact come to the rescue by reducing fuel consumption in new models of vehicle. England with its winding medieval road patterns is no less of a beneficiary from such developments.

6.3.4 Packaging

Modern packaging reduces the effect of distance and time on the cost of products. In former times it used to be necessary to transport fresh

The Scale and Scope of Economics

food each day from the producer for more or less immediate consumption. The economic food chain had to be geared to the instant rate of local consumption because the food would not survive long time-consuming journeys in edible condition. Stocks of food were impossible to hold for any length of time, as the seamen of Elizabethan times knew only too well.

The first change in this situation came with the invention of glass jars and tin cans. Canned foods could be kept for years. But the most fundamental changes came with plastic containers and films. Not only are they almost as protective as cans but they are lightweight, flexible and transparent, so that the contents can be seen and the package handled without contamination. The result is greater shelf life, variety of products and freedom of display, which have transformed the distribution system in advanced countries, making possible the supermarkets and self-service stores and a general reduction of the costs of such wide availability. Packaging has changed the scope of distribution and consumption, and brought major economies.

Packaging in the form of containers has also transformed shipping. By packing goods into rectangular boxes it has been possible to protect them from damage and loss, and made them easy to load and stack mechanically. If the boxes should also be designed as the load for a lorry, the cost of handling is reduced even further, an economy of scope on both shores as well as on board ship.

Perhaps the most astonishing new form of "packaging" is the VLCC or very large crude oil carrier, which is used to ship oil from the middle East to all parts of the world, but especially Europe. When the Suez Canal was closed, the smaller vessels of the time were inadequate to bring oil around the Cape of Good Hope to Europe, and so a new breed of tanker was invented, the VLCC with ten times the capacity. When the canal opened again, the ships were too large to pass through. Many such ships were built in anticipation of increasing oil demand, but when the price rose and demand first halted and then began to fall, there was a surplus. There are not many uses for a ship big enough to house a cathedral in one of its main compartments. As a result there was an excess of shipping i.e. scale which was strictly limited in scope. The results were still being felt around the world a decade later. Many such ships rusted away at anchor in distant waters, never to be used. Such are the vicissitudes of the economic process.

6.4 The Scope of Energy

If the economic process consists of temporarily re-arranging some of the earth's resources, energy is what brings about and characterises the change of scope. It enables man's arm to reach much further than before, thus increasing his power to influence the natural environment. One of the features of recent decades is that energy has become popularised to the point where the use of the word has become careless. We have administrators of energy, as of drought, and the newspapers talk, or used to talk of the energy crisis. But energy is a concept, a way of measuring change. It is not a marketable commodity; no one has ever seen any. What is important in the economic process is not just the scale but also the scope of the available sources of energy.

To understand the role of energy in the economic process we must return to fundamental definitions. Every day the earth is bathed in radiation energy from the sun i.e. sunlight. The sun's energy provides man with varying degrees of warmth, depending on the climate and the season, and some of it is captured by vegetation and drives the biological cycle which leads to the growth of plants and so of animals and man. Far more energy falls on earth as sunlight than vegetation can capture. Much of it simply warms the earth where it falls and hence the atmosphere. Much is reflected away from earth again as "earthlight", or re-irradiated invisibly if it can penetrate the cloud cover, witness the chill on a clear night.

But the characteristic of sunlight is that it falls fairly evenly on all areas at a low intensity. Its scope is such that it gives a low "energy density"; otherwise the extremes of heat and light would probably not permit life to exist at all. Nature has responded by dispersing vegetation thinly over the surface so that each plant can get sufficient light, and then hanging out the collectors, the leaves, widely on a framework of branches and twigs, rather like washing, to giver the optimum scope or configuration for solar collection. The radiation thus captured activates the biological processes, producing stores of "energy" in the form of carbohydrates.

But agriculture apart man has arranged the scope of his economic process in such a way that he requires energy in high density forms.

The reason is fundamentally that he requires much of it for eventual transformation into motion, whether for transport or in fixed installations. His concern is to get it in a form in which it is easily carried either with him in his car, say as petrol, or to his factories. It needs to be in a concentrated and tangible form. Whatever its scale, the radiation of the sun has a diseconomy of scope as an energy source for the non-agricultural part of the economic process. Much the same is true of other energy sources which are "renewed" by the sun, the earth and the moon. What is more, they have the fundamental disadvantage that they cannot be easily stored for later use or transportation.

Stores of energy which have a high density come in a limited number of forms: firewood, coal, oil, gas and nuclear. They may be transmitted in other high density forms, what we have termed utilities, for example, electricity, especially at high voltages, steam, especially high temperature, and radiation such as infra-red or microwaves. Each of the primary sources of energy has its own characteristics which determine the scope of its use: coal is a solid, with all its problems of handling and abrasion; oil is most easily stored in vessels and transported by pipe or tanker; gas is readily transmitted under pressure and convenient to use, but it is difficult to store and needs an expensive network of pipes for distribution; nuclear plants are massive, fixed installations suitable only for generating electricity or heat, which can then be transmitted. They all have their own diseconomies of scope, therefore, both for producer and user, oil as a liquid probably having the least.

For oil, gas and coal the process of concentration into high energy form was carried out many years ago by the sun; their diseconomy as fossil fuels is that they lie in inaccessible and hidden places. For nuclear there are the additional diseconomies that the fuel has to be concentrated into suitable form for the reaction to occur, which itself consumes much hydrocarbon and other energy, that the by-products are radioactive for many years and that the installations themselves must be left in place for a century or more, because they are too dangerous to dismantle.

Energy and economics are linked by costs which reflect the various economies and diseconomies of the energy sources described above, but energy is the fundamental variable because it drives all conversion, and forms the economic energy content of materials irrespective of the

Economies of Scope

price. Man has become steadily more clever at producing what he wants from the economic system with less and less energy consumption through the continual differentiation of products and processes. This continual change of scope in production allows a greater proportion of the population to move into the provision of personal services, which require little energy. As a result of all these fundamental changes there has been a secular trend for reductions in energy consumption per unit of gross domestic product.

Figure 6.1 is a graph of aggregate figures for the OECD over the last 42 years. It shows a marked and progressive decrease in the quantity of primary energy required to produce a US dollar's worth of GDP in real terms. There are occasional blips, but the trend is unmistakably down. This is entirely consistent with the systems interpretation of economic processes. One would expect a system to try to achieve its goal with the minimum expenditure of energy. A system which learns, which is an accurate portrayal of economic systems for all the reasons described in this chapter, would continually find new ways of achieving this end.

The trend emerges in spite of the approximations involved in collating such a wide range of economic data over such a long period of time, for example: collection of data on production in different countries; translation to a volume basis with changing compositions of production, which are the reason for the calculation, and during a period in which there was unprecedented growth; choice of exchange rates for conversion into US dollars, during a period which saw the end of the Bretton Woods agreement etc. The source relied on for this analysis was OECD Main Economic Indicators. There are similar problems involved in converting changing mixes of energy sources into comparable primary energy units. The source used in this work was the BP Statistical Reviews of World Energy. Since the absolute levels are of little significance over such a period, the energy/GDP values were turned into relative indices with the 1960 level as 100. Nevertheless the trend was unmistakably down. It would probably hold over much longer periods still, indeed the whole of the industrial period of the world or indeed the life of the economic process so far, if the interpretation is correct, and if the data were available, could be collated in suitable form.

The Scale and Scope of Economics

The same calculations were done for the oil component of primary energy i.e. the oil used per US dollar of GDP in real terms across the OECD in aggregate 1950-92, and they were also expressed in the form of an index with the 1960 value at 100. The result is simple and expected, which suggests that it is valid, in spite of all the approximations mentioned above. The curve is bell-shaped with its peak in 1973, the year of the first dramatic oil price rise. From 1950-73 there was a steady increase in the proportion of oil in the primary energy mix, up to 54% for the OECD in 1973, because of its convenience as a fuel. After the uncertainties of the 1973 upheaval there was a steady decline back to former levels at about 43%. The decline took about 12-15 years, the OECD's response time for investment.

All this was driven by strategic considerations. Anything further from the predictions of price/quantity equilibria would be difficult to imagine. There is no reason why such a trend should emerge for primary energy under neoclassical theory, any more than for wood pulp or tea, since it is treated like any other commodity. Moreover, as far as oil is concerned, the simple bell-shaped curve covers a period when world primary energy consumption increased by 500%, when OECD oil consumption increased by 50% between 1966 and 1992, and dropped back by only 7% between 1973 and 1992. Meanwhile the oil price was roughly constant for 40 years up to 1973, increased fourfold overnight and threefold in 1979 and then dropped back in real terms to about its pre-1973 level. It is much simpler and more satisfactory to conclude that the OECD simply responded to all this as an intelligent system with appropriate response times related to new investment.

The response of less developed countries or LDCs to these to these changes was quite different. LDCs were defined for the period of this analysis as the world less the OECD and less the centrally planned European countries. Additional data were obtained from the IMF World Economic Outlook. Indices were calculated, based on 1960 = 100, as above. The LDCs converted to increasingly energy intensive production in the 1950s, and their primary energy use per US dollar of GDP increased rapidly until 1973. This compares with the steady downward trend for the OECD.

Economies of Scope

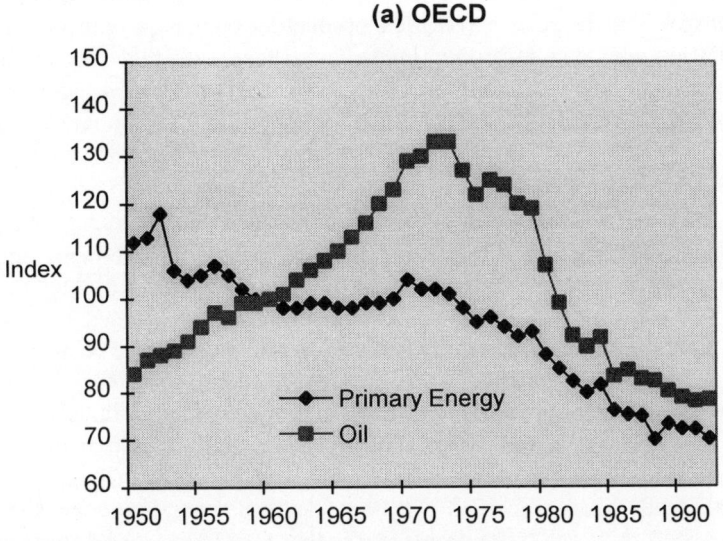

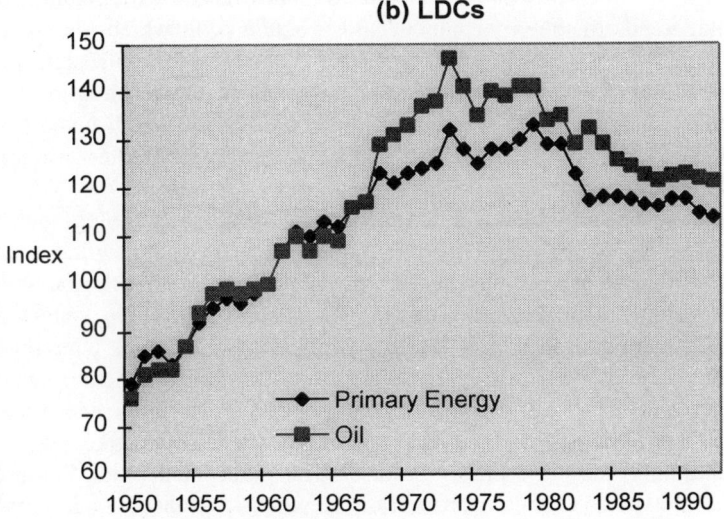

Figure 6.1 Energy Intensities of GDP of the OECD and the LDCs 1950-1992

The Scale and Scope of Economics

After 1973 the index stayed at a high level; LDCs remain energy-intensive with respect to recorded production compared with OECD countries who can afford to invest to differentiate their economic systems and obtain economies of scope. The trend for the oil index for LDCs is very similar to that for primary energy.

6.5 The Effect of Information Technology

When the telephone was invented, a group of eminent and knowledgeable people estimated that the only likely users in the USA would be a few hundred businessmen, because they needed to pass information routinely and quickly. Why should anyone else want one? Much the same happened with the first electrical computers in the world which were invented in the UK to crack German military codes in the Second World War. The post-war UK requirement for computers was put at about half a dozen by a group of officials who had actually been concerned with their development. How could they have been so wrong? The problem was that for reasons best known to themselves both groups based their estimates on the extrapolation of scalar trends of the environment and products with which they were familiar. The results underestimated the adaptability of the societies in which they lived, and perhaps the potential of the technology too. What in fact happened was that in the course of time both inventions changed not the scale but the scope of society, and they brought economies accordingly.

It is often said that the emergence of information technology out of computing, robotics and telecommunications presages a new industrial revolution. If this comes about, the concept of scope shows why: information technology is changing the scope of the main factors of the economic process i.e. labour, land and capital, and with them energy. Hard work can be handed to robots who do not tire, eat or sleep. They can work in toxic and dangerous environments, and if they should be damaged they do not have to be sustained by the community; they can simply be discarded or recycled. What is more, man always consumes a proportion of what he produces, but robots need only electricity and a little maintenance. Man's share of the economic harvest therefore increases, if he can avail himself of it.

Economies of Scope

Computers can accumulate skilled routines and reproduce them accurately and effortlessly time and again. Telecommunications can make their services available anywhere on earth. Distances are shortened by satellites, cables and television. Man's response time to events is equally shortened.

Economies of scale change, and capital can be set to work in different patterns, as it becomes possible to transmit manufacturing expertise and control processes remotely. Nearly stockless production reduces the need for working capital. The accumulation of expertise which becomes available globally promises to reduce the energy content of the goods and services which make up the economic process. Ease of control reduces the cost of differentiation and brings the products increasingly closer to the individual needs of each person.

Industrial societies are indeed undergoing fundamental change. The industrial revolution was largely a change of scope which depended on the harnessing of new and abundant forms of energy. Information technology offers economies of scope which are also great for those who can grasp them. However the impact on production and consumers which brings the benefits must also of necessity force social adaptation. These are different aspects of the same effect. Just as the change offers economies of scope, it also confers diseconomies on those who fail to adapt. The costs of their goods and services will not fall in the same way as their competitors'. Their capital investments will become obsolete sooner. For makers of goods which are subject to international competition this will be damaging indeed. But those who do adapt may suffer too. The cost of adaptation may be that they lose what they value more than the economic gains they make, not least their social stability. It is a question of proceeding with balanced judgment, as always.

6.6 The Underlying Assumptions

6.6.1 Mathematical Representation

The use of mathematical equations is that they enable predictions to be made i.e. the outcome of changes can be calculated, preferably before the commitment of resources. The basis of the calculation is that the equation incorporates what is known about the relationship between the important parameters. The problem of representing economic

The Scale and Scope of Economics

processes in this way is how to express the progressive differentiation which takes place over time.

We saw in the last chapter that the cost of the output of a firm had two components in the scale model; one which was "fixed" or constant over a wide range of production, and another which was "variable" and increased with output. This was expressed by the equation:

$$C = a + f(q)$$

The composition of the fixed and variable categories was to some extent notional; rent was fixed, raw materials were variable but labour could be either, depending on the nature and social environment of the firm. So for a given level of output, the unit cost of the product could be calculated.

Planners recognise that the conditions for which they make their estimates might not obtain in the event, and so they calculate the sensitivity of the results to changes of capital costs, wage rates, material prices etc. Similarly selling prices and hence the net revenue might turn out different from what is expected. When all these factors are considered together, the expected net revenue which would result from the investment of capital in the project must give a satisfactory return. Once the investment has been made, the assumptions are part of the algebra of the fixed and variable costs, and the profitability of the enterprise.

The tacit assumption underlying this scalar analysis is that the aggregates used are homogeneous through time; changes which occur are attributed to prices in known markets settled on the basis of supply and demand. Cost is said to vary with the quantity of output at a particular point in time, and the result is taken to be general i.e. the cost/quantity variables are homogeneous through time. If this is true, the uncertainty of the future can then be discounted by scaling down of aspirations as to the outcome by applying probability factors .

The result can be misleading in a number of ways. It may underestimate the extent to which conversion process can be adapted and improved by the application of skills, which will be developed in time, whether by one competitor or another. It ignores, because they cannot readily be accounted for in economic aggregates, the options for profitable investment related to but outside the remit of the particular conversion process under evaluation which may arise in future. Such options may be turned to advantage only by those who are

Economies of Scope

aware and have learnt from experience in a particular conversion activity. These are part of the information flows which are essential to the operation of the economic process. Indeed they are the skills and experience which have improved the process from its very beginning.

Furthermore it may underestimate the extent to which the cost structure is dependent on its environment, that is the external changes which may bring economies and diseconomies of scope, as they affect inputs and outputs. This also includes the changes in competitors' costs which may result from their internal and external changes of scope, and which are eventually reflected in prices. Costs and revenues, and hence net revenue which is their difference, need to reflect differentiation, not just quantity but time.

A first step would be to consider the monetary flows associated with all of the inputs of materials, information and energy into the conversion system as functions of time, and the same for the outputs. Instead of $f(q)$ there would be $f(t)$, $g(t)$ and so on for the flows of money. Each flow represents an interaction with the environment, but there is the possibility that they too will interact with each other. The costs will be a function not just of the sum of $f(t)$, $g(t)$ and so on, but of their cross products i.e. $f(t).g(t)$ etc. Net revenue will then be the difference between inflows and outflows as functions of time, and so the total net revenue from the project will be obtained by integrating these functions over the lifetime of the project.

A similar technique could be used for the whole economic system which is the network of conversion processes.

When the economics of a conversion process are set out as a function of time, the complexities of the evaluation become clearer. It is not just the magnitude of changes which is important but also their phasing over time. Nor is it just the first order effects which change but also their multiple interactions. This may occur when the interacting factors are themselves correlated with some major underlying variable.

Such multiple interactions become apparent when the system is given a shock. When the price of crude oil increased dramatically in the 1970s, though it was not very large in relation to the Western economies, the consequences surged through the economic process in different ways and at different rates. The increased price of oil reflected immediately in the price of oil products such as heating and transport fuels, and hence eventually in the cost of all materials and utilities. Governments felt obliged to deflate, which reduced the spending power of consumers. Inputs into conversion processes therefore rose in price while production decreased, a double pressure on costs. Conversion processes were soon differentiated into high and low energy users. The whole range of industries had to adapt and many became prematurely obsolete. Some failed and disappeared, and their products, which might have been a vital input into concerns which were still going, also disappeared. All the relative revenue and cost structures were thus shaken by the oil price increase directly and through multiple interactions in some way over the following 5-10 years. To complete the shift, the oil-producing governments began to spend their new found wealth in Western countries, but of course on a completely different range of goods and services from what the previous owners would have bought.

There was hardly an element in the competitive cost structures of conversion processes which was not disturbed in a way which differentiated country from country, industry from industry and firm from firm. The effects rippled through the banking system and made themselves felt in various complex interactions over the following decade. This was an extreme case selected for the sake of illustration, and the results were particularly difficult to interpret, but it is no more than a compressed version of what is happening anyway, much less dramatically and over much longer timescales, throughout the economic process.

This example points up the difficulty of representing economic processes at all mathematically. Algebraic equations are by their very nature homogeneous through time. They assume that the processes which they represent are also homogeneous through time. Probabilities may be introduced to indicate that outcomes are not guaranteed, but they always contain the assumption that, if nothing else, the source of the variability can be known in advance.

In the real world, however, this is not so. Many changes which will have a major impact on the costs and revenues of conversion processes cannot be known or even guessed at in advance. They simply cannot be forecast, and so they cannot be represented by equations at all. They are in the words of Keynes in the quotation at the beginning of this chapter not "homogeneous through time". Back to judgment and experience!

Economies of Scope

Finally, some at least of the incalculable occurrences which will affect conversion processes will provide opportunities for further investment, perhaps in very different areas. The corollary is that they will accrue only to those who are in the business. Economies of scope are all the various aspects of differentiation of learning systems. As they provide a barrier to entry which newcomers must overcome, so they facilitate recognition of opportunities when they come along.

6.6.2 Elasticity

The term elasticity is applied to supply and demand curves to describe the proportional change in the quantity of a commodity bought in relation to a proportional change of price. In some senses it is therefore a measure of the sensitivity to price of the quantity passing through the market. Elasticities however are not unambiguous because they depend on time. There will be a short term elasticity, a long term elasticity and so on.

Elasticity is a term drawn from static physical models in which springs or perhaps rubber bands are stretched "elastically". It is however being applied to dynamic systems, as we have seen from the model of the "perfect" market. The different elasticities may therefore be considered as the response to the expected markets to changes with different response times. The difference between them reflects the adaptations with time which are going on in the supplying and customer networks i.e. changes of scope. The above treatment has dealt with costs rather than prices, but in the long run prices must reflect costs if there is any semblance of competition. There is thus a direct link between elasticities and economies of scale and scope on the supply and demand sides. A particular elasticity is in effect a measure of the sensitivity to change of scale within a given scope.

6.6.3 Implications for Firm Size

The "perfect" market implies that anyone can enter a market and survive, if they can command similar efficiency in the conversion process. The outcome should therefore be a large number of firms of similar size, since none can gain sufficient advantage to outgrow its rivals. If some disappear, others spring up to replace them, so that the balance is maintained. Since the number of firms is large, they will all be relatively small. If there are economies of scale in a conversion process, the competition to enter the business is more restricted. The struggle is between converters who can lay their hands on sufficient capital to lay down their conversion process on the same scale as their competitors. If it is quantity which determines cost, there should be no problem; anyone with capital should be able to match General Motors or Nissan. The result should then be a smaller number of large firms of equal size.

However it is manifestly untrue that anyone with sufficient capital can succeed in those businesses, and the reason lies in economies of scope. It is not simply a question of money, but of people, experience, skills, design, technology, location, layout, flexibility of manufacturing, organisation, politics, preferences and so on; in fact all the components of scope acting over the lifetime of the asset. The population of potential manufacturers is therefore much more limited than "perfect" markets or even economies of scale indicate.

Furthermore, once a firm has achieved economies of both scope and scale, the problems of dislodging them become almost insuperable. Capital investment alone cannot achieve it. The need is for a change of scope, but money can buy economies of scope only if it goes hand in hand with time, so that the investment is even more risky than scale suggests. The competition is changing and learning all the time.

These are barriers which impede potential entrants into any but the simplest of businesses. The result is that there is likely to be a relatively small number of firms which can capture economies of both scale and scope. These will grow large. The rest, which will comprise the great majority, will be closer to the "perfect market" size i.e. small. The predictable outcome is a bimodal distribution of firm sizes, with the middle being fairly sparsely and temporarily occupied.

Scope also explains why economies of scale cannot be extrapolated ad infinitum, whatever the paper calculations say. As the scale of operations increases, further economies of scale may be achieved, but diseconomies of scope begin to arise (Figure 6.2).

At some scale of operation these increasing diseconomies begin to outweigh any economies to be gained. The firm in question has then reached the optimum size which it can attain. Whether this is enough for it to survive against the competition, only time will tell.

Economies of Scope

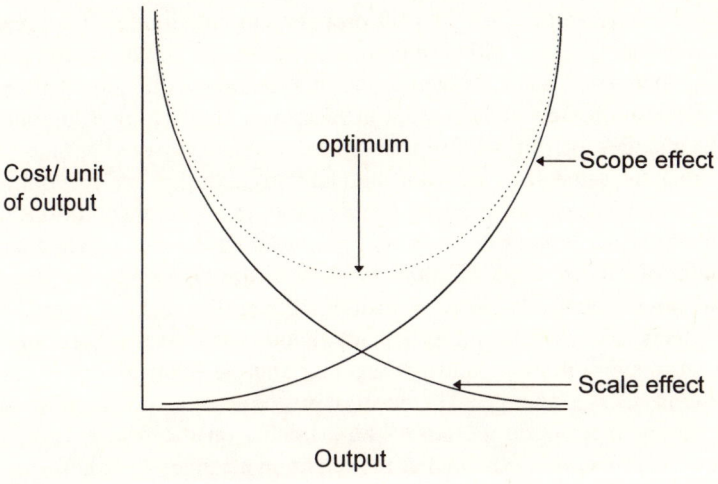

Figure 6.2 Optimum Size of a Firm

6.7 Conclusions

The revenue flowing back to a conversion operation, which in a money economy is the reason for its existence in the long run, can be increased by two means which are specifically excluded from orthodox, scalar, economic analysis. First the product may be improved or made more suited to the needs of its potential customers than the products of its competitors, thus commanding a higher price and/or selling a greater quantity. Secondly the process may be improved to make the product more efficiently, that is with less of the inputs which it requires, especially energy and materials. Both of these means of improvement may be called changes of "scope", either of the product or the process. Continuing changes of scope are the normal state of affairs, as a look around any real shops and factories will confirm. Indeed many people are permanently employed to bring about such changes, because of their vital importance.

Improvements brought about by such means are called economies of scope. Diseconomies of scope occur when changing circumstances cause the economics of products or processes to deteriorate. There may two reasons for this: either their consumption of inputs, especially energy but also materials which are not readily available, may be excessive in the new environment in relation to their required outputs; or the changes may be so abrupt that they have no way of adapting. Or of course the same may occur through bad initial design and planning.

Economies of scope are irreversible under the normal conditions of exchange. Once good processes and products have been designed and introduced, it is unlikely that they will disappear. Only global catastrophic change is likely to dislodge them, and even then only if the effects are uneven, and by chance favour some over others, since otherwise every producer suffers together and the relative competitive positions do not change. The technology expressed in the form of economies of scope is therefore like a ratchet on the advance of the economic process; in effect what is once known cannot be unknown.

Economies of scope thus confer permanent advantages. They bring in more net revenue than their competitors can muster, and reinvestment of this brings still more economies and still more revenue. The process is in principle endless, because there is no limit to the changes which advancing technology can bring about.

Competitors can match economies of scope only by investment in all the various aspects of products and processes described in the text. All changes and improvements in scope require the investment of new resources. Reshuffling the existing assets is not by itself enough; even linking existing assets together differently needs new investment. While all this is going on, of course, time is still marching on, and economies of scope are being extended still further by those who have them; the target is moving.

The cost of the investment needed to obtain comparable economies of scope may be called the "competitive advantage" which one producer has over another. It presents a barrier to new entrants. In the absence of funds, which must be additional to those required simply to run the existing business, there is no reason short of incompetence on the part of those who have the advantage why their competitors should

Economies of Scope

ever catch up under the normal conditions of exchange through even imperfect markets, provided buyers make rational decisions as individuals about price and quality, since economies of scope produce what buyers want. After all, it is the producers who have economies of scope who are better able to produce what buyers want.

The result nationally is likely to be a bimodal distribution of firm sizes, with a small number of well established large firms and the rest much smaller. (Size is of course a relative term, and depends on the nature of the business). Internationally the result is likely to be a perpetual, gross imbalance between producer nations, once economies of scope have been established, by whatever means, unless extraordinary measures are taken to counteract them. The converse of this is that economies of scope, once lost, are almost impossible to re-establish when exchange is through the normal market mechanisms.

Compare this with the neoclassical world of "perfect" markets and the general "equilibrium" to which all economic activity would automatically return, if it were not for the intervention of people as learning systems. Since scalar analysis is misleading, all the conclusions which flow from it are likely to be false. In fact the comfortable view that there is some underlying economic balance is misguided; economies of scope lead to increasing polarisation. Competition is no longer simply a question of reducing input costs per unit of output. Differences are reinforced, especially as economies of scope lead to the possibility of much increased scale, and hence economies of scale too.

Competitive advantages are not the same as comparative advantages of which conventional economics speaks. Comparative advantages are generally thought of as some kind of natural advantage conferred by ownership of raw materials or favourable location or geography. People then make the best of what they have; if they cannot grow their own wheat as cheaply as their neighbours, then perhaps they are better at fishing etc. Even then it is assumed that everyone will have the chance to be good at something. If not, then what?

Competitive advantages by way of contrast are built up by planning and organisation, and perpetuated by reinvestment in further economies of scope, later reinforced by scale. Products and processes are targeted which are particularly likely to yield economies of scope.

The Scale and Scope of Economics

These are areas of high added value per unit of output and high volume, e.g. cars, not agriculture where the value added is often comparatively low. Then resources, especially research and engineering, are concentrated on improving these products and processes, in order to obtain a competitive advantage. Through competition among the limited number who can afford such activities, products and processes are continually improved, which benefits buyers. This is almost always an incremental process, so that none of the producers gains such an advantage that he can never be caught. Thus they all improve together, for the benefit of all.

Economies of scope are another way of describing the differentiation of an economic system in response to changes in its environment. Predicting the course of this process is difficult because the future is uncertain, and understanding, awareness, experience, skill and vision are better guides than mathematical calculations; it is the only safe way to put to sea. Essentially this is because economic systems are not homogeneous through time, but it is only factors which are homogeneous through time that are amenable to calculation. However two things are certain. First, low energy processes are a better bet than high energy competitors, because process energy is pure loss; energy efficiency is always an advantage. Secondly, you have to be an operator of conversion processes to reap economies of scope. Instantaneous or on-off commitment is not sufficient; experience and expertise are all.

Development of economies of scope requires a planned succession of investments, whether in a firm or a country. Planning and execution of such a sustained investment pattern is called strategic management. In the absence of strategic management economies of scope can be achieved only by chance, because they require a consistent response to competition. Strategic management applies to decision-making for a whole system, whether a firm or a country. Foreign investment in effect shifts the locus overseas, quite possibly to competitors; countries which rely excessively on foreign investment forfeit strategic control.

In Anglo-Saxon countries the pursuit of economies of scope, sometimes called "synergy", often takes the form of mergers and acquisitions. This amounts to rearranging the nation's share portfolio. The problems of achieving economies of scope in operations, where it counts in the competitive race, are much greater. In the UK much

Economies of Scope

emphasis has been placed on changing scope by centralisation, and on curbing the power of trades unions, who may rely on diseconomies of scope to attain their objectives. These are essentially the priorities of politicians, and they have drawn attention away from real national assets.

Meanwhile in South East Asia much bigger things are afoot. National strategies, often aided at some stage by protectionism, copying and even counterfeiting, have been directed towards gaining economies of scope through technology, followed by economies of scale with exports the priority. If they had followed orthodox economic analysis, they would have stuck to activities which used their "comparative advantage" of cheap and plentiful "labour", like growing rice.

One of the best examples of a country which makes the most of its scope must be Switzerland. A small country in a large continent heavily marked by frontiers, it seems to have little in the way of economic advantage. Two thirds of it are Alpine rock, the other third has been too accessible to other nations for comfort. For much of its history its people had to fight as mercenaries in its neighbours' armies in order to scrape a living.

Consider how it has matched its scope to the economic environment. Forbidding mountains have been opened up to the outside world as an asset. Climbers pit their wits against rocky precipices with the help of Swiss guides. Skilifts operated by Swiss carry winter sportsmen up to carefully marked slopes for some of the finest ski runs in the world complete with Swiss instructors, chairlifts carry summer visitors to the mountain tops, and at the summit of each is a Swiss restaurant to give sustenance. In the summer the cattle feed on the high mountain slopes and in the winter they are sheltered below. In each valley there is a village of hotels, and each is reached by a network of ever improving roads and railways, diligently kept open for as much of the year as the snow permits. No earning asset is out of use for long here.

But this is not enough to buy abroad all that the Swiss need to keep them as well fed and provided for as they would wish, and so the rest of their assets are fully used too. The third of the country which is plain is fully clothed in farms and even vineyards. In the towns industries have grown which sell special products such as chemicals and pharmaceuticals, high in skills so that they are not easily matched by competitors, but low in imported raw materials. Other industries make the most of the timber products produced in the mountains where the trees serve the purpose of protecting homes from avalanches.

But the shrewdest move has been into banking, where nothing need be processed but information, whence no pollution and no (imported) energy consumption. Even banking has its own special economy of scope afforded by secrecy. All this is backed by a social and political structure which encourages the total use of available resources, gives every man, though perhaps not yet every woman, a voice in the community and eschews violent changes, economic, social or political. Everything points in the direction of sustaining long term economic growth by earning in world markets, minimising its own total costs by making maximum use of its scope and safeguarding its indigenous economic activities as necessary.

Underlying the argument of these last two chapters is the question of economic growth. Economies of scale and scope reduce the real cost base of GDP. They allow an economy to produce more and more output from less and less input, which is economic growth. To obtain such economies requires planning and organisation, or they can happen only by chance. Growth takes place when these come to fruition in the form of investment in production systems. The improvements which are continually built into new equipment, for instance, are alone enough to give an economy a certain buoyancy. The process by which these, as well as the more spectacular changes which catch the public imagination, come about is called technological innovation.

Chapter Seven

THE PROCESS OF TECHNOLOGICAL

INNOVATION

There is nothing more difficult to arrange, more doubtful of success, and more dangerous to carry through, than to initiate a new order of things ..... Men are generally incredulous, never really trusting new things unless they have tested them by experience.
Niccolo Machiavelli, The Prince

..... he that will not apply new remedies must expect new evils. For time is the greatest innovator.
Francis Bacon, Of Innovations, The Essays

The term "innovation" is used here to describe the deliberate process by which a new product or process comes to be sold in the market. Technological innovation applies to conversion processes, which require the use of energy, or their products, which have an economic energy content. It is therefore a function of all the forces which shape markets: manufacturing, processing, technology, buying, selling, information, prices, costs and so on. Since by this definition it is not a matter of pure chance, it requires a degree of organisation. The innovating organisation may be a whole company or it may be an individual. The above analysis of economies of scope suggested that it is more likely to be a team effect. Other forms of innovation relate to the sale of services within what we have defined as the facilitation system. That sort of exchange is not specifically considered here because it involves different adaptation processes and response times, and does not of itself add to the quantity of goods or utilities sold.

Innovation is to be distinguished from invention, which we describe as the process of discovering something completely new i.e. a new fact or relationship, which may turn out to be an important scientific advance or a piece of ingenuity. Invention enlarges the scope of man's awareness, but it does not necessarily have direct economic value in itself. If it is sold, it is the sale of an idea, an exchange of a little creativity for an incentive within the facilitation system. It is not marketed as a product of a conversion process. No energy of conversion is involved. The great majority of inventions do not enter into the economic process, and they do not become innovations until that happens.

The first point to note is that this definition of innovation excludes the normal effects of competition envisaged in "perfect market" theory. Such competition requires that there should be a continual stream of firms entering or leaving the market, as prices are driven relentlessly down towards costs. The new entrants believe they can achieve a lower cost structure by more efficient operation of the given conversion processes, because their entry will by definition drive down prices still further. Those who leave the market have been unable to compete in this limited form of efficiency, and so they are driven out for lack of net revenue.

Simply running up and down the scale of production of the given process is similarly excluded. That is the normal effect of competition, albeit this time in an "imperfect" world, away from the theoretical "optimum" output level. Nor does it count as innovation if it simply involves investment in larger factories using the given processes. In both cases the goods or utilities are already being sold by the firm in the market, and changing the scale of supply by these methods simply affects price by changing the quantity available.

Innovation is therefore a scope effect. It may be defined as the process by which a firm succeeds in achieving new sales in the market place by changing the scope of conversion processes rather than the scale. This change of scope can take one of two forms; a cheaper method of making a commodity product or the development of a new differentiated product.

If the change of scope results in a new process for making a product or utility which is already being sold, this cannot be differentiated from the existing product or utility in the market concerned. To be successful the new process must therefore make it at a lower unit cost than the existing processes. The result then is that either the price of the product falls, and pressures to improve are imposed on competitors, or more net revenue is accumulated, which allows investment in even more cost-reducing measures.

Alternatively the change of scope may take the form of developing a new product or utility i.e. one which is not already available. This will be a new market by the definition of the "perfect market". What the firm is in fact doing is either to attract new money which might otherwise have been saved, or to attract the expenditure of buyers away from markets for other goods and utilities, which they might otherwise have bought. Innovation then includes competition between markets for goods and utilities which buyers may consider to be alternative candidates for expenditure i.e. differentiated. This is closer to the common view of innovation, which is that it implies step changes or "breakthroughs" in new technology.

The broad categories of innovation are therefore:
- the introduction of a process for making at a lower unit cost a non-differentiated product which is sold into a commodity market, and
- the development and sale of a differentiated product which will draw buyers away from other markets, or draw money into the market which would not otherwise have been spent.

We saw that buyers make their production decisions on the basis of maximising the net revenue R_N which they expect to earn over the lifetime of the product, where

$$R_N = R - C$$

and R is the revenue earned in the market and C is the costs. The parallel for buyers would be that they expect their purchase which costs them R to bring them maximum net benefit B_N over the lifetime of the product, where

The Scale and Scope of Economics

$$B_N = B - R$$

and B is the total benefit. Putting this in the form of an equation implies that B can be quantified in some way, but this need not be so; in any case there must be as much uncertainty for a purchaser as there is for the supplier at the time of investment, and so this is common to expectations in both equations. As long as the purchaser thinks that the benefit will outweigh the costs, the principle holds good.

More important is the requirement that buyers are prepared to take the risk of buying something new. It implies an informed buyer, a recognition that things could be better and an intent to pursue possible solutions; otherwise innovation simply cannot happen. It is not enough for buyers to wait for innovations to float by or drop like plums off a tree. Nothing ventured, nothing gained on either side. The only other attribute which might inspire a buyer is curiosity, which is useful, and perhaps even vital, but may not be sufficient.

There is no reason to postulate that decisions concerning innovation involve anything more than expectation of B_N as far as the buyer is concerned. In the case of a cheaper commodity, he will have no way of knowing, nor will he care, whether it is made by a new process or not; the price will simply fall and the buyer will accept it as his due. In the case of a new differentiated product or utility it will also provide what the buyer wants to buy at a lower cost than before; since it did not exist, the cost may be considered to have been infinitely high until it became available. As soon as identical products appear from other suppliers at a lower cost to him, he will according to market theory buy those instead. Similarly if yet another new product appears which tempts the buyer away, it is in effect providing something which the buyer likes even better in relation to its cost. In each case the basis of the decision is cost relative to the benefit which the buyer expects to receive in the long run (1): not cost alone, or potential benefit alone, but the two weighed against each other. It requires an understanding of both elements, and it is a more rational process than is commonly believed.

The total cost to the buyer of a new product is not necessarily as simple as the market price. Its purchase, which is in effect a response to the pressures transmitted by the exchange of the market place, may have significant implications for both the buying and selling organisations. Any increase in costs beyond what is paid in the market place must therefore be deducted from the benefit derived from the purchase.

This is the crux of the problem of innovation. It requires a change of scope in all those affected by it, sellers and buyers alike, and hence a readiness to change. Innovation is a force for renewal which is brought to bear on economic and therefore social and political systems. If it causes pains of growth and adjustment, these must be borne within limits, while mitigating the effect on people as much as possible, because it re-invigorates the social processes. The alternative for most people is economic stagnation and eventually decay. The proviso is that the rate of change should be within the ability of society to adjust to, and the direction should be useful i.e. not simply change for change's sake, or the whole process will be destructive.

The goal of technological innovation is therefore the introduction of economies of scope to obtain new benefits. This chapter examines the complex nature of technological innovation, discusses the origin of some of the observed phenomena, and demonstrates the formidable obstacles facing the innovator, especially in an uninformed or uninterested society: the same obstacles which resist any change of scope.

7.1 The Nature of Technological Innovation

The process of technological innovation is the arrangement of materials in a new way to produce a new result which is of economic value. This may be the arrangement of materials at the elementary, say atomic or molecular, level; or of components, as in the design of new machines; or of the relative positions of components, for example the location of nodes in networks. These are the three levels at which the scope of the economic process may be changed.

Technological innovation cannot occur without some change in the way materials are ordered. It follows that all technological innovation flows initially from some change in a conversion process. Thus technological innovation is the result of investment in conversion processes, where investment is defined as laying down fixed assets, and so it requires a change in the use of energy consumed during conversion to make useful products. Not all investment produces new conversion processes; some may be simple replacement of worn equipment. Investment is therefore a necessary but not sufficient condition of innovation.

At the elementary level there are many examples of changes in materials which have been innovations. Each new material in the ages of man has been a fundamental innovation: stone, bronze, ceramics, iron, steel and plastics and rubbers. With the advance of technology the list has become never ending: stainless steel, nylon ropes, polyethylene films, rubber tyres, high tensile steels, ceramic engines, polyaramid sails, antibiotics and so on. The basis of the latest technological revolution is the silicon chip, extremely refined crystalline silicon, having atoms perfectly arranged with only one part in a billion of impurity. The electronic properties are selected by controlled diffusion of other atoms into the silicon structure. There are also different substrates such as gallium arsenide with different atoms diffused in for special effects. Lasers are the stimulation of materials through ordering in a particular way at the molecular level. Optical fibres which carry pulses of light are extremely pure glasses atomically arranged to give optical gradients. New chemical processes are appearing based on catalysts which are atomic or molecular arrangements of materials such as platinum on silica. All are continuously improving.

The next step up is the design of manufactured components. The common element in design is the use of materials, or their relative arrangement, to give the desired result at minimum cost. That is not to say that designers work down to the lowest possible cost, but that anything added which does not contribute to the effect that the buyer wants, is superfluous and therefore increases cost without benefit.

The essence of good design is that it makes itself felt throughout the lifetime of the component, no less than arrangements at the atomic or molecular level. Apart from the obvious knobs which fall off, the corners which get chipped and the joints which come loose, all of which are materials problems, there are the complex fabrications like the fascia panel of a car. These have now become single plastic mouldings which replace dozens of separately formed components and the screws that held them together, and worked loose during normal use or were taken out by the mechanic and never replaced. The more expensive moulding gives an economy of scope measured over the whole lifetime of the vehicle. Other examples abound. Tin-openers

The Process of Technological Innovation

with a smooth cut have largely replace those which left jagged edges at untold costs to the user in cuts and scars. Controls of all sorts of equipment are more economically arranged and seats more comfortable to work from, at little or no extra cost, with fewer backaches as costly consequences. Heating and ventilation systems have controls which perform better and save energy. Video screens are being changed to reduce eye fatigue of operators, which reduced their effectiveness and induced mistakes. Electric light bulbs are being designed for longer life. Lead acid batteries are being designed which do not spill sulphuric acid during use and corrode and burn. The progress to better components under the pressure of competition in the market is never ending. Indeed it is intensifying in markets which are becoming more international.

The most significant change which is occurring at this level of innovation arises from flexible manufacturing systems or the first step towards them, the sharing of design and manufacture of components, and the increasing use of robots and automated handling, which takes basic materials and turns them into whichever components are needed at the time. The system contains all the necessary information, and switches from one to another without delay and without tiring. The speed with which the system can respond to instructions will itself accelerate the innovation process by increasing the scope of possible changes in the design of components and reducing the time needed to introduce them.

Flexible manufacturing systems themselves are examples of the third level of innovation, the spatial arrangement of components and hence the link between them. Patterns of communication have changed and are continuing to change as a result of new technology in the use of energy and the convergence of computing, data manipulation and telecommunications. Flexible manufacturing systems manufacture components in situ rather than having them made by supplier industries and transported to an assembly plant in batches. New configurations of satellite factories begin to emerge. The new arrangements reduce both the time of response to market changes and all the stocks of components which are needed to give flexibility of response in conventional systems i.e. they give economies of scope.

Networks of all sorts are potential sources of innovation at the spatial level because they allow new arrangements to be made which reduce costs or introduce new benefits, whether in the form of components or a conversion process. The introduction of electricity allows machines in factories to be arranged much more efficiently and safely with respect to each other (2). Belts and pulleys imposed severe constraints on the physical location of machines in relation to the old steam engines, if too much power was not to be wasted in transmission. Availability of electricity from a grid promoted the same improvements universally in every home, factory and office, in the streets and the highways. In the same way major opportunities for innovation are occurring now with the launching of communications satellites and the replacement of copper communications cables by optical fibres. New roads have similar effects.

Every one of the above innovations stems ultimately some improvement in materials, the way in which materials are engineered together in new systems or the networks into which they are formed.

The other spatial element of innovation concerns buildings, that is the internal arrangements of structures, which may be considered as components which house people. It is not generally recognised how much architecture influences behaviour. Buildings house not simply people but organisations, which function in different ways according to their spatial distribution (3). Behaviour is an important aspect of innovation: to bring people together in new ways may have a considerable effect on their productivity and creativity. A brand new office tower block may in fact be much less conducive to effective operation than a ramshackle collection of huts on the ground. New technology may also make possible new arrangements of offices whether advantageous or otherwise. New building technology was imposed on the tenants of local authority housing with disastrous results for some, a social innovation with repercussions far beyond what the local planners envisaged.

Technological innovation, by definition, can only make itself apparent with the passage of time. Time must elapse while new arrangements are being set up, and even more before economic benefits can be demonstrated.

7.2 The Stages of Innovation

The layman's view of innovation is that a bright idea occurs to someone who rapidly turns it into wealth, rather like the exchange of groceries for money in a shop. Innovation is thus perceived to be simple and quick, a matter of individual perspicacity and motivation.

As a general rule nothing could be further from the truth. Innovation is chiefly about the matching of organisations in pursuit of a goal. The market place provides a medium through which this can happen.. The innovating organisation is usually a team. Only in exceptional circumstances does it consist of one person; the complexity of modern technology is such that it is comparatively rare for a single person to be sufficiently widely versed to be sole innovator. Even when that seems to be the case, further investigation usually shows it to be a misconception. The initiator of the innovation marshals a team around him as soon as he has time.

Consider first the innovating organisation. The individuals who form the teams which are engaged in innovating cannot all act simultaneously because the outcome of the various contributions cannot be foreseen. Innovation is therefore a multistage process, where the stages are often sequential, and so the leadership passes from one to another as the emphasis changes. It may move from one creative individual to another who has a different and more fruitful approach to a particular part of the problem. Almost certainly it will move from function to function as the development proceeds, say salesman to R and D to engineering to marketer etc.

What actually makes this happen behaviourally is a common, agreed perception of the need for a new product or process. The implications of this are far reaching indeed. First someone must perceive and convince colleagues of the need. The diversion of resources in the form of time and money away from competing projects must be achieved. The resources must include a sufficiently multidisciplinary team to be able to cope with the range of nearly insoluble problems which beset most worthwhile innovations. The team must be fully committed to making the innovation work, at a risk to themselves personally and perhaps to the whole company. This aspect at least is not too far from the popular perception. In addition resources must be protected from marauders from other parts of the

The Scale and Scope of Economics

organisation or from outside competitors during the long drawn out period of development. The project must have a protector at a high level; certainly it must have the support at some level of involvement of all those whose withholding of resources could prevent it from being successful. Even a simple project may involve a substantial proportion of a company's resources in some degree. All these are vital, but on them must be superimposed the technical risks, which most people consider to be the real problems of innovation.

The behavioural part of this process is in effect the interaction of two systems, the innovating and the purchasing systems. This is essentially a mathematical description, but it represents the dynamics of what actually happens. Both innovating and purchasing systems are composed of subsystems. The innovation process begins when one of the subsystems, whether in the supplying or the buying organisation in effect generates a new goal for itself; it sets out to do something new.

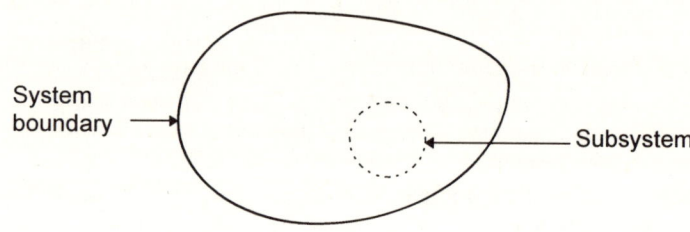

Figure 7.1 Inception of Innovation in a Subsystem of a System

It may not fully realise that it is doing so; it may be a recognition that something could be better than it is, and there may be a need to change. This may be any subsystem, from researcher to purchasing officer, salesman to office manager, but essentially it is anyone who is in a position to make the creative step of identifying a new goal in response to his or her perception of the environment. This may be represented as in Figure 7.1, where the irregular shape is the boundary of the system, like the skin of a biological entity, and the circle inside is the subsystem in question. The rest of the system consists of subsystems which are not yet involved.

The next stage is for contact to take place between the subsystem which has the problem and another system which has a potential solution. It tries to generate a response in a subsystem belonging to this second system. This is written in such general terms to avoid the popular misconception that the innovator dashes out to sell his new idea, because it is quite misleading to label the subsystems at this stage. It may be that someone recognises a potential need for a new product or process which they could bring to commercialisation, so that they seek possible users. It is equally likely that a user recognises the limitations of what is currently available, and sets out to find an alternative. Some users of industrial equipment modify anything they buy to suit their own particular circumstances; they add some safety feature or replace part of the machine or its control system to improve safety, productivity etc. A wise supplier would take note of such customer feedback and prepare his next model accordingly.

However it comes about, if the contact succeeds in generating a common interest between the subsystems in the two different systems, the process of innovation is under way. The system which will eventually supply the new process or product is the "innovator", and the system which will eventually buy it is the "purchaser". The course of the innovative process from this point may be represented as in Figure 7.2. If the subsystems involved are A in the innovating system and B in the purchasing system, the course of the innovation spreads out from them until it involves the whole systems.

Not all parts of the innovating organisation need be committed to the same extent, and the process does not follow the organisation's hierarchy. Nevertheless all are involved, even if only to counter the natural resistance in any system which can have an "antibody" effect on anything new. The managing director may not need to know the detail in the same way as the technician, but he needs to understand and actively agree with the implications, and seek to gain the potential benefits for the organisation, while accepting the difficulties. Otherwise he might inadvertently cut the support in mid-development, say by reallocating resources. He needs to understand that the difficulties themselves prevent competitors from following too closely, and may eventually turn into advantages. Above all he needs to be aware that if the innovation is significant and successful, it may well require the adaptation of the whole organisation by sucking old cash flows and creating new ones, thus changing the balance of power in the organisation; some will gain at the expense of others, while of course taking the risk of failure.

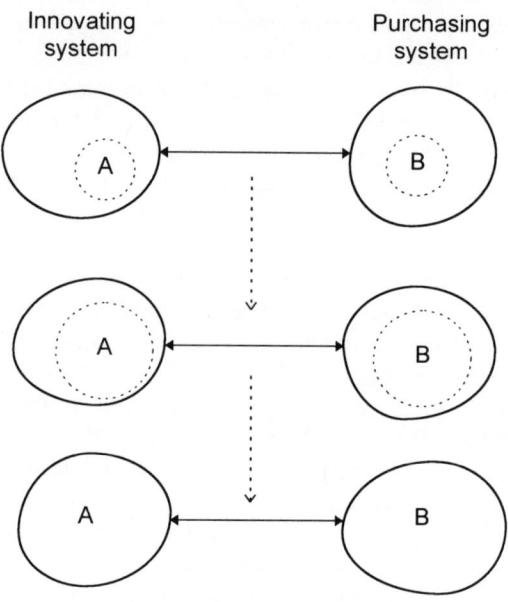

Figure 7.2 Innovation Process Spreading through and between Systems over Time

Similar considerations hold good in the buying organisation. Buying the product or process is not simply a transfer of money. It changes the balance of resources in a company or other organisation, and forces adaptation of the whole organisation to varying degrees. One could always have allocated capital expenditure to something else, which might have strengthened another part of the company in preference. The new purchase influences the performance of the purchasing organisation throughout its useful lifetime. At the very least it denies the organisation another opportunity, which may be crucial in a competitive environment. It will also make further demands on revenue through the need for maintenance etc, which limits the revenue available to others.

Nor are such effects confined to large companies. They may easily be recognised from one's own experience as a consuming organisation venturing to buy, say, domestic appliances for the first time; purchase of a car or a microwave cooker or an automatic washing machine can change the whole schedule of a family and the balance of interest between its members, for better or for worse.

This process may also be expressed in terms of goal formation. At the outset neither of the subsystems A or B can develop a goal for the whole system of which it is a part, but it can persuade other subsystems to formulate their own contributory goals, until there are sufficient to generate a goal for the whole system itself. The goal in the innovating system is to bring the innovation to the point at which it can be sold commercially. The same process of interaction takes place in the purchasing system, until it too reaches a goal, which is to acquire the potential innovation for its own advantage. The two systems are then interacting to achieve the same goal from their different perspectives, which makes the potential innovation much more likely to succeed.

The whole process is rather like the spread of an infection or lighting fires in the subsystems until the whole systems are taken over, but of course in a positive, constructive sense. The result is effectively the formation of a new innovation system in which both systems interact in pursuit of a common goal, which they see from opposite but complementary viewpoints: to complete the innovation successfully, in order to benefit one party from selling it, and the other from using it (Figure 7.3).

This is very different from the conventionally held view, where innovations somehow just happen spontaneously. Subsystems must have the opportunity and ability to pursue something unforeseen, uncertain and risky; an environment which is precluded by tight "control". Nor is it compatible with conditions of "necessity"; if all resources are devoted to survival, there will be no room for experimentation. It is a sequential process with contributions coming from different subsystems at different times. Indeed time runs through the whole process, as through all systems. It requires subsystems which can initiate even if only on a small scale i.e. self-starting.

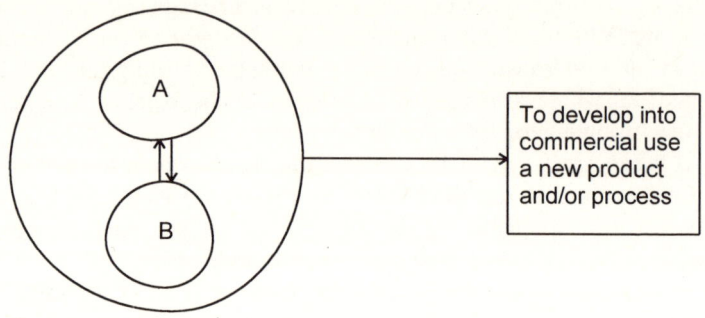

Figure 7.3 Innovating System formed from Innovator System A and User System B

It requires a system in which risk-taking is not penalised, because most attempts will fail. It requires a system which learns from failure and improves next time, in other words a learning system. Particularly in the innovating system it requires the sort of flexibility that allows it to pursue a product or process, but change direction to another which it recognises as more likely to succeed, if it comes across it en route. This is the sort of flexibility which turned an electronic switching device into a desktop computer, and a discarded billet into stainless steel. It requires an ability to live with uncertainty. How different from the concept of innovation as something which takes place in the designated department!

All the elements of systems are there: goals, time, subsystems, interactions, information, feedback; and the essential assets of awareness, understanding, stores of information to draw on, and experience. The common goal plays the same role as a blackboard for prices and quantities in markets. It provides the extra degree of freedom that allows individuals to operate with their own independent initiatives, without which the innovation is unlikely to happen, but at the same time permits them to focus on a common objective. Moreover there must be a means by which subsystems may interact with each other. They cannot innovate by sitting in their own offices or laboratories, though the very organisation which believes it is trying to innovate often requires them to operate in this way

The innovation process at work was well illustrated by the home computer industry in the UK. Potential suppliers hoped to sell at least one to every home, pointing out its virtues in controlling the central heating and checking the finances. Closer contact suggested that the needs of many of their potential customers, the children, revolved more around electronic amusements than cost savings, but the purchasing power which governed entry into the market remained in the control of parents. Sales and hence innovation were slow. Parents, however, as controlling buyers did in fact have need of home computers, mainly to educate the children and help them to get jobs. But how could this be reconciled with the triviality of computer games? And even if the computers were alleged to be able to do more serious things, how could one be sure that the sellers were not simply toy merchants or even fly-by-night operators? Nevertheless the innovation system was slowly being established and the government helped by initiating a large programme of education which suggested that industry could not survive or children expect jobs unless they got to grips with the microchip revolution. However, residual doubts inhibited the whole process.

Into the breach unintentionally stepped the BBC, which is renowned for its impartiality in commercial matters. It launched a series of educational programmes for television on how to come to terms with computers, and as an afterthought it commissioned its own home computer to accompany the series, the BBC Microcomputer. Parents knew that if the BBC put its name to them, and the technical review incidentally turned out to be good, these unfamiliar machines were safe to buy. The innovating system was complete, and included manufacturer, government and the BBC on the supplying side, and parents and children on the buying side. Demand for the BBC Computer grew so fast that the manufacturers were hard pressed to keep pace.

It is not altogether easy to discern who initiated the innovation, as is often the case, but the commercial beneficiary was the fortunate company which happened to produce a better design for the BBC at the right time. It was inundated with orders, and the whole system was so powerful that the UK soon became one of the most heavily populated with home computers in the world. And, for better or for worse, one of the most expert in computer games!

7.3. Response Times in Technological Innovation

In the terminology which we have developed above, the behavioural effects may be considered as adjustments of the scope of the seller and buyer organisations as the process of acceptance of the innovation in the market proceeds. Because of this need to adapt, technological innovation can scarcely be a rapid process, and the more radical the innovation, the more difficult it will be to make that adaptation occur. It is not surprising therefore that innovation moves slowly in all except the simplest cases.

Just how slow is not commonly appreciated. Most processes and products take 7-10 years from concept to initial acceptance in the market. Innovators being by nature optimistic people, like to think that it takes rather less, but that view does not bear scrutiny. Large complex products such as aircraft may take twice as long. Not a few automotive internal combustion engines which are around today have their origins in 20 year old designs and concepts. The new designs of cars coming onto the market in the nineteen eighties were sparked off by rises in the price of oil which occurred over a decade before. Even quite small modifications to products or "technical service" are likely to take 18 months to conceive and implement.

An exception to this may appear to be the pace of development in microchips, where the adaptation of materials and techniques seems to be extraordinarily fast. But even then the basic elements of the technology go back over a couple of decades, and the microchips themselves have a capacity which far outweighs the pace of adaptation on the part of the purchasers. A personal computer is likely to provide ten times as much as most users are ever likely to be able to use. Most of its facilities remain untouched. This has undoubtedly moderated the rate at which still more capabilities of chips can be turned into effective innovations in the hands of the user.

The time needed for the economic system to respond positively to a would-be innovation is related to the response times in markets as described above. It cannot respond in the immediate or stock-related senses. It begins to match organisation-linked response times for the reasons indicated, but it is much closer to investment-linked response times i.e. 5 years with the additional complication that it requires not one but two investments: the first in teams capable of producing the innovation, and the second in the fixed assets needed for production, which must by definition lag behind the first investment.

7.4 Costs and Risks in Technological Innovation

Innovation requires the commitment of resources over a long period, and it is therefore subject to the same kind of risks as any investment in conversion processes. The most obvious risk is that the technological difficulties inherent in the initial concept will be insuperable, with the result that no returns will be earned and the resources sunk in the investment may have been wasted.

There is however a set of market-related reasons why technological success may not result in an innovation. By the time the new process or product is ready for the market, the demand for it may have receded or may never have materialised. This may be the result of fulfilment of the potential users' needs by another technology i.e. the innovation may be technologically obsolete before it has seen the light of day, or it may be because of a change of fashion or styles of living. These are both changes in the scope of the environment in which the innovation must gain a footing that have occurred during the period of its development. They are the natural hazards of the innovator. Another of course is that the need may never really have existed. (There is the facile view that supply creates its own demand i.e. Say's Law, in which case these sorts of failure cannot happen, because products can always be sold if they are cheap enough. However we do not consider this to be a serious proposition).

Most important is a different sort of risk which depends on the innovators themselves: costs relative to those of competitors. The difference in costs will be a barrier to entry into the market if it acts against the innovator. We can sharpen the argument by analysing innovative processes and products separately.

7.4.1 Processes

Consider first the case of a new process for making a commodity product, such as a bulk chemical. The potential gain to the innovating organisation is determined by the net revenue which it stands to make, that is the difference between revenues and costs. The commodity will fetch the same price in the market as its competitors' products, and so its revenue is simply a function of the quantity of the commodity which it sells. Competition in process innovation for undifferentiated commodities therefore rests on costs alone.

The relevant total input cost to be considered by the innovating firm in deciding whether to enter the market is made up of the materials, fuels and operating costs. The net revenue which it expects to make must be sufficient to repay the capital which it is obliged to sink in the new process plus interest, and also to give a return, provided there are other avenues of investment open to it. (And if there are not, as a firm it has no real choice; it either invests or disappears from the economic process.) The capital repayments, and interest we shall combine to give a single capital charge. It can be expressed in terms of money per year at design output or of ton of commodity produced, whichever is appropriate. Here we use money/ton.

However the competitors, who have already sunk their capital in their investment, have a different decision to make. Sunk capital is no longer part of the cost of production; it cannot be influenced retrospectively by decisions made now. It remains sunk whether there is any production or not, and the aim of producing and selling product is to make enough money to repay it, at the very least.

If the new entrant comes into the market and prices are depressed to reflect the new supply, they must decide whether to continue to operate or not. Their decision depends on whether they can earn more by continuing to operate or by leaving the market. If they stay in the market, they have a chance of earning positive net revenue, which will help to pay off what they borrowed to finance the project, and they can also avail themselves of any opportunities which accrue to operators. If they leave the market, they might be able to derive other revenues which will consist of whatever price they can sell the operation for less the capital still outstanding, plus the income which they believe they

The Process of Technological Innovation

could obtain from the sum realised, whether interest on a loan or return from another capital investment opportunity.

The problem for those involved in making decisions may be illustrated in bar chart form (Figure 7.4).

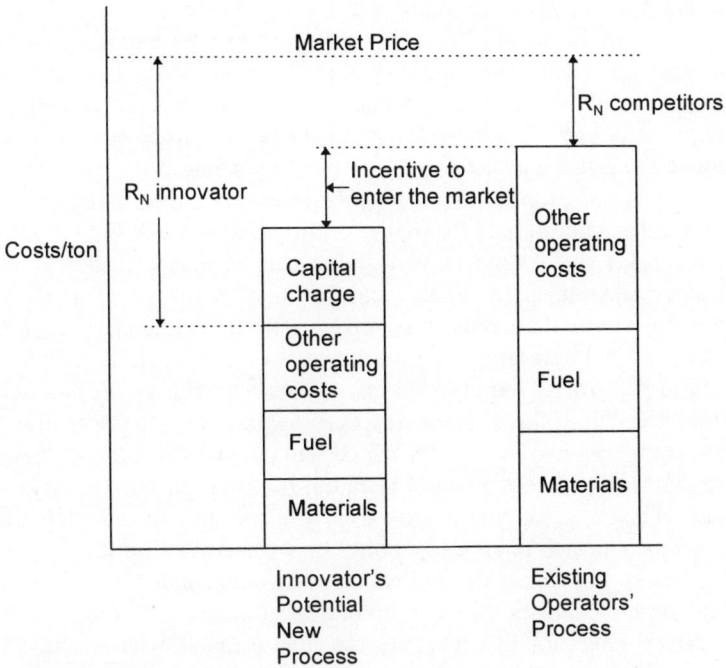

Figure 7.4 Cost Structures of Existing and Potential New Processes

Assuming it behaves rationally and independently, the innovating firm will decide to enter the market if the unit cost of its product, including an allowance for getting its money back, is expected to be less than that of its competitors. The difference between its cost/ton and the revenue/ton which is earned in the market is the net revenue/ton, designated R_N.

If the innovator enters the market, he could expect to make net revenue R_N (innovator) at current market prices. Provided he operates the process at design throughput, this should be enough to pay the capital charge per ton produced as calculated over the required payback time, and still leave some over. This "surplus" would be the return on the capital invested.

At the prevailing market price competitors could expect to make net revenue R_N (competitors) per ton, but it is most unlikely that the market price of the commodity will stay at that level. As soon as the new process begins to produce, the price can be expected to fall. Neoclassical economics will say that this is because the increased quantity available must be associated with lower prices, the result of the curvature of the supply/demand schedules. Larger quantities will reduce the price, and the lower price will generate extra demand, but not in the same proportion, or it would otherwise expand indefinitely.

Another interpretation is that existing producers will fight to retain their market share, especially if giving ground means shedding staff, closing plant and so on. To this end they may go on reducing prices if necessary until they only just cover their total operating cost i.e. materials, fuel and other operating costs. Any net revenue they make goes to pay off the capital charges, and so they can go on producing while it is still positive. They may even begin to reduce prices to deter new entrants, a barrier to entry which will benefit customers at least in the short term without a single extra ton being produced. The situation may change when the existing producers are forced into new investment as their plant wears out, if they can still afford it.

This is something the innovator must anticipate. He must try to estimate his competitors' cost structures, and anticipate the reduction in prices which might occur. He can then estimate what net revenue this would leave to pay off the capital charge if the worst occurred. What is left, the return on the capital invested, is a measure of the incentive to make the investment. It has to be large enough to justify the risk, because there is still the possibility that something unforeseen will occur and render the whole project unprofitable e.g. a succession of mild winters or a war.

7.4.2 Differentiated Products

Innovation in products requires differentiation, the creation of a new market which attracts buyers away from the markets for other products. If the product is not different, it can compete only on the basis of cost as in the previous section. The fundamental difference is that a commodity earns the same market price whatever its source, but a differentiated product operates in a different market and commands the price obtaining in that market.

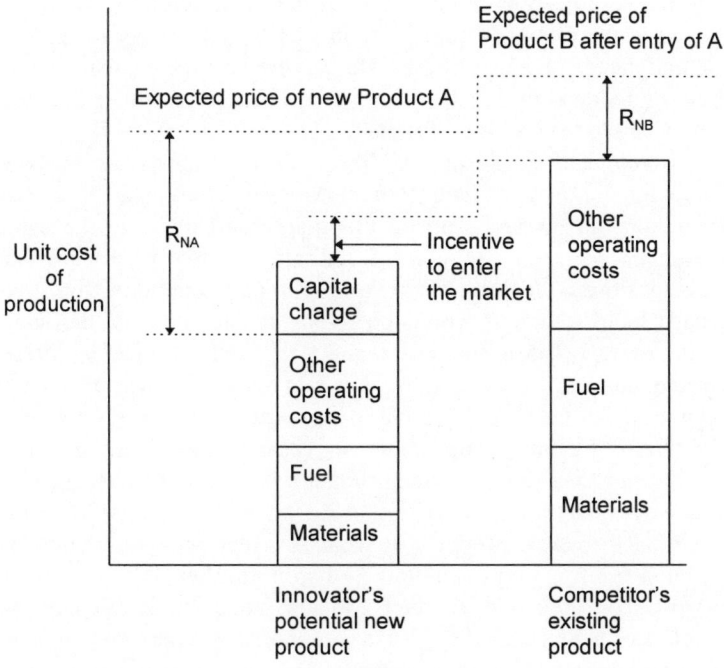

Figure 7.5 Cost structures of a Potential New and an Existing Product

This price may be higher or lower than that of the competing goods, depending on the demand for the new product i.e. the extent to which buyers prefer it to the alternatives. The decisions to be made by the potential innovator before committing his capital depends on his assessment of the net revenues (Figure 7.5).

The expected price of the new product A has been set lower than that of the existing product B for the purposes of illustration. However it might equally be greater if buyers prefer A's distinctive features. The innovator can calculate the net revenue per unit sold on the assumption that the price of the established product will remain unchanged. His competitors' unit materials, fuel and other operating costs could be estimated to determine how far they could reduce their price in response to the entry of the new product. The new product might have to be priced correspondingly lower to gain a foothold in the market and sell in the proposed quantities, in which case the net revenue per unit and hence the contribution to paying off the capital charges, would be reduced too. If the return is still satisfactory after this, there is an incentive to enter the market.

Differentiated products are likely to be knowledge intensive. Before the innovation even came into view, there may have been expenditure on research and development comparable to the capital investment required for commercialisation. This is a sunk cost resulting from a decision to look in this particular direction, taken perhaps long before. It would be wrong to include it in the capital charge now, because the past cannot be influenced. The present decision concerns what can be done to earn as much revenue as possible in future. If it is a good investment, it may make enough to cover not only capital charges but also research expenditure too.

However for a differentiated product price is not the only response. Competitors may introduce a further differentiation still which entices buyers back to their products in what is effectively yet another new market, a leapfrogging operation. And so it goes on. They may reduce the price of their old product too for good measure. This also complicates matters for them because not all customers may be happy to abandon the old product, Product B; they will certainly want it serviced. The result is that they may be obliged to have two models in production at the same time, until they can phase one out.

7.5 Rates of Innovation

Implicit in the analysis is the continual annihilation of invested capital through technological obsolescence. Each successful new process or product diminishes the income to be made from existing assets by reducing the revenue potentially available to them in their markets. This is quite different from wear and tear which assets undergo during use i.e. entropic degradation. Even brand new assets may be made uncompetitive by a change in international markets, whether in inputs, novel conversion processes or products, or in sentiment, say a more critical perception of risks and dangerous by-products.

Two conclusions may be drawn. First a good deal of foresight and understanding is needed when undertaking projects which consume large amounts of capital, or it may result in gross waste, because the future is always uncertain, however clever the analysis. Secondly, there is a limit to the rate of constructive innovation in an economic system, the rate at which the system can accommodate; abrupt changes are likely to be particularly destructive. Neither should come as any surprise on reflection; balanced development is usually more fruitful. But it is extremely important for a society, as for a firm, that the rate of change should not be such as to destabilise the whole system itself.

The dramatic increase in energy costs in the mid-1970s is thought to have made a significant proportion of new assets technologically obsolete almost overnight by exposing them to increased competition from more energy-efficient foreign processes which had previously had no particular advantage. The same might occur with any process or product which depends on the price of a particular input for its advantage over competitors. By the same token, if prices drift back again to their former level, the "obsolete" products and processes can enjoy a revival, until next time. In the long run energy efficiency must have the edge, (other things being equal !).

These are manifestations of the economies and diseconomies of scope of conversion processes over time, as discussed in a previous chapter. The analysis of costs cannot assume homogeneity through time, and the assumption would be particularly misleading if applied to the innovation process.

7.6 Product Life Cycles

There is the further problem with the above analysis that it is based on a snapshot, as in traditional economic methodology. It begs the questions: costs when, revenue when and so, most important, net revenue when? We said earlier that no one sows except in the expectation of harvesting more i.e. the two events are separated by time. Innovation is an unusually risky form of cultivation. Not only is the harvest uncertain, but even if it materialises we have only the most approximate idea of when it is likely to happen, and the weather can change for the worse before it is gathered in.

To mix the metaphor slightly, new products have been observed to go through a sequence of changes which can be described as their life cycle. The aggregate revenue from the product sold tends to follow what is called the S-shaped curve, which is typical of growth and decay in living things. Hence the term "life cycle". Product revenue is then thought to pass through various stages of growth and decline as in Figure 7.6. Net revenue, which has been the focus of the analysis so far, also reaches a maximum during maturity.

Such a curve is strictly applicable only to a single homogeneous product. If it is applied to a range of products or industries, it may be like trying to describe the lives of a collection of different creatures on a single curve; even if each follows the same pattern, the span of each life is different, and to aggregate them into one life will obscure the meaning. If the qualification is not made, the concept is suspect because the life of an economic system can be prolonged indefinitely by continual and perhaps perpetual transmogrification into something new.

Nevertheless the concept of a product "life" brings time into economics in a way which is important in answering the questions posed at the beginning of the section. It is the common experience of everyday life that new products appear, that many die young but others survive, that these grow in volume until they reach all the available purchasers and that they tend eventually to be overtaken by newer products and so decline. It is this evolution in response to markets which extends and renews the economic process itself.

Even though it is expressed in terms of simple revenue growth, implicit in the S-shaped curve are changes which occur not only in scale but in scope. In the early days of the innovation process experience shows that there will be many firms trying to make very similar products by different manufacturing processes. Developing and marketing a new product may be very expensive, and the real cost of a prototype may be many times what the mature product will cost. Revenue is most unlikely to be proportionately as large and so net revenue will almost certainly be negative, but costs should fall rapidly as more units are produced, because economies of scope are obtained as skills and understanding improves.

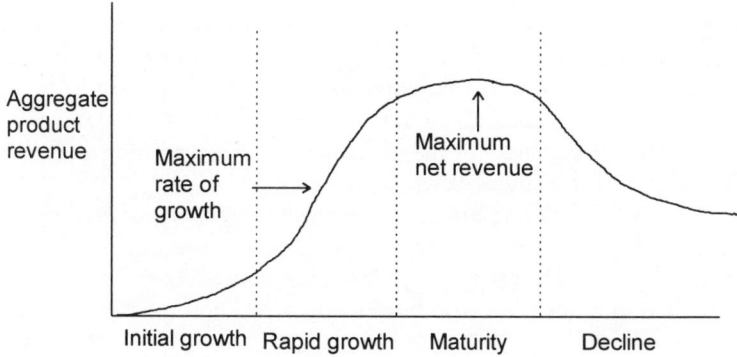

Figure 7.6 Product Life Cycle

Nevertheless costs may exceed revenues for much of the initial growth phase, and the innovating firm has to decide whether to continue in the market. There are three basic considerations in arriving at the decision: whether demand for the new product will grow or has already reached "maturity", and is set to peter out; whether with continuing development the firm's own process is capable of reaching unit costs as low as those of competitors' processes, which are also being continually improved; and finally, whether the company is in a healthy enough position financially to endure such an indeterminate period of waiting for growth to accelerate and then invest to match its competitors. These are major uncertainties which face the innovator, and many drop out at this stage while the going is good. Better to exit early, albeit at a loss, than to imperil the very existence of the business by failure in the next stage. The range of competing processes thus narrows early on.

The initial growth phase requires the commitment of skilled people and enough money, some of which may be borrowed, to finance a relatively small conversion process. However as soon as demand for the product takes off, there is the opportunity to obtain economies of scale and scope. The sheer volume of product permits the scale of manufacture to be increased to that which is most economical by spreading the cost of major capital items such as furnaces, presses or computers over many units of output. But it is most unlikely that the revenue generated in the initial phase will have been sufficient to make these heavy investments. The company may hope to finance its expansion out of increased revenue as it goes along, but the total demand must outstrip its capacity to supply by this route, (or why consider new investment?), and the result will be that competitors will take an increasing share of the available revenue, and ultimately deny the company the economies which it is seeking.

The only solution in the period of rapid growth is a heavy influx of funds from outside the project to finance the assets required for the greatly increased output, either by cross-subsidisation using funds generated in other parts of a business and retained for investment, or by heavy borrowing. The result is that revenues are high and operating costs are high but decreasing, so that net revenue is high and increasing. But much of the net revenue is absorbed in repaying debt and interest charges, or the equivalent, restoring its retained funds for future investments. The firm is reaping very little net reward at this stage for taking the risk of innovation, whatever the appearances. It is having to sow even faster than it reaps. If it should falter and the revenue fails to materialise in sufficient quantity and at the right time, it may find itself caught in a cash flow trap which could result in the firm's eventual demise.

In the midst of all the mounting revenue the company may easily forget economies of scope. Yet it is these which will determine how large a net harvest will eventually be reaped. Throughout the periods of growth the manufacturing process must be improved to obtain the benefits of the experience curve. Fixed assets must be laid down not just fast but in a configuration which minimises costs. Distribution

The Process of Technological Innovation

networks must be rationalised etc. The quality of the total asset base must be improved continuously. All this must take place at a time when the emphasis is on output at almost any cost to capture as large a share of the available revenue as possible, because it will too expensive to restructure entirely in the next stage.

The key to what happens in the later stages of the life cycle is unit cost. If all the competitors in the market have managed to obtain a comparable share, there is nothing to choose between them in economies of scale. They may all manage their assets with maximum possible efficiency for their particular firms but they have arrived at their position by very different routes, and so the contest will be settled by their basic cost structures i.e. by the economies of scope which they managed to build in on the way. Superior technology, less costly designs, better disposition of assets, cheaper distribution etc give a cost advantage which may be small for each unit but amounts to very large sums when multiplied by the number of units sold. Further economies depend on further investment; lower costs result in more net revenue, more to invest, and so on.

Such a cost advantage is termed a "competitive advantage". It is a broader term than the "comparative advantage" of traditional economics because it does not depend on a favourable climate or an abundance of natural resources or some other divine endowment. It is developed and maintained entirely by the skills and ingenuity of the people in the firms which are involved. The difference may be readily understood by analogy with a race: some win races even without the track being physically tilted in their favour, and even though they are not stronger or better endowed than their competitors. They win because it is a race over time, which gives them the opportunity to plan and carry out a winning strategy. This should come as no surprise to nations which habitually seem to win only one battle in a war: the last one.

Eventually in the life cycle maturity is reached and revenue stops growing. By this time costs have reached a minimum for each company and so net revenues are at a maximum. There is no longer a major need or an opportunity to invest; debts can be repaid, profits reach their maximum. This is the harvest which has so long been awaited. But different companies will have reached different cost levels, depending partly on scale of operation, and partly on the structure inherent in the fixed assets representing the culmination of economies of scope through technological know-how etc. Different conversion processes will therefore bring in different harvests. Strong competitors increase in strength as the weaker are inhibited from improving their cost structure by the risks of committing additional resources at this late stage.

This is all important in the final stage which is decline. Revenues decline for two reasons: the quantity demanded may decrease slightly as a result of substitution by other products in what is by now a fairly profitable area of business; and price also declines under pressure of competition, as firms seek to increase their share of a market which has stopped growing. The result must be contraction in the industry. The weaker succumb and are either swallowed by their stronger competitors or adjust internally to a smaller operation. Contraction is extremely painful because it is not simply a reduction of scale which is required. It is a change of scope, turning a frog into a princess, or vice versa, which is much more difficult. Alternatively there might just be a long slow decline, and a transfer of as much of the assets as possible into another line of business. Lucky the firm which can afford to cut its losses and concentrate on a market in which it is likely to be more successful. Even the successful firms will eventually have to invest much of their reward in something different, while putting just enough into their successful business to keep it efficient and the competitors at bay.

Nothing is ever quite as clear cut as the life cycle analogy suggests, and many product lines linger on profitably for many years at reduced levels. The problems facing the innovator may be formidable, but it happens all the same. It is just as well for our economic health that hope springs eternal in business as in life itself.

But there is no doubt whatsoever about the main thrust of the argument: there is no possibility of standing still for long, because the economic process is perpetually changing and evolving. The neoclassical analysis which recognises only the scale of operation is extremely misleading in this respect. Time changes the nature of the economic process itself.

7.7 The Role of Competition

The theoretical "perfect" market economy, to which there is complete freedom of access, would provide the opportunity for innovation through its system of conversion processes and exchanges, as described in an earlier chapter. Anyone who could compete could break into the network with something new.

However, the preceding analysis of the stages of innovation sheds quite a different light on the effect of competition on innovation itself. To continue the metaphor of the life cycle, competition is primarily about survival, not reducing prices. Prices are a mechanism for expressing competition, but those who do not survive for whatever reason to compete another day are eliminated from the economic process for ever. If a firm is trying to introduce something new, it may find that prices of competitive products are reduced. This may be a pre-emptive bid by competitors, which has the effect of raising a barrier to entry, and also benefiting buyers, which is the object of the system in the long run. But it may well be in response to the mere threat of increased quantities in the market i.e. part of the bargaining process, a card in the hand of buyers; seeking potential alternative suppliers is part of the bargaining process, even in the conditions of the "perfect" market. Once the innovator has committed his capital, it becomes self-fulfilling, the normal operation of real markets.

Furthermore with a brand new product there might be many competitors in the initial stages, and some must inevitably suffer in the subsequent shakeout. Those who survive ought in principle to be healthy, but to stay in the next stage of the game they must borrow heavily, and in effect competitively, or else cross-subsidise from another activity in their firm. They are then committed to compete in every aspect of their organisation, marketing, technology and finance to achieve the economies of scale and scope necessary to survive.

But there may be a host of other problems too. The total market system may not be equally accessible to all, say because it is divided by national barriers, not only economic but perhaps cultural. Firms may then use the ploy of differential pricing, which is selling at cost or low net revenue in the market which is available to the potential innovator, while recovering their capital in another, probably the home market. There may be subsidies at home to allow firms to surmount barriers to entry abroad, and limitations on access to home markets to allow economies of scale to develop among home producers.

An example of this is the technique which seems to have been used by Japan and other South East Asian countries. Japan built its car industry by buying technology from firms abroad, including British Leyland, and making available to a range of firms in Japan, so that they could compete vigorously with each other. Such competition brought about economies of scale and scope for those who survived, but for a period of 5-10 years while the indigenous producers were establishing themselves, access of foreign companies to the Japanese market was severely restricted. The import quota on foreign cars into Japan is said to have been $600000 worth in 1954 (4). But even without a quota it would be quite possible for cultural antipathy towards imports or, to put it positively, loyalty to home manufacturers to produce the same result. People are not obliged to buy foreign goods if they prefer not to, even in neoclassical economics. It is a form of product differentiation.

When the Japanese industry had developed to the point at which it could compete on a world scale, it launched itself into world markets. The economies in its cost structure, brought about not only by scale but by the scope effects inherent in its industrial make-up and the attitude of its workforce to quality control, for example, gave it a cost advantage which was almost unassailable anywhere else in the world.

Japanese companies thus surmounted the barrier to entry and then proceeded to develop a competitive advantage over American and European companies which was hard to match. Given the cost advantages which it had now attained, the industry no longer needed protection or subsidy. It could more than compete on equal terms with other manufacturers, and needed only access to world markets to prove it. Not that its problems stopped there. Its models of car were often unsuitable for Western tastes, and they had to be modified to local conditions. However this was just a continuation of the process which had stood them in good stead at home: learning, adaptation, investment, economies of scale and scope etc. Other countries in SE Asia have followed suit.

This illustrates the difference between Ricardo's comparative advantages, which he discerned in a largely agrarian society, and the competitive advantage which has appeared in manufacturing more

The Process of Technological Innovation

recently. Japan has almost no comparative advantages in the making of cars: no iron ore, no oil, no gas etc. If it now has a competitive advantage, it is the result of skill, technology and above all national strategic management, which has directed its investment towards human and fixed assets with more efficient production capability than its competitors'.

Much of the difference between Japan and its competitors used to be ascribed to low wages. That may have been true while it was building up its investment, but not later. The difference in costs became such that its competitors found it difficult to respond, even if their workforces were paid very little. The Japanese economies of scope were now too great for its competitors to be able to counteract them by reducing wages. By the mid-1980s it even used less capital per vehicle than its competitors. In open markets, therefore, once the competitive positions were established, and providing the Japanese did not lose their strategic direction, as the Europeans and the Americans did, there was no reason why they should not always succeed in this kind of business.

Not that there is anything immoral in all this. Japan simply used its breathing space to accumulate the learning necessary to compete, and managed to attain a position in which it could hold its own in the world market, having started from behind. After all there was nothing pre-ordained about the differential economic positions of nations in the early years of the industrial revolution. The same processes occurred then, but over a much longer period. Many sleeping nations may awake, if they can shake off their inhibitions and make the necessary adjustments.

If a balance is to be reached, it will not be by the operation of some global market, but by a change of scope resulting from investment, not only in fixed assets but in people. In the UK where the car industry was racked by internal strife, as if the only competition was between managers and workforce, where little account was taken of customers for many years and where the industry was turned on and off like a tap to prevent the economy "overheating", the cost position was difficult to retrieve, however hard everyone worked.

Surgery is not a cure. If there is a solution for the UK, it must be through strategically sound investment. Even now the economies of scale in manufacturing industries seem to be changing, as the discussion on information technology showed, if only one has the economic strength, wisdom and foresight to create the necessary investment base.

7.8 The Rate of Return on Innovation

There is a further inhibitor of innovation which lies in the distribution of the rewards between the innovator and the rest of the market system in which the innovation is made. The innovating system's reward is the net revenue which it makes in the market place over the life cycle of the product, and may be designated the private rate of return. But there are three other groups who benefit as well: suppliers, imitators and not least buyers.

Any technological innovation requires material, equipment and services from the markets which would not otherwise have been bought. Thus the suppliers to the innovating firm benefit from increased sales. Furthermore the employees of the firm share in the net revenue derived from the innovation and spend much of this on consumer goods in the locality, thus spreading the benefits to shopkeepers and others.

All innovations soon give rise to imitations, some of which may be illegal, but many of which may be perfectly legitimate. It is much easier to make something new if someone else has shown that it can be done, and that it will sell to boot. Imitations soon cut back the revenue available to buy the product of the original innovator, which is the normal effect of competition, but at a particularly hazardous time for the innovating firm.

Finally buyers of the innovation expect to derive some benefit from their purchase, and, as described above, are seeking to maximise their net benefit B_N, where

$$B_N = B - R$$

B is the benefit and R the market price. Why else should they buy? What is more, some buyers are so conservative that they will not buy anything new unless the reward is very high and the risk very low.

The result of all this is that, according to some analyses (5, 6), the innovating firm captures less than a third of the total benefit which arises from the innovation. Thus all the risks of failure and pains of adjustment bring in less than a third of the reward. The other two thirds go to the suppliers, buyers and imitators.

Whatever the reason, the relatively small return to the innovating firm must limit the rate of innovation because it is obliged to make its calculations on the basis of what revenue it expects to recover. The less net revenue it expects to make, the less its capability of surmounting the barriers to entry erected by costs sunk in competitive technologies.

The other side of the coin is that successful innovation may be considered to have a multiplier effect on the rest of the economy. The benefit to the community as a whole will be, say, three to five times the apparent benefit derived by the innovating firm to the extent that it adds to and does not merely substitute for another activity. The innovating firm is therefore of great benefit to society by helping to reduce costs and improve products and processes for a whole range of users.

Firms which do not innovate, but simply wait for others to do so, will gain to some extent from the general improvement brought on by innovation, and with less risk to themselves. But they will derive no cost advantage over their competitors, because by definition they will be able to buy the innovation only along with everyone else who wants it. They will be forced to adapt willy nilly, and the chances are that they will be worse placed to do so through lack of experience in the new technology than if they had been active themselves. Not that everything in a firm should be subordinated to a perpetual, headlong race to innovate. Moderation in all things; some stability is also vital. It is simply that in the long run, there is no substitute for a positive attitude to change.

7.9 Cycles of Innovation

It has been observed that innovations tend to occur in clusters at around the same time. Some believe that this reveals an underlying pattern of long waves originating deep in society with peaks which occur every thirty or fifty years (7). This view is particularly associated with the name of Kondratieff. Some even extrapolate this to the gloomy view that there is nothing to do but to sit and wait until the next peak comes along. Small consolation to the thirty million or so

The Scale and Scope of Economics

unemployed in the OECD. Other explanations are that the apparent cycles mark stages in global industrialisation.

The analysis of this book suggests that peaks of this sort may be considered to have their origins in economies of scope derived from cost interactions between innovations. If economic development is considered as a scalar process, there is no reason why the rate of innovation should not be relatively smooth over long periods of time. It will simply increase or decrease with the general business cycle. If however scope plays a part, one can imagine that potential changes of scope i.e. innovations may accumulate for long periods until finally they are sufficient in concert to bring about a quantum economic change. This may then be likened to establishing a new pathway through the economic process from earth to earth, or building up enough pressure to burst the dam.

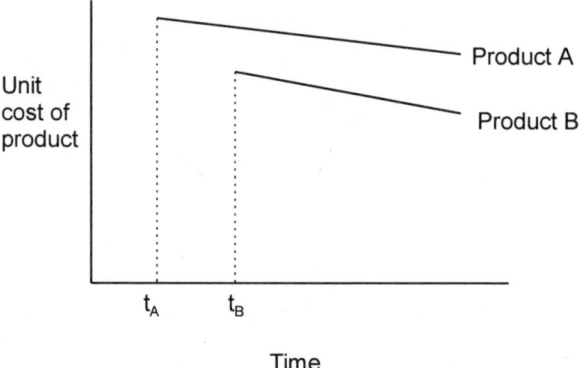

Figure 7.7 Reduction over Time of Unit Costs of Products A and B in Isolation

Each innovation has its cost structure, which we know changes over time because of experience effects, competition etc. So, for instance, the unit cost of innovative product A might change as in Figure 7.7, where t_A represents the time at which A is introduced. The unit cost of product B might tend to do the same, but starting at a later date, t_B.

The Process of Technological Innovation

If products A and B are synergistic economically i.e. they interact positively in an economic sense, when they both become available in the market at the same time, consumption increases dramatically and costs fall accordingly. The result may then look more like Figure 7.8.

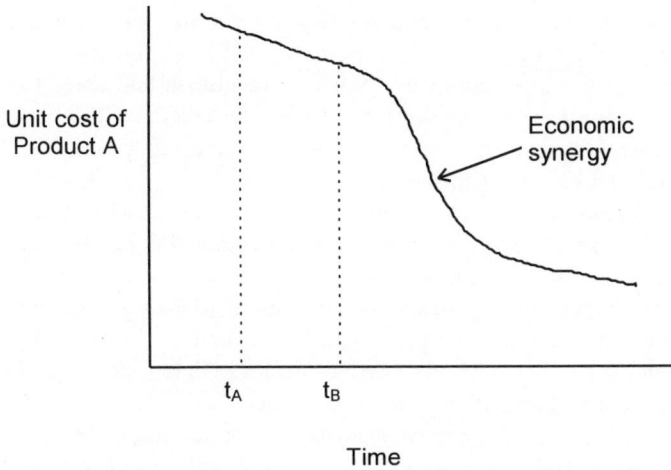

Figure 7.8 Reduction over Time of Unit Costs of Product A in Economic Synergy with Product B

Such cost interactions are in fact happening all the time (1). Cheaper integrated circuits and cheaper colour television tubes make cheaper television sets. This increases demand which permits economies to be made in the manufacture of the circuits and the TV tubes, and so on around the cycle. Such interactions are likely to occur not just between two but between many product and process innovations. Once innovations are earning net revenue, this can be used to develop processes and products still further, thus generating more revenue and so on. Success breeds success until eventually some limit is reached i.e. maturity. This sort of interactive process seems to be going on at the moment in the field of information technology e.g. between computer software and hard disc storage.

The Scale and Scope of Economics

The underlying dynamics of such a process depend on rates of change of scope. We have seen that innovations take a long time to reach fruition in the market place. Apart from the technological development, there is the period of adjustment of the supplier and buyer organisations to acceptance. But it is clear that changes of scope in an organisation contemplating an innovation will be greatly facilitated by the prospect of new products from other suppliers which will also increase the demand for theirs. One may be considered to precipitate the other. Or it might be compared to a critical mass effect except that the interactions are much more diffuse and spread out in time than the physical analogy suggests. The length of the period of adjustment depends not only on the incentives to change in both supplier and buyer organisations, but on the climate for change in the general environment. This may be the reason why peaks of innovation tend to coincide with periods of national upheaval. Any sort of crisis is likely to precipitate innovations which have reached different stages of this process i.e. innovations in the pipeline. War is a well known example. Another is the frontier activity of the sort which has energised the USA for two centuries. Under these conditions organisational barriers are reduced, which facilitates the necessary changes of scope. The common goals of supplier and buyer are more readily perceived. Barriers to entry drop. All routes to victory over the enemy are pursued, and competitive advantages are allowed to be tested in the field. Not that innovation is plain sailing even then; there are plenty of examples of armed forces rejecting new weapons which would win the war for them, and each innovation has to be protected and fought for as in peace time. Jet engines, airframes, radar and computers are examples from the UK alone in the Second World War. It is just that innovation becomes slightly easier under those conditions, with the result that they seem to bunch.

It would be a dispiriting conclusion that only a war is sufficient to change the scope of an economy and allow innovation to flourish. The alternative is a regrouping of resources under the direction of an overall strategy. Since the objectives then have a strand in common, whether competitive or synergistic, successes in different fields tend to reinforce each other by increasing rates of acceptance. This is a manifestation of interactions of cost, where different innovations may influence each other's economies of scale and scope e.g. rubber tyres and internal combustion engines, or radar and jet engines, radio and computerised signal decoding, and hence computers.

The elements of success are the same ones which have been described above: common challenges, strategic foresight and a willingness to adapt at all levels from the most exalted to the lowest. Surely these are not beyond the wit of man to achieve.

7.10 Conclusions

Technological innovation consists of differentiating or changing the scope of conversion to produce new products or processes with lower unit costs, and establishing them in the economic scheme of things. It always involves energy and materials, whether at the molecular or structural level, or through improved designs or layout. From the economies of scope which result, it may be possible to increase scale of operation considerably, thus reinforcing success.

It is essentially a team effort, perhaps most simply described in terms of spontaneous creation of a new goal in a subsystem, often in response to a customer need, and spreading it through the innovating organisation until it becomes a goal for the whole system. The same sort of process takes place in the buying organisation, until both innovating and buying systems interact in the pursuit of compatible goals out of mutual self interest. It is a long drawn out process in spite of popular misconceptions, since quite apart from the technology, which may itself prove to be an insuperable barrier, it involves the accommodation of two behavioural systems i.e. long response times comparable to those characteristic of investment.

The innovation process is much more rational than is commonly believed, and it is driven by the prospect of advantage through acquiring net revenue, i.e. revenue expected to be earned less the costs expected to be incurred. This is an even more risky calculation than for ordinary production, because costs and revenues are both more uncertain and out of phase. Costs are incurred early in the life of the conversion process, long before revenues start to flow in, and throughout the life of the product or process modifications are being incorporated through heavy investment to give further economies of scope. These accumulated investments constitute a barrier which potential new entrants into the market have to climb to enter the competition. Such barriers are an inescapable part of market economics, and cannot be wished away to suit "perfect" market theory.

If the stage is reached when further differentiation is not possible, a small number of producers of nearly identical products will be left occupying the same market and commanding the same price. The winner then will be the one with lowest costs, which will be determined by economies of scale and scope. Losers will not necessarily disappear; they just have to settle for an inferior position. The final stage of the life cycle may then be said to have been reached.

Only a third of the total benefits of an innovation accrue to the innovator, who bears a disproportionate share of the risks. The other beneficiaries are suppliers, buyers, imitators and the general public. Technological innovation is therefore important for the whole of society, not just processors. If technology is the ratchet on the economic process, then technological innovation advances it notch by notch.

Some governments, especially in SE Asia understood this deficiency in "perfect market" theory early on, and managed their economies so as to give their industries economies both of scale and scope, based on advancing technology. As a result, these industries have gained competitive advantages with which it is difficult to compete in international markets, advantages which could to all intents and purposes be permanent. More are adopting the same strategy.

Innovation renders existing capital investments obsolescent, unless they can adapt, and so there is a maximum rate of innovation which an economy can bear, its rate of accommodation, if it is not to be destroyed. Innovation may be particularly destructive if it is imposed abruptly from outside, say by a flood of innovations which have been developed and nurtured through the early stages of the life cycle in another economic system, decoupled from the economy into which it is sold, and therefore not bound by its constraints. The existing assets will have no chance of responding in time.

It has been observed that innovations tend to come bunched together, often in time of war. Extreme circumstances help to sweep away some of the barriers which have been holding them back, and so they all come flooding through together. This is reinforced by interaction between them, so that once one innovation has managed to jump the barriers to entry and reach an acceptable cost, others which depend on it also have the opportunity to come forward, and so on. Some have interpreted this in terms of waves i.e. a regular phenomenon, perhaps linked to regular social upheavals. Still others draw the conclusion that there is nothing to do but wait for the next wave to arrive.

What a counsel of despair that would be, if it were true! However the experience of the countries which have enjoyed such spectacular growth during the last few decades suggests that it need not be so.

Not all a firm's or a country's resources can sensibly be devoted to innovation. Technology supports our present status, but innovation only inches it forward. Anything faster would be too disruptive to be beneficial, which is after all the aim; society in general and those employed in industry need a basic stability on which to build. But there can be no doubt that the limited lives of products and processes drive economic change, whatever the rate at which it can be accommodated. Time and the differentiation that human ingenuity brings about thrust themselves into economics, in spite of the inconvenience to neoclassical theory. Change will occur, and to achieve the best outcome from the process of adaptation we need to plan and organise for it.

Chapter Eight

ORGANISATION AND INNOVATION

IN THE ECONOMIC PROCESS

One of the most surprising aspects of conventional economics, after the treatment of technology and hence technological innovation as exogenous, and after ignoring time, is that there is no mention of organisation and the information flows which are necessary for decision-making. The concept which pervades its analyses is generally one of atoms in collision, or bulls and bears pursuing their own individual interests. Yet it is clear that all economic activity revolves around organisations, and in the absence of organisational structures change, growth and innovation will occur only by accident. Indeed they account for much of the delays in responding to the environment, as described above.

This chapter examines organisation in relation to the economic process. Organisation is defined here as the skill of group perception, learning, decision-making and response. Markets may be considered as particular types of organisation, in which exchange of goods takes place. Conversion processes also require complex organisations for making and executing their operating and strategic decisions. Innovation, we have shown, depends on teams i.e. organised

Organisation and Innovation in the Economic Process

individuals. The whole economic process therefore depends on and responds to organisations which include in one form or another all who take part in the process. Even personal services are seldom sold on a completely individual basis. Doctors and lawyers form group practices. Skilled advisers form consultancies. Hairdressers form partnerships etc. In every case the nature of the organisation affects its response to its economic environment, and so its costs and the revenue which it can capture.

Organisation in the sense of this definition is the acme of man's achievement. It is manifested in his families, tribes, nation states and alliances. It has made possible his science and technology, his schools of art, architecture and sculpture, his religions and philosophies. Organisations have permitted individuals to develop their talents more widely than they ever could in isolation from their fellow men, and co-operation and learning in groups, in which each may benefit from interaction with the others, have enabled all mankind to rise however slowly to a higher plane of existence. This is civilisation, the skill of being a citizen, a member of a nation, a community. It in no sense contains a moral judgment, even though the balance of man's organisational achievements has been tilted naturally towards the greater good of large proportions of mankind; many effective organisations have been directed towards quite other ends.

Organisations are behavioural systems; the individuals of which they are composed have at some level a common purpose or goal. The parts which make up the system, individuals and subgroups, exchange some of their freedom to act as totally free agents for the benefits of being part of the system. They are free to act within this constraint. A system in which all parts are free to act totally independently is a contradiction in terms, a free for all, in short chaos.

The economic system is no exception. Economic competition is largely between organisations, within which individuals play a co-operative role. The distinction between the organisation, the whole, and the individuals of which it is composed, the parts, is by no means pedantic. Organisations develop a character of their own, which truly makes the whole greater or less than the sum of the parts, because of the multiple interactions between the individuals concerned. The organisation may then perceive, learn, make decisions and take action in its own right in response to its environment. Or, just as likely, it may fail to do any of those things in spite of the efforts of individuals, and pay the price. Organisations seem to have a life and death of their own, a cycle of growth and decay, with time running as surely through them as it does through other elements of the economic process.

Organisation always presents a paradox. The interactions between individuals form as a response to an environment which threatens them or promises opportunities at a particular time. These interactions tie them into a unit which is capable of a more appropriate response than they could achieve individually or by simple addition of their efforts. Interactions between individuals are therefore vital to organisations; they are what makes organisations behavioural systems.

But the self-same interactions or bonds and structures within the organisation, which are appropriate in the environment of the time, may prevent it from changing from its original form and adapting as the environment changes. Once they have settled down in such a way as to produce, say, a gazelle of an organisation, they may prove very difficult to transform into a workhorse, still less a tiger should the predators arrive. The bonds which give the organisation life may also bring about its ultimate destruction, which is an exact parallel with life itself.

This chapter describes the elements of operation of an organisation, the sort of structures which have developed to meet particular needs, including learning and decision-making, the direction in which organisations seem to be evolving, the role of information and the effect of new technology. In particular it sets out to demonstrate what is involved in changes in the economic process, that is technological innovation. It is in fact an analysis of behavioural systems, but since systems concepts are often difficult to represent in two dimensions, the general ideas are described in terms more susceptible to graphic representation.

8.1 The Individual

There are no organisations without people, a fact which is easy to overlook. Individual people are the fundamental parts from which organisations as whole systems are formed. Individual behaviour is apparently the simplest aspect of organisation to study, and so a great deal of the literature is devoted to the role of the individual.

Organisation and Innovation in the Economic Process

Economists tend to describe economic behaviour at the level of individuals as microeconomics and that of whole systems as macroeconomics, thus recognising the difference between the parts and the whole, though with what success in reconciling the two is still a matter for debate.

Individuals in many countries are often free to decide at least in principle whether or not to belong to organisations. This is the exercise of their free will, though they are not free to opt out entirely even if they retire into the wilderness, as long as they identify in any way with a nation or culture. Once they have decided to sacrifice some of their freedom of action in return for the benefits of belonging to an organisation, their contribution to it depends on their commitment to help it towards its goals. They must have the ability to interact and communicate with other members of the organisation. Their effectiveness as members of the organisation depends on their use of skills and understanding, derived from education and experience in a co-operative way.

Motivation, skills and an energetic approach are not, however, the full contribution of people to an organisation, because they are individuals each with his or her own characteristics. In particular they vary in their ability to be creative, and what is related, their attitude to risk. Some may be efficient performers in the situation in which they find themselves, that is they make the best of what is available as they perceive it. Others may be dissatisfied with what they find and set about redefining the problem to find new solutions. The former, the processors, work within the system as given; they operate on scale not scope. The others, the innovators, remodel the system itself; they change its scope (1).

Innovative individuals, because of their personal make-up, are willing to take risks and expose themselves to criticism in the particular field of endeavour in question. They seek to find solutions and even problems by an experimental approach involving a large proportion of failures in pursuit of a few successes which will outweigh them.

Individuals are certainly not homogeneous through time, and corporations and organisations of all sorts run into problems when they classify them as anonymous posts, or try to beat them with sticks or entice them with carrots as if they responded like donkeys and had no understanding or, an even bigger mistake, memories. Economists make the same mistake when they fall into the trap of manipulating figures which represent collective nouns such as labour.

People change with time because they learn. Their awareness, consciousness and hence priorities are aroused by observation of their changing environment and by communication with each other. Their own circumstances change. They get married, have children, age. Their physical as well as material attributes wax and wane with time. It is not clear why their propensities to innovate differ initially, but these too change with time, and not always predictably, often decreasing but sometimes increasing with age.

These are some of the factors which affect the willingness of individuals to try a new purchase in the market place or attempt something new in conversion processes or respond in unexpected ways to the incentive system. They may even enable people to perceive the possibility of something new in the first place. Different cultures seem to influence the factors in different ways at different periods in their history, some encouraging a spirit of adventure and others stifling any tendency to change as dangerous. It is remarkable that individuals from apparently stultifying cultures have suddenly been transformed into risk-takers when thrown into new environments. Many of the European countries were example of this in their early days of empire, though they soon lapsed into bureaucracy.

8.2 Information Systems

The power of individuals to create change is greatly magnified by an organisation, and the lifeblood of organisations is information. Organisations take on an existence of their own and may therefore be considered as behavioural information systems.

The first skills we attributed to organisations were those of group perception and learning. An individual makes his own perceptions of the external environment and stores it within his own head. but as soon as there are two people, say A and B, they constitute an organisation and the process becomes potentially more effective but also twice as complicated. Each makes his own perception and analysis, but a new interpretation AB may well emerge when the two communicate with each other, making A, B, and AB and their point of reference. It is the

Organisation and Innovation in the Economic Process

factor AB, that is what A and B can achieve together that they could not separately, which is the synergy in the organisation, the difference between the whole and the sum of the parts. Quite simply two heads together are better than two heads not communicating with each other.

The information flows may be more complicated still in the short term, if the initial response depends on who first communicates with whom, because they may introduce a bias for a short time. However this in the rational world of economics ought to be a passing phase, and a full two way interaction may be assumed to emerge eventually. This admittedly would be the simplest possible outcome, and in some behavioural systems (such as marriage for instance!) full two way interaction is by no means assured within the lifetime of the "organisation".

When there are three people in the organisation A, B and C, the number of information flows doubles yet again. Each makes his own perception and analysis as before: A, B and C. Each then communicates with one of the others i.e. AB, AC and BC. All three then confer together i.e. ABC, and then measure the information against the common yardstick, making 2^3 or 8 information flows in all. The minimum number of flows if all information is to be shared with all members of the organisation, doubles for every additional person i.e. it is 2^n for n people.

Passing information in this way takes time. For a large family the process can be cumbersome, for a small company intolerable and for anything larger, impossible. The world will have moved on before what was perceived in the environment has been fully registered in the consciousness of the organisation as such. The organisation will suffer what is in effect a diseconomy of scope, a paralysis. But if it is to function in an organised way, it must succeed in detecting what threats and opportunities present themselves in the wider environment in which it operates. Moreover in the competitive environment of the market economy it must be better than its rivals; its very survival may depend on it.

The solutions to information paralysis fall into a number of categories. The first is to present information obtained from outside in a way which makes it available simultaneously to all. This may be a joint meeting of all members of the organisation, such as a tribal gathering or an assembly in the forum as in the classical world. Or it

The Scale and Scope of Economics

may be a notice to all staff, or a report in a newspaper. Or it may be the blackboard as described in the particular organisational system of the "perfect" market. This category of solution requires that everybody concerned has the time, experience and understanding to appreciate what is being communicated. It may be more appropriate therefore to broad issues of principle which are important to the organisation than to specific details.

The second "solution" is to make the organisation small. This is not really a solution at all, because its size at any time should be what is appropriate to its long term survival in a competitive environment. Its appropriate size will be determined by its competitors, because resources and the ability to use them depend on size. It is no solution to slim down to featherweight and sap your strength in the process, if your rivals are heavyweights. If the organisation cannot compete at a size which is appropriate for the competition, its solution must lie in internal arrangements for handling information rather than dieting. A reduced size may just make it easier to capture and swallow.

The third "solution", which courts disaster but is all too common, is to reduce the quantity of information coming into an organisation by limiting its sensible contact with its environment, or even preventing it entirely, while the organisation concentrates on its internal politics and other things which it believes to be its prime concern. But the very raison d'être of an organisation is a common response to the environment, and if it has no or only a limited perception of the environment, it may become irrelevant or disappear entirely.

For instance the economic environment for a company includes not only market prices or labour relations or wage rates but also competitors, who may be predators or just steamrollers. Companies who fail to keep a watch on their competitors may wake up one day to find that, although they are still trim and prosperous, they have been swallowed lock, stock and barrel by another concern. it is not much consolation to end up as a meal for someone else.

Nor is it simply a question of preying in that sense. The market system enables an innovator to pull revenue away with a superior product or by-pass whole conversion processes entirely, and so the threat may come from a most unexpected quarter. Mechanical systems may give way to electronics, steel to plastics, and plastics to better plastics, as sail gave way to steam, coal to oil and ocean liners to air travel. Awareness and understanding at least give some chance of survival or adaptation or salvaging of resources.

Other solutions to the problem of handling the necessary quantity of information are the division of the labour of observation and interpretation by levels of abstraction or function. These are attempts at real solutions, as opposed to shying away from the problem, and are described in the next sections.

But the problem is not just one of the quantity of information. It is also one of information storage to provide the "yardsticks" or "reference points" against which to measure new information. In the absence of such storage, there is no learning; each new perception comes as a surprise, and its evaluation starts from scratch. Organisations which do not learn find they need vast information flows to interpret what is going on around them.

The essence of an organisation, which is a learning system, as opposed to one which is simply reactive, is therefore continuity of information systems: that is continuity of perception, communication and storage of information. In an individual these requirements are obvious, because they are part of everyday living. In organisations they are frequently ignored; individuals fill "posts" which relate to specific activities. This is thought to be an efficient way of reducing wasteful overlap. But overlap is vital for learning and communication. Language is a form of overlap, and information gathered by sitting, watching and interpreting, though not apparently an active pursuit, may turn out to be a life saver when the need arises.

Learning systems are repositories of skills, experience, technology etc. Organisations which do not learn cannot innovate except by chance. But information is not enough; it must result in making good decisions and executing them at the appropriate time.

8.3 Levels of Abstraction

There may have been a time when one person could cope with every requirement of an organisation. For instance it may have been possible for one man to know how to build his own ship, weave his own sails, navigate his own passage, buy his own cargo, catch his own food etc, though it seems unlikely. But in the modern world almost everybody must depend on others with specialised knowledge, because this gives economies of scope.

So it is within organisations. If two individuals A and B form a business partnership they will soon reach a situation in which A looks after one aspect of the business and B another. Partner A will obtain and analyse his own information from the world outside and develop the related store of information i.e. learn about his specialisation. Partner B will operate in a slightly different sphere. Neither will have the time or expertise to cover all the available scope with equal effectiveness. If they can, the partnership is not making use of the full scope which was the reason for setting it up in the first place.

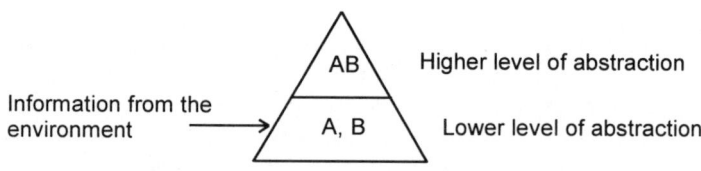

Figure 8.1 Two Levels of Abstraction

If however they are to be an organisational unit, A should be influenced by the information coming to B and vice versa i.e. they interact as above. But there is insufficient time for all to receive all the pooled information and analysis, and so the interaction is restricted to information which has been abstracted to summarise the essentials. The interaction may then have been said to take place at a higher level of abstraction. This may be depicted as in Figure 8.1.

This is a symbolic way of describing the nature of the information flows. A and B communicate and learn from each other at the higher level of abstraction. If there were three, A, B, and C, the interactions would be more complex again and there would be three levels of abstraction (Figure 8.2). For four people A, B, C and D there would be another level at the top of the pyramid and twice as many interactions, and so on.

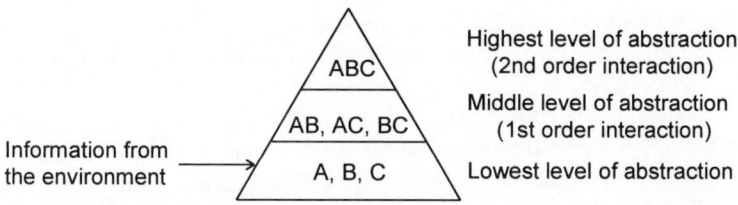

Figure 8.2 Three Levels of Abstraction

In a modern organisation the pyramid can contain many levels, because products are so complex. Take for instance a car manufacturer. The levels might be as follows:

Top level	Share holders, public, government, regulatory bodies etc
next and	Board of Directors
next	General management functions i.e. manufacturing, marketing, finance, planning, research
etc	Functions by country e.g. UK, Germany, US etc
	Factories within the UK, research units in the UK etc
	Individual factories, research units etc
	Departments within factories e.g. assembly lines, stores, maintenance etc
	Component supply
	Individual suppliers
	Individual components
Lowest	Materials for components etc.

If an organisation is divided into levels of abstraction in this way, instead of all participants now having to know everything, the flows of information between them are now concentrated into the interactions at higher levels of abstraction which are required for each of them to make full use of the organisation's power of perception and analysis. But the success of this kind of decomposition depends entirely on being able to predict what each should communicate to others at the next higher level of abstraction. If each has to receive all the information to know whether he needs to know, the object of the decomposition is defeated. If important information is withheld for any reason, this may be equally dangerous. This often happens in organisations which consider themselves to be efficient, having cut out "wasteful" information flows, so that the left hand does not know what the right is doing.

There are two further points. First, valuable information may in fact often come to the organisation at the higher levels of abstraction. Secondly, interactions can occur only if communication takes place internally between the various levels of abstraction. The pyramid of information flows is therefore more accurately illustrated as in Figure 8.3.

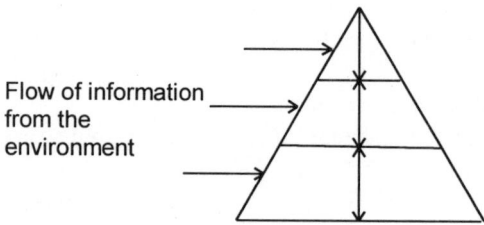

Figure 8.3 Flow of Information into and between Levels of Abstraction

Organisations frequently fail to make use of all the flows of information, external and internal, available to them at all appropriate levels of abstraction. Indeed if there are many levels the interactions may become so bland as to be virtually useless, with all the risks to the system which that entails.

8.4 Architectures

Decomposition of the system into parts offers a solution to the problem of dealing with the volume of information generated by interactions. By exposing the interactions it allows a proportion of specific interactions at the higher levels of abstraction to be eliminated, so that those left are only a small fraction of those theoretically possible.

Inherent in the method is the assumption that the loss of interactions between the parts eliminated, and between these parts and those which remain, is outweighed by the benefit to the whole system (2).

The structures which remain may be classified into three main groups: hierarchies, matrices and co-ordination matrices.

8.4.1 Hierarchies

Hierarchies are what most people have in mind when they think of organisation. They are particularly prominent in some priesthoods as the name suggests e.g. a hierarchy consisting of priests, bishops, cardinals and a chief priest at different levels.

In the example of an organisation consisting of four people or subsystems A, B, C and D we saw that there would be four levels of abstraction associated with sixteen information flows. These may be reduced by restricting the contact between the A and B pair and the C and D pair to give the simplified pyramid in Figure 8.4.

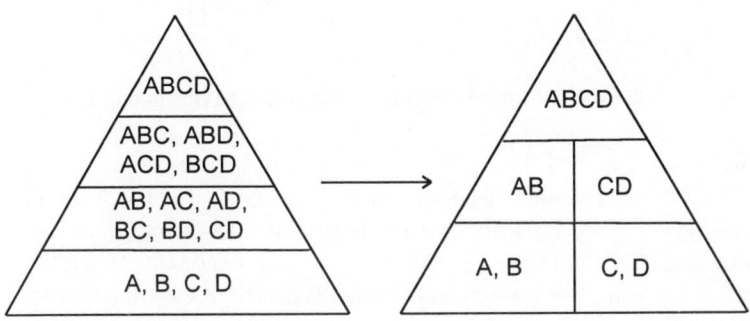

Figure 8.4 Elimination of Interactions

The number of information flows is then halved from 16 to 8. However this also means that half of the interactions are lost, in this case AC, AD, BC, BD, ABC, ABD, ACD and BCD. It is assumed that these interactions are either less important or that they are picked up sufficiently in ABCD, where in principle they all come together, though by the time they reach the highest level of abstraction it could be a vain hope.

This may be more easily recognised as the familiar organisation chart on which we may mark information flows up and down (Figure 8.5). The nodes X, Y and Z which we have introduced into an otherwise unstructured system of four components prevent A or B fromreaching C or D i.e. all the interactions listed above. The nodes X, Y and Z may also be represented by people or other subsystems i.e. positions in the hierarchy.

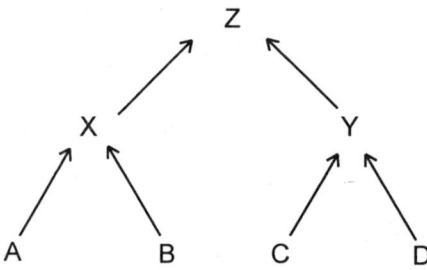

Figure 8.5 Flows of Information up a Hierarchical Organisation

This is the simplest decomposition, but some are much more complicated than that, with five or more flows into one node e.g. Figure 8.6. The number of interactions, and hence the potential information flows from which learning takes place are then much more limited still.

The hierarchic architecture is most suitable where the most useful interactions or flows of information can be foreseen and allowed for. The others can then be discarded without penalty. Some Western religions have been quoted as examples. Others can be drawn from military situations. For example a general cannot afford to wait for all the members of his armed force to interact in case a swift decision has to be made. The permitted interactions or information flows are set out in advance in a mandatory rule book.

Organisation and Innovation in the Economic Process

It is usual but not necessary for different branches of hierarchies to represent different functions or some other entities. This itself provides information about who does what. For instance in a large company they might represent finance, planning, marketing and manufacturing. Each of these might then be divided at a lower level by region or manufacturing site and so on. However such an arrangement puts individuals in functional or geographical pigeonholes on the assumption that they do not need to interact except in a limited range of prestructured and hence foreseeable situations. This may of course be correct, but the first time the branches may actually meet may be at the level of abstraction corresponding to the board of directors, supervisory commission, general council, heads of government departments, national defence committee and so on. As a result those who operate at the highest levels of abstraction may have very little idea of what information passes at lower levels and in other functions of the organisation, which has implications not only for policy-making but also creativity and innovation.

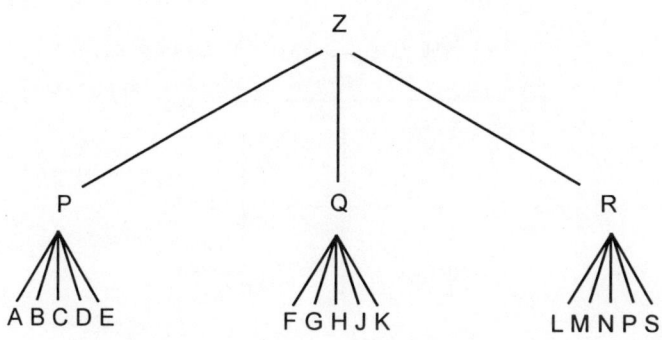

Figure 8.6 Hierarchy with Five Flows into Some Nodes

8.4.2 Matrices

Matrix organisation attempts to mitigate the functional divisions of hierarchy by selecting a range of interactions on a different basis. We reduced the number of interactions between A, B, C and D by collecting them in pairs: A and B, say two types of craftsmen, and C and D, two types of designer. The architecture is set up as follows.

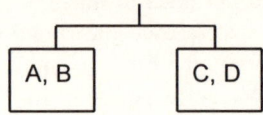

The result is that there is no provision for craftsmen and designers to interact as functions.

If it is considered that there is something to be gained by a structured information flow between the functions in the form of an interaction, a matrix might be set up as in Figure 8.7.

		Design posts	
		C	D
Craft posts	A	1	2
	B	3	4

Figure 8.7 Simple Matrix Organisation

In this representation it is the boxes which represent people, and each then finds himself as the focus of two information flows. Person Number 1 deals with the A type of craft and the C type of design, person Number 4 deals with the B type of craft and the D type of design etc. Some of the advantages of specialisation in the hierarchy

Organisation and Innovation in the Economic Process

have been sacrificed for the interaction in the matrix. On the other side of the coin, some of the disadvantages which may be inherent in the matrix are thought to be outweighed by the advantages of the interaction. In any sort of organisation some element of matrix is inevitable.

Because it sacrifices many interactions there is no more opportunity for learning in the matrix than in the a hierarchy. It simply covers a different set of learning possibilities, which are deemed to be appropriate to the particular situation. The two factor matrix is a relatively simple structure but as soon as more functions are introduced, say four or five such as manufacturing, marketing, planning, personnel, safety and so on, it becomes extremely complicated and the chance of missing important interactions increases rapidly in the ensuing confusion.

8.4.3 The Co-ordination Matrix

The co-ordination matrix is the conventional structure for overcoming some of the deficiencies of the hierarchy without the complexity of the matrix. It consists of adding a staff function i.e. one which is outside the direct line, with a remit to establish information flows with any part

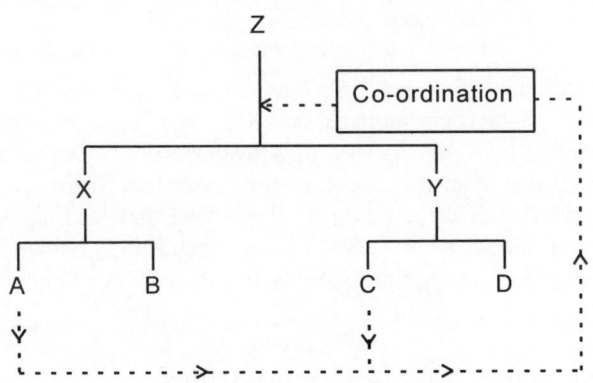

Figure 8.8 Co-ordination Matrix

of the organisation as appropriate. This type of co-ordination function is shown in Figure 8.8.

In effect co-ordination sets up specific interactions which are different from and additional to those built into the line structure, and so it represents an additional matrix element. Co-ordination cannot deal with all the information flows in the system by definition; it applies to a set of information flows selected for a particular purpose. It therefore embodies a different set of learning capabilities which is complementary to that in the line.

A variation of the co-ordination function is the task force, but whereas co-ordination is usually a permanent feature of an organisation, task forces are temporary structures set up for a particular task (Figure 8.9).

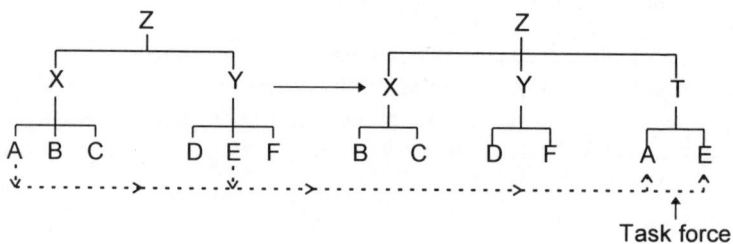

Figure 8.9 Establishing a Task Force

Task forces are often set up where a dedicated multidisciplinary approach to a problem is necessary, and the scope for learning is correspondingly broad and fruitful. However task forces must be the exception rather than the rule for an organisation, because their use deliberately breaks the continuity of purpose and learning which is essential to its long term health. An organisation which consists entirely of task forces has probably been structured wrongly in the first place.

8.5 Decision-making in Organisations

A decision is the formulation and execution of systematic response by an organisation to its environment. The need to make a decision is determined by a change in the relationship between the organisation and the environment in which it operates. Such a change may result from the appearance of a threat or opportunity in the environment i.e. exogenous, or it may be caused by a relative deterioration or improvement within the organisation itself i.e. endogenous. The organisation can only judge by what it perceives at the time. Whether these perceptions are correct and whether the developments which it expects in fact materialise, only time will tell.

The only information absolutely necessary for decision-makers is that a decision needs to be made. But the more information available to them, the better these decisions are likely to be on the whole. Even so, just as there cannot be perfect information about what will happen in the future, so there cannot be perfect decision-making; there is always an element of risk that decisions will turn out not to have been optimal.

Information about the environment comes into the organisation through the awareness of individuals. It ought to be captured at all levels of abstraction at which it appears, because only those who are operating at each level are likely to understand the significance of what they see at that level. Nevertheless information gained at one level may be of great importance to another. For instance information obtained by a clerk that someone is taking an unusual interest in his company's shares may be of great interest to its chairman. Awareness of patent applications by an unexpected source may alert business managers to the emergence of a new business competitor. On the other hand news that two companies are merging or another going bankrupt may have great significance for an engineer who is relying on using their materials or technology.

So even though information may arrive in the organisation at different levels, it must be disseminated from each level to higher and lower levels in order to put them on the alert. All the interactions described above must come into play, or else the organisation will fail to make the most of its chances. It will in effect fail to use all its faculties. Its problem is that its competitors may not.

All who receive the information can judge its significance only if they have a yardstick against which to measure it. Their criterion is what they have learnt from previous experience of similar situations. This is why it is so important for an organisation that it should collectively learn by experience i.e. it should be a learning system.

Moreover if it is to function as a co-operative system, the criteria should be common at all levels of abstraction though expressed in different terms. If people at one level perceive a situation as a threat, but those at another level try to ignore it, the result is likely to be chaos in the long run. These common criteria are inherent in the organisation's goals.

Having appraised itself of the situation and analysed the options for responding, the organisation must have some way of deciding who should make the decision i.e. choose between the options. There are organisations where, even if the gathering and analysis of information are efficiently carried out using all the available faculties, decision-making is permitted at only one level; the top, or in only one part of the organisation, the head office. The result is that some good decisions may be made and swiftly executed, but many will be suboptimal because the centre does not understand the information which should guide the decision, either because it does not have the capability or because it does not have the time.

Some go to other extreme in which many different parts of the organisation are taking decisions in complete ignorance of one another. When each tries to optimise its own position independently, the result is likely to be conflict and far from optimum performance for the whole; in fact chaos, as long as there interactions between the parts, which there must be if they are one organisation.

These are the age old problems of whether to centralise or decentralise. Centralisation brings order, and a case can always be made on paper on the grounds of cost; concentrating activities in one place can always be calculated to eliminate duplication, and reduce overheads, rent, secretarial help, paper work, lighting bills etc. All of which may or may not be true in a particular organisation in its present situation, but ignores completely the diseconomies of scope which will occur when subsystems find it more difficult to operate and costs to the whole system increase in time, as circumstances turn out not to coincide with assumptions and the system lacks the flexibility to respond. Above all the calculations take no account of time, and the changes it will bring. They are based on scale but not scope.

What matters most is that an organisation should be able to respond to its environment. It has no other reason for existence. The bonds of centralisation may bind it so tightly that it cannot move or sometimes

Organisation and Innovation in the Economic Process

breathe, even though it is aware that a response is required. While bound and tied by its own rules, it may be overtaken by disaster from outside, and at the very least it will miss opportunities which come its way. its order becomes a diseconomy of scope. What is the cost to it then?

Evaluation of costs must take account of the time the organisation has to respond, which is dictated by the environment in which it must operate, and will depend on the nature of the stimulus from outside. If it is simply a matter of control, that is one which concerns the efficient operation within its existing structure, the decision can be made swiftly because it requires no special accommodation. The decision may, however, be sufficiently weighty to necessitate adjustment of the organisation i.e. a change of scope. This begins to break some of the interactions and form others, which takes longer to happen, because more people's interests are affected.

But the longest response time is when a significant investment in buildings or equipment is needed, because this will change the scope of the organisation in the long run. Some parts will be favoured at the expense of others, and the decision may even influence the well-being of the organisation itself. Decentralised organisations may find it difficult to respond to this kind of situation. These are effectively the response times described previously in relation to markets.

Both centralisation and decentralisation have advantages and disadvantages. The structure of decision-making should be whatever is appropriate to the system and the environment at the time. It will probably change with time i.e. it will not be homogeneous through time. In general decisions should be made at the lowest level of abstraction which spans the necessary information flows, what has been called the Principle of Subsidiarity (3). Each level will look after the functions which only it can, because no other is at a high enough level to span the necessary range of functions. The role of the centre is directing, watching and restraining as the occasion and necessity demand. The parts should be free to operate within the exposure limits set by the centre. The art is then to find a way of achieving such a decomposition into parts.

In making its decisions the organisation will take account of the risks to its own welfare, but it must also take account of the risks run by those to whom decision-making is delegated. In the West, especially in the English-speaking world, there is a tradition of lone decision-making where those who achieve high enough positions to do it carry the whole burden on their shoulders in self-imposed isolation. Anything else would be considered as shirking one's responsibility, or even worse, it would be seen as weakness. Moreover everyone knows and tacitly accepts the penalty for failure.

Yet in the modern world the complexity of important decisions is such that the widest possible range of information and interpretation is required, even if the ultimate choice rests with one person. Moreover making mistakes is a prerequisite of experience, though preferably they should not be too serious. It is fundamentally a question of trust. The West has much to learn from the Japanese approach to industry in which there is collective acceptance of responsibility for wrong decisions, and factory managers can learn from the shop floor and vice versa without loss of face.

Finally, allied to risk-taking is motivation. In the culture of the English-speaking world it is believed that motivation is a personal characteristic. Incentives are applied to individuals to encourage them to increase their personal contribution. But economic competition is usually between organisations, and these either are or consist of groups. It is the group which needs incentives, and those who form and manage groups who are the key individuals. Excessive effort for personal reward may achieve advancement for the individual but detract from the optimisation of the group effort. Most of us have experiences of people whose idea of leadership is domination. There are other ways, typified for instance by the saying attributed to Lao Tze that he who would lead the people should walk behind them, a very un-British concept.

8.6 Creative Problem Solving

Implicit in many descriptions of information-gathering and decision-making is the assumption that the problem can be uniquely defined and is capable of exact solution. Such problems undoubtedly exist, but they are specific problems of computation, however sophisticated, rather than the rule in economics or societies or behavioural systems in general. The more important a problem, the less amenable it is likely to be to exact definition or solution; sacrifices will be necessary in some aspects to achieve optimum results in another i.e. trade-offs. Since economic decisions are made by members of groups of one sort or another, decision-making also requires a degree of explicit or tacit consensus within the group. If a problem is wrongly defined, the appropriate solution for a system can be found only by pure luck. As the saying goes, garbage in, garbage out. But a lone decision-maker in isolation from the rest of his system may well define a problem inadequately, because of restricted view and interpretation. The result may be that the decision which is made relates more to the symptoms than the disease, or worse, actually treats the problem optimally for one part of the organisation to the severe detriment of another.

To some extent uncertainty and risk in decision-making are inevitable, but they are minimised if all the faculties which the organisational system has at its disposal are used. This is the purpose of the process known as creative problem-solving (4, 5). This process is a structured, group approach to solution of a problem brought by a member of the system. It begins with a check that the problem really exists, a necessary step because many apparent problems are the result of miscalculations or misunderstandings and dissolve when exposed in the appropriate forum. These tend to be the problems which are capable of exact solution, if someone devotees sufficient time and effort to them. Once the existence of a problem is established, the next step is to define it as different individuals within the group see it.

For instance, suppose the agreed problem is that the returns made by a company on its operations are inadequate to finance the new investments needed to keep it in business. The problem may then be perceived by various individuals in a group drawn from the company's members, shareholders and advisers in different ways e.g.

- how to raise the prices which its customers pay or
- how to produce a larger volume of product from its factories or
- how to reduce prices paid for raw materials or
- how to reduce wastage of raw materials or
- how to reduce manpower costs or
- how to convince trades unions of the need to do this or
- how to change managers' attitudes or
- how to change managers or
- how to change the board of directors or

- how to convince the bank that a loan for new investment would be repaid or
- how to rearrange existing assets to reduce long run costs or
- how to develop new, lower cost processes or
- how to develop new, high added value products or
- how to convince the bank that the recent loan for new equipment will lead to better returns   soon or
- how to keep the creditors from the door or
- how to forecast the business cycle better or
- how to forecast government actions better and so on.

Each of the definitions of the problem will require a different solution. The difficulties of the firm may be caused by a whole raft of problems, some of which may be soluble, some not. Some will be important immediately, because the wolf is at the door or the golden opportunity is beginning to fade. Others may be a matter of life or death, but in the longer term. First staunch the bleeding.

Against this background of different perceptions of the problem and the ensuing wide ranging discussions, the decision-maker has the best possible analysis of the nature of the problem confronting the system and the extent and implications of the solutions open to it. Moreover the system itself will be better prepared to respond when the decision needs to be implemented. The operators may have to accept flexible rostering, the finance director may have to go cap in hand to the bank, general managers may have to go, better early warning systems may have to be evolved etc.

Such a process of problem solving does not have to be formal or all in one place, provided it takes place. In effect the group chosen to take part subsumes all the levels of abstraction relevant to the problem in hand from nuts and bolts to finance and theology, if that is required. If information cannot be interpreted or solutions agreed at one level of abstraction, they are kicked up to the next as a base from which to renew the process of solving the problem.

The value of the method is that it addresses problems on a systems basis so that all the necessary interactions can take place. It is independent of the structure of the organisation itself which by its very nature inhibits interactions across functions and between levels. It requires that those who take part, and their selection is vital to the success of the process because they must span the necessary interactions, suspend judgment of each other's contributions until a full understanding of the problems and potential solutions is reached. If confrontation is necessary, it needs to be about decisions not the range of definitions of problems and potential solutions.

Creative problem solving processes can be applied to very difficult problems of widespread public and industrial concern (6). But they are almost never used in the West, particularly the English speaking world, because the nature of the process is to expose ambitions, prejudices and perceptions which many would prefer to keep to themselves in the interest of optimising their individual positions, though this must be at the expense of the system as a whole.

But similar techniques seem to be used to considerable economic effect in Japan, where the culture is that the individual yields in public and in private to group interest. The Japanese way is to spend a great deal of time and money gathering information world-wide, so that problems can be recognised early. They then spend a considerable time analysing and debating the problems and opportunities which the information suggests, and the possible strategies which could be adopted. All this takes an intolerable amount of time in Western eyes, but when the strategy has evolved it is already understood and agreed by all those who need to contribute, so that decision making and implementation can then be very swift indeed.

The Western way is to spend much less on systematic gathering of information about the competitive environment, and much less on exploring problems and debating the range of solutions, but to reach and start implementing solutions as soon as possible. This is thought to be hard nosed and business-like. Asking for information and advice from others may be construed as weakness and vacillation. As a result decisions on complex problems frequently are not based on the use of all the faculties of the organisation, fail to consider the total effect on the system and are not understood or supported by all those needed to implement them i.e. devote resources to them. What is intended to be a swift response may turn out to be very slow indeed.

The process of identifying the need for a response and available options has become confused with the responsibility for making the final decision i.e. choosing between options and its successful implementation. The role of leadership is to ensure that the process takes place and the decisions are made by those best placed to do so.

One does not have to go as far as restraining individual identity as Japanese culture requires in order to achieve an optimum result to which everyone contributes. Perhaps the most obvious manifestation that the West knows that it has something to learn from this approach is its flirtation with co-operative effort at its simplest, the quality circle.

8.7 Strategic Planning

Planning is the preparation of an organisation for an event, whether a threat or an opportunity, which it expects to occur at some time in the future. a plan is an attempt to form a yardstick by which the significance of new occurrences can be measured in order to minimise the organisation's response time as a system. It leads to the decision to invest resources, which may eventually include new buildings and equipment, in anticipation of the expected event, since time is needed to prepare them for use. It may for instance take a decade to build a power station to meet an unexpected increased requirement for electricity.

The planning process has to take place at all the levels of abstraction at which action will eventually be required, and so yardsticks are needed at all levels. All yardsticks in the system must be compatible or else different interpretations may be put on external events in different parts of the system, leading to a confused response. There is no universal time horizon, though the nuts and bolts level will probably have a shorter time horizon than, say, mobilisation of an army. This is not necessarily so; the army may have to be mobilised tomorrow.

Moreover planning applies to all future events, even though the more time there is to respond and the shorter the system's likely response time, the less pressing it is to plan for the event. It is not permissible therefore to omit planning for a period in the middle distance, say at the lower levels of abstraction, or to start planning in two year's time at the highest level. The enemy may invade tomorrow. The future begins now.

Strategic planning is the part of this process which occurs at the highest level of abstraction. This is where all the interactions come together, and so it is the most critical level in the long run. It concerns the relation of the whole organisational system to its environment. It is

Organisation and Innovation in the Economic Process

the function literally translated of the general i.e. in industrial terms the relationship with shareholders, competitor companies, governments, administrators, the public etc.

Because of the interactions the behaviour of the total system is not simply the sum of what is going on at lower levels i.e. the strategic plan is not just the sum of the lower level's plans. The plans of component parts of an organisation are necessary but not sufficient for strategic purposes. However the strategic plan will depend critically on all the sources of information available to it at its level of abstraction. These will be not only external but also internal in the form of information coming up from inside, so that the optimum result for strategic purposes is a combination of both (Figure 8.10).

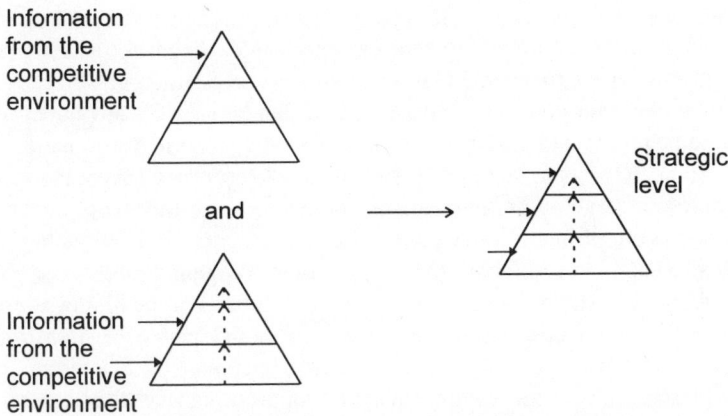

Figure 8.10 Information Flows for Strategic Planning Purposes

But if useful information is to be distilled up through the organisation and not lost in the hurly burly of everyday operations, all parts of the organisation need to have yardsticks by which to measure the importance for each part of the organisation of what it perceives, so that it has a criterion of what information to push up to the next level. The role of yardstick is fulfilled by the organisation's goals.

The Scale and Scope of Economics

The goal is the position which the organisation is going to attempt to reach at the furthest planning horizon, ten or even twenty years into the future. The time chosen will depend on the nature of the change envisaged and the response time of the organisation. The change itself will be dictated by the competitive environment, since the competitors will also be changing. By its very nature the goal must be chosen wisely since it cannot easily be altered in the short or even medium term. For a general it is like deciding which war he is really fighting, looking beyond the battles and skirmishes on the way. In the economic process the nature of the competition is by no means easy to decide and the goal is much more likely to be questioned, so that it needs deepseated support in the organisation.

There will be a range of possible routes to achieving the goal. The one which is selected, after due consideration of the capability of the organisation and the enemy and the lie of the land, is called the strategy. The strategy will determine the underlying pattern of allocation of resources at the organisation's disposal. Milestones reached in the course of pursuing a strategy are strategic objectives. Unlike the main goal, strategic objectives can be sacrificed if they turn out to be unattainable, and an alternative strategy can be formulated.

Since strategy is about the allocation of resources according to a pattern, strategic planning relates to changes of the scope of the organisation through its sequence of investments. It is planning to achieve economies of scope relative to one's competitors over time.

Although strategic planning must by definition be done at the highest level of abstraction i.e. on behalf of the whole organisation, and it is therefore the most important element in achieving its adaptation, not all the commitment of resources can be directed from the top, and so the strategy gives rise to goals at every level. Everyone in the organisation makes a contribution to planning the optimum commitment of resources to the extent available to them. For this to happen the goals of the whole organisation must be available to all parts of the system at the appropriate level. In this way the goals fulfil the same role as the blackboard in the "perfect market". In the absence of such common ground the various parts of the organisation could all be facing in different directions. or even working against each other.

In economic organisations the strategy always conflicts with someone's interests within the organisation, since it relates to changes of scope. If it is to be worthwhile, it must therefore involve compromise among the leading players. A strategy must be understood and agreed by all those required to commit resources to make it work, which also implies an agreement with, or at least an acquiescence in, its goals. In the absence of agreement it may be only a pious hope.

Formulation and implementation of a strategy is a matter of leadership. The major task of a leader is to get his organisation to respond at the appropriate time in the appropriate way and to the optimum extent. A sound response which comes too late, or one which is unnecessarily premature, may put the organisation itself at risk.

Planning has in the past been misconstrued as prediction or indeed calculation of the future. Such an approach is doomed to failure and has got itself a bad name. Planning must relate to the preparation of the organisation for possible future events; it cannot possibly relate to preparation of the environment.

When organisations become very large, there may be so many levels of abstraction that the top becomes very remote from the bottom. Neither understands the other, and so information must pass through numerous middle layers in its passage up and down. Thus those at the highest level are unable to direct what is happening lower down. Nor can they simply wash their hands of it, because it is essential to the strategy. They need a plan to communicate.

Two other major elements in strategic planning are trust and confidence. Players at all levels need to be confident that the strategy is well founded. They must trust their leaders not to abandon them to their fate when the going becomes hard, as it always does in the course of a campaign, and to share the spoils when the war is won.

Failure to formulate sound goals in the aftermath of the era of gifted amateurs; lack of confidence in such as do emerge and in the ability of leaders to carry them out; and the absence of trust in the more fortunate parts of the community not to abandon the rest; these are some of the failures of leadership in our society today, when others who are better organised in all these respects are inching past in the economic competition.

8.8 Innovation and Organisation

We now have the necessary elements to build up a picture of what innovation involves in terms of organisation. We need to bear in mind that innovation is the deliberate process by which a new product comes to be sold in the market or a new process comes into commercial use. It is not invention, though this involves a related set of problems.

The organisation gathers information about its competitive environment at all levels of abstraction. Not only must information come in at all levels but it must distil up and down internally to allow the various elements to be related, thus maximising its usefulness. Since there is no way of knowing in advance what information will be useful, the gathering needs to be systematic. Prices are clearly part of the information to be gathered, but much of it will concern technological, organisational, financial and social change. For many products the best source is the user.

The architecture of the organisation is a major constraint. Products and processes which can be encompassed within one line of a hierarchy are soon identified and developed. But most new opportunities cross the various divisions, and so they do not appear of their own accord: they must be made to surface. This function is facilitated by co-ordinating groups, and it can often be reinforced by individuals, sometimes called gatekeepers, who make contact and talk across the organisation in a way which may appear to be casual, because it does not seem to stay within the line of the organisation chart.

The organisation needs some way of analysing what it learns, measuring it against a yardstick and synthesising it into options for action. The yardstick is provided by a strategic plan which allows preparation for innovation even if it is not known what specifically it will be. The strategic response may be explicit but it may be instinctive in the organisation. Much of the preparation is really overcoming in advance the reactions against changing the scope of the organisation, thus reducing the time it takes to respond. It makes sure all the troops are facing in the same direction, or helps to suppress the antibodies which always set to work on something new.

Analysis alone is not enough; the other side of the coin is synthesis, the creative development of options for response. Synthesis requires

Organisation and Innovation in the Economic Process

stores of learning from previous situations, which might be called feedback about the effect of previous decisions. Apart from creative individuals it may also require a minimum number of contributions from different sources, a critical mass effect.

Finally the organisation must be prepared to adapt in response to its environment. Interactions must be broken so that other more appropriate ones may be formed. This may be an uncomfortable process and often takes place when a small number of individuals are willing to accept the risk of acting as agents of change.

An organisation cannot produce an orderly response without some form of structure, and yet most of the factors which favour innovation cut right across the structure. The art is to find a modus operandi which manages both order and freedom, as Schumacher observed (3), or to be both loose and tight according to other descriptions. There can be no innovation if there is no slack in the system, since all resources are directly and completely tied to the present output. This is the usual result of tight budgeting. To change metaphors again, what is required is a creative ferment, which may be chaotic, and some means of pulling order out of it as appropriate.

The very nature of innovation is that the outcome is uncertain. It is making an investment without being able to define precisely what the resources are being invested in, because it may well change as time goes on. It requires some way of allowing the organisation as a system to experiment. If the system refuses to accept this, the whole of the risk falls on the individuals involved, and many initiatives will therefore be stifled.

In Far Eastern cultures it seems that the risks of innovation may be carried collectively by the system, whereas in the West we pin the responsibility on individuals. But we have shown that the whole of an organisation needs to be involved in innovation, and only leadership can break the interactions which prevent a flexible response. These are some of the factors in the management of change, which is badly done indeed in Western countries, not least in mine.

Research and development is usually set up as a separate division in large firms. This has the advantage that it can form a sort of innovative or primordial soup without contaminating the structure of the rest of the organisation, whose major priority must be to run its operations efficiently. But it may also prevent the very interactions which are necessary to the one to encourage innovation and to the other to survive in the long run. The result all too often is that each side views the other with suspicion.

One attempt to impose some control over this was the introduction of the customer/contractor principle in government scientific establishments in the UK. The customer was supposed to say what he wanted and the contractor would then say what it would cost. If they agreed, a bargain was struck in the manner of the market.

Consider the assumptions which this made. First the market idea was a complete nonsense, because the "product" fulfilled none of the conditions required by the theory, especially that it should be well-defined. Indeed it was not known what the outcome of the work would be; if it could be predicted, experimentation would not be necessary. What was being bought was so much skilled time and measurement, backed by experience i.e. man hours. The customer almost certainly had only the vaguest idea what he wanted, not least because he did not speak the same language. Nor did he have any incentive to bargain in the manner of the market, because he could do no more than spend the money, very often as an insurance policy to show he had done his best. He probably simply dictated what he would spend, and the rest was up to the researcher. It was not unknown for a customer to spend most of his time counting the expenditure of his single contractor, one on one with a vengeance!.

In short the system absolved customers from the responsibility of decision-making and strategic commitment, because these could be left to the accounts. It generated a vast and costly flow of information to allocate resources in place of what should have been a management decision, without influencing the total strategic effort at all: a generally counterproductive result, an unnecessary diseconomy of scope.

The researcher for his part almost certainly had no option but to accept what was on offer, whether it was "sufficient" or not, because the alternative was not another customer, but probably no customer at all. The result all too often was short term working, broken teams, destructive competition for work and loss of expertise; certainly no vision or creativity. This was accountability which was no accountability.

The solution is quite straightforward. The customer should be pursuing a plan or strategy which includes a research element, and for the success of which he is accountable, not just the budget. The size of the commitment depends on how important it is to fulfil the plan or beat the competition, and when. If it is not very important, why do it? If it is important, then agree the priority with all concerned and proceed, until the task is finished i.e. a long term commitment.

Parcelling out the payments on a hand to mouth basis is expensive in useful time, employs too many in the capacity of clerks, achieves "control" which is more apparent than real and defeats the objective of having a skilled research tool or weapon. It hands what should be a strategic management decision over to an accounting device. What is more it is almost certainly a positive feedback mechanism, reinforcing yesterday's successes. Better to get the strategy right and leave it to a competent management, and educate the customers too, so that they actually understand the language.

A further extension of the "market" concept was that the customer should have the right to buy his service outside "on the open market", so that competition would bring down the "price". This was a particularly destructive application of these severely flawed "market" principles, because the money might be buying the same manhours, but it could not buy the same experience. What is more, it prevented the in-house "contractor" learning and adding this experience to his store of knowledge. It is like hiring a mercenary; possibly all right in non-strategic areas at times of peak demand, but dangerous as a routine.

Probably the only virtue of the system was that the customer and contractor were required to communicate at least once, perhaps for the first time. But there are other, cheaper and more effective ways of achieving this.

Sadly the concept has taken root and is now being extended to other functions for which the "market" analysis is equally inappropriate, in the name of accountability. It will prove to be just as misguided in these too.

8.9 The Economic Costs of Behavioural Effects

Organisation and information flows may be seen as just another exogenous distortion, but they do in fact have a very real effect on both input and opportunity costs, as the following examples show.

The Scale and Scope of Economics

Domestic rates in Britain were a tax levied locally on housing. Their apparently inexplicable variations aroused considerable controversy, at least among a vociferous minority. However they had the merit of making use of two important pieces of information. First, those collecting the tax always knew where the houses were. Secondly, owners almost certainly had the wherewithal to pay. In any case there were always the ultimate sanctions against property disowned for the purposes of evading the tax. Information flows were therefore relatively simple, which is essential if tax is to be collected at low cost. This is one reason why virtually all modern industrial countries, whether European or North American, have property taxes.

The political response was to replace the domestic rates with a tax on people as citizens, a poll tax, abandoned in Europe hundreds of years ago. This immediately divided individuals into a range of categories: those who could pay, but with no more enthusiasm than before; those who could scarcely afford to pay, but might in the end, though it would take much effort on the part of the authorities and perhaps even involve the courts; and those who simply did not have the wherewithal, whatever action was taken to make them pay. Even the minority groups were substantial in numbers as a proportion of the whole. In addition there was a significant proportion of people at any one time who were moving around, and were quite legitimately difficult to trace for tax purposes. The quantity of information required to collect the tax at satisfactory levels rose dramatically as frequent notices had to be issued, special departments had to be set up to trace and encourage those liable to pay the tax, the law became involved, the government machinery started to pick up the pieces and so on. Not only this, but the system was so widely perceived to be unfair that a proportion of people refused to pay at all, and fought it every step of the way.

All this amounted to a vast increase in information flows and hence the cost of collecting the tax. It was calculated to have cost several billion pounds more to collect than the local rates, which is an estimate of the cost of the quantity of information needed to operate the system. The cost was still rising at its abandonment, and could probably be shown to be heading for infinity. (It was estimated that it had cost £10000 to try to recover £40 of unpaid poll tax in a recent case, and from someone who simply could not afford to pay anyway). People are not static for tax purpose. Their dwellings are, and their places of work probably are, or at least they move slowly enough to capture for tax purposes, which simplifies information flows enormously. People as individuals are not, and the costs of assuming they were became all too apparent both in money and other terms.

The second example also concerns housing. When the housing boom of the eighties came to an end, the demand for housing and house prices both decreased together, in complete contradiction of the "laws" of supply and demand. The reason seemed quite simply to be that people were too uncertain about their circumstances to move house. If this had applied to a few individuals, the outcome might have been more in line with neoclassical predictions. Indeed complete independence of action amongst buyers and amongst sellers, leading to a sort of stochastic exchange, is an assumption implicit in that analysis. But in the system as a whole, the buyers and the sellers were for the most part the same people. Uncertainty applied to the whole system, not the parts, in exactly the same way as the boom had applied to the whole system, which might even be considered the definition of a boom. People do not have to collude over prices to invalidate the "perfect" market response; they simply have to be subject to the same influences as a body, a not infrequent occurrence.

The net result was that many were left with debts which exceeded the value of their houses. The cost to them was the opportunity cost of the capital invested, expressed as higher interest payments than they might otherwise expect to pay. For those whose worst fears were realised when they lost their incomes, the costs were much higher: their homes, the money invested in them, the improvements which they had to leave behind and perhaps their families and self respect.

A third example relates to the analysis of earlier chapters. It began with a classification of the elements of the economic process including incentives, which were defined as everything to do with money. It was shown that the incentive system could be considered to act as feedback into conversion processes (Figure 2.6). In later discussion the incentive was crystallised into flows of money (Figure 3.13), or specifically the net revenue R_N accruing to converters (Figure 4.6). As an extension of this the incentive for innovators to enter markets was shown to be the net revenue per unit of output they were likely to earn (Figures 7.4 and 7.5).

The Scale and Scope of Economics

Pound notes are much crisper than behavioural concepts, especially in diagrammatic form, but incentive is the more comprehensive term. It is people and their behaviour which determine outcomes; the money measures the effect. Thus it is perfectly reasonable to equate the two as feedback for conversion processes when considering the short term responses to sales in the market. It is very likely that converters will make all they think they can sell, if it increases their net revenue without fundamental changes to their processes. If it means some kind of upheaval, they may be a little more circumspect, and perhaps hang on to some of their earnings a little longer, which to an extent accounts for longer response times. If however they need to make investments in new equipment, they will deliberate longer still before making a decision. This is the normal effect of competition for individual converters. They may be right to delay, and those who rush to invest may come a cropper. On the other hand they may miss the boat. It is a question of individual appraisal.

If however all converters decide not to invest, the situation is quite different, because one converter's investment is another's output. The result is that production is constrained within the limits of existing capacity. The system as a whole runs down through entropic degradation and technological obsolescence, which eventually affects everybody's output. This will be exactly reflected in the flows of money through the economy, because they measure the transactions which take place. But it will be the behavioural response of converters which determines the flows or revenues, not vice versa. The decisions of individual converters which may be perfectly rational responses to their specific situations coincide to have an unwanted and deleterious effect on the system as a whole. The costs of this are not simply the lost output, but the unemployment which ensues, the taxes which are not paid, the public services which are not affordable and so on. On the other hand when confidence is high, the exact reverse can occur. It is all part of the system's response.

As this suggests, not all behavioural effects are adverse. It is just that the costs when things go wrong are easier to identify than the benefits when they go well. It also fits in with conventional analysis more easily when applied to whole systems rather than the parts.

The final example shows this other side of the coin. Much has been made, and quite rightly, of the problems caused by some of the high rise housing constructed with the best of intentions to provide good accommodation for the poorer sections of the community at affordable costs. The estates too often degenerated through unsociable activity such as vandalism and petty crime, which were facilitated by the way in which they were planned and assembled. Poor construction did not help, but too much of the available resources was devoted to cleaning up the mess to be able to effect improvements. Things sometimes reached such a pitch that the local authority could no longer afford to maintain them i.e. real input costs, and the only course of action was to raze the buildings and start again, that is more capital investment.

Another approach which seems to be succeeding is to enable the people on the estates to form more coherent communities, that is a behavioural response. Money is spent on new or perhaps first time facilities for children to play with adequate supervision. Someone is designated and funded to encourage sociable behaviour with the authority to enforce it through sanctions if necessary, and either live on the estates or visit frequently enough to make his or her presence generally noticed and accepted. In short money is spent to change the scope of the investment, albeit very small in comparison with the total capital already sunk.

The results, which may all be considered as opportunity costs, are a transformation of people's lives. Children can play safely, women can go about their daily lives more freely, old people are not robbed, windows are not smashed, lifts are not destroyed and so on. Every one of these is associated with a cost which will no longer be incurred, a saving which can be offset against the investment required to change the scope of the problem in this way, with who knows what benefits to society in the long term. The problem for calculators and neoclassical market enthusiasts is that the costs and savings, where identifiable, occur on different budgets. But that does not prevent them from being real; it simply illustrates the problem of representing the dynamics of the real economy by static methods. A look at the whole system soon shows the limitations of that approach.

8.10 Conclusions

All this is a world away from markets for undifferentiated "labour" and "perfect" markets in which buyers and sellers are seen as isolated individuals. They are almost always organisations or their representatives, and the complexity of their economic function is such that many of the decisions which have a fundamental effect on prices and quantities have been taken long before market day.

Organisations are behavioural systems. They have the usual systems inputs and outputs of information, materials and energy, and they are more than the sum of their parts. An organisation is essentially a system for handling information flows, and using them to make and implement decisions. Revenue-earning conversion processes are systems which operate in a competitive environment, and so they need strategies to succeed in the face of competition. Hence strategic management and planning. They require much more than "stewardship", or looking after the silver.

It is a misconception to consider behavioural systems as regimented like an army on parade; they are much messier. If one must use a military analogy, perhaps a real war situation would be nearer the mark. In fact they require different modes of operation in different situations: sometimes command, sometimes participatory, very often as teams. It is a question of judgment.

Teams are an essential characteristic of modern organisations, because of the complexity of modern economic life, and the problem of setting up organisations is how to promote the formation of teams, and reward them, while maintaining the structure which is necessary to the integrity of the organisation. Special arrangements have to be made to separate information flows from decision-making.

Management of change is one of the most difficult problems of organisation, and it lies at the foundation of technological innovation and growth. The interactions within the organisational system are what gives it identity, but they also prevent it from accommodating to new environments i.e. threats and opportunities. Since economic organisations are in a continual process of development in order to obtain economies of scale and scope, these interactions are continually being broken and new ones remade, which affects individuals. Without this it is impossible to grow and innovate. Such adaptation needs leadership and people who are willing to act as agents of change, but for these to be effective a culture of trust is essential. If everyone is constantly engaged in a struggle for personal survival, there is no room for adaptation, and so flexibility is vital. Otherwise it is like trying to move a jibsheet from winch to winch under tension.

Organisations need to be constituted as learning systems, so that they accumulate expertise. This is what allows them to obtain the economies of scope, which are necessary to their economic survival. They need contacts with the outside at all levels, sensors and yardsticks which allow them to recognise what incoming information is important. They need a means of processing this information and a stock of knowledge against which to compare it, so that rational decisions can be made. Above all they need continuity. Contracting out functions, which is fashionable at present, mainly in response to accounting, is a particular form of limited interaction which runs counter to the learning system concept; it is another organisation which does the learning, and as mercenaries they may not always be on your side. It is not suitable for more than routine work, and then only in time of peak demand, if the state of competition allows it. Even baggage handlers and office cleaners may affect the performance, and certainly affect the perception, of a corporation. It is ultimately a question of trust.

Decision-making is not the same as information flows. One of the functions of leadership is to make sure that all the faculties and experience of the organisation are used to best effect in evaluating responses to changes in the environment, before the most appropriate options are selected. The time taken for this process to take place is part of the response times of conversion processes to changes in net revenue, which act as feedback to the system.

Handing decision-making to accounting devices is an abdication of responsibility, though it is often considered to be "efficient". Setting up organisations which require excessive information-processing in the name of accountability is wasteful. It is like trying to win a race by continually measuring your pulse. We have shown that cash flows provide feedback which is vital to the economic functioning of conversion processes. The problems arise when costs, which can be allocated internally only by the use of conventions, are estimated at every turn in an organisation, because the quantity of data multiplies with every node at which "measurement" is made. What this brings to the problem of adaptation is a matter of conjecture.

The Scale and Scope of Economics

The quantity of information to be processed by an organisation and the rate at which it needs to be done are vital considerations in the economic process, although they get scant mention in orthodox economics. Information costs money to acquire, process and keep. Just how much depends on the goal which the organisation sets itself and the architecture which it adopts. Poor choice of either may give rise to unsustainable costs. On the other hand failure to gather information may impair the organisation's response, which will incur opportunity costs.

Information may suffocate at one level, or precipitate abrupt changes at another. Abrupt changes are destructive. Rates of change are all important because behavioural systems are full not of things but of people, who need trust, membership and continuity. They are certainly not the abstraction of "labour". One particular form of accounting device, the customer/contractor relationship, managed to be short term, suffocating and bring about abrupt changes all at the same time, a destructive use of spurious "market" economics. Its use is being extended in the name of efficiency.

As behavioural systems economic organisations can react in predictably irrational ways. Armies who check the rations and count the ammunition meticulously have been known to reject a new weapon which will win them the war. Similarly corporations have regularly rejected "goldmines" offered to them, even in their own line of business. This is not simply mistrust or incompetence, though there is always a chance of both in innovation, as in all organisations. It stems from the interactions which bind the organisations together in pursuit of their goal. They exclude anything which does not fit their current perception, because this is a condition of the system's survival. An extension of this is the vested interests which hold determinedly onto interactions which suit them, to the detriment of the system as a whole. All sorts of vested interests may inhibit, as well as promote, change: certainly politicians, but also professions, class, religion, caste, old boy networks, trade unions, cultural antipathies to industry and technology etc.

The free flow of reliable information is essential for all economic systems, especially in the delicate phase of innovation when cash flows are critical, and mistakes are likely to be heavily punished. Information is what allows them to change and adapt, to succeed or, if it is not

Organisation and Innovation in the Economic Process

heeded or acted upon, to fail. They need statistics which are as complete, unbiased and reliable as possible. If statistics are biased or unbalanced at the national level, there is the potential for disaster for all who use them. "Information management", the fixing of statistics to suit one political ideology, the packing of institutions, business, and "quangos" with supporters of a single view bodes nothing but ill. It means that the national system is using only a small proportion of its faculties. In an international competitive situation, this is a disaster in the making. Balance is essential, if the response is to be informed.

There is a peculiarly English (not British) characteristic, party political in origin, of destroying anything which is systematic, especially if it successful. The market is considered the only valid form of organisation by supporters of this view. They espouse a free market in everything but ideas. The result is an approach to economics which is confrontational, and anything but co-operative. It is not simply a right or left wing view, because it does not happen on the left or right elsewhere in Europe, for instance. This selfish individualism goes back at least 150 years, and it is not surprising that it breeds an attitude among the workforce which is its mirror image. This concerns the fundamental organisation of society, and it has profound implications for the economy. Systems which cannot hang together in the modern world, will find that their subsystems will certainly hang separately. Or more formally, you cannot optimise the whole by optimising the parts!

Chapter Nine

CONCLUSIONS

If a man will begin with certainties he shall end in doubts; but if he will be content to begin with doubts he shall end in certainties.

Francis Bacon

Classical economics and its genetically related offspring, neoclassical economics, emphasise the role of markets to the near exclusion of everything else. Great importance is attached to the theoretical "perfect" market on which the whole edifice is founded, and much effort has been expended on trying to determine how close to "perfection" particular markets are. "Perfect" markets are linked to each other in the universal network of markets, which has the amazing and satisfying property of being in "equilibrium", given the chance. This property is derived from the "perfection" of "perfect" markets; just as they settle down to a unique, "equilibrium" price for a product, so the network which links them all together, if displaced from its "equilibrium" point, returns to it automatically. "Perfect" markets which are in "equilibrium", are in "equilibrium" with each other.

Thus the whole economic system is thought to rest on the effort of individuals pursuing their own interests in a world of market prices which respond only to quantities supplied and demanded. Everything which is produced is sold, because the "equilibrium" price clears the

Conclusions

market. In this world individuals collide atomistically like billiard balls on the supply/demand schedules. If they pursue their own interests to the exclusion of all else, then they have done the best they can by the economic system. It will adopt a position of "equilibrium" which cannot be improved upon. There is no point in trying to change the status quo. Everything is for the best in this best of all possible theories.

If the real world does not respond like that, it must be the real world which is at fault. Markets must be freed from "imperfections", a continual battle requiring many maids and even more mops, but it is worth it, in spite of the damage caused to ordinary people's lives, because at the end of this particular rainbow lies the "equilibrium", the thought of which soothes away all misgivings. If "equilibrium" does not seem to be quick in coming, it must be through lack of application, and the pursuit is redoubled, the "remedies" administered even more forcefully.

To the non-believer this presents an astonishing picture. If we take the conditions specified for the "perfect" market and examine them rigorously, we see that they could never work to any serious extent. First there are the problems of information during bargaining. You can postulate perfect information before bargaining, or even perfect foresight, though this would seem a curiously unstable base on which to build anything practical. But surely you cannot postulate perfect information during bargaining, or why bargain? Then there is the sheer quantity of information during the bargaining process. For the system to work at all there must be a display of the progress of bargaining for all to see. For "equilibrium" to be reached, there must be displays for all markets, and everyone in the economic process must watch all of them all of the time, so that they can intervene as they wish in exercise of their individual right to optimise their own positions.

Then there is time. There is no time in classical economics or in "perfect" markets. Time does not appear as a variable on supply/demand schedules. But how do they bargain, if there is no time? If there are many people involved, does not time run out before the process is finished? If they are bargaining for eggs or tomatoes, will they not have gone off, or the customers have lost their appetites, by the time the bargaining has come to an end and the unique price/quantity relationship has been reached? It is no use thinking of

The Scale and Scope of Economics

each additional participant as a marginal addition to the process; the information to be handled during bargaining doubles if he is to play his role, as he surely must be allowed to in a "perfect" market.

Finally there is energy, which is conspicuous by its absence from classical economics. Even to mention it is thought to be wicked. It is all to do with Marx, who by the way was himself a classical economist. Mention energy, the theory goes, and before you know where you are, subversion, revolution and worse must follow. If only the man in the street realised this, he might from loyalty be expected to think long and hard before filling up his car with petrol (hydrocarbon energy), or switching on his lighting (electrical energy), or using his cooker (heat energy) etc. Or would he? At this point, even if not before, one begins to smell a rat; no time, no energy. Could this be because they do not fit the theory? One wonders how it accommodates its perfectly valid branch called energy economics. Presumably it talks only of price and quantity of energy, though energy itself does not exist, and it comes in a wide range of inconveniently differentiated forms: oil, gas, coal, electricity, firewood, sunshine(!), and so on.

The consequence of all this is that in orthodox economics, which seems to be largely Anglo-Saxon, others being more pragmatic, everything can be substituted for everything else. Banking substitutes for coalmining, hairdressing for petrochemicals, economics for agriculture etc. The reason is that money itself substitutes for everything e.g. money is equivalent to machine tools or aircraft, as it may seem to be, if you confine your field of view to reckoning up after market day. Indeed this is a requirement of reaching "equilibrium". The unspoken corollary of this would be that manufacturing was superfluous; money would suffice to meet all needs.

In a concession to the real world, analysis is made of the output functions of conversion processes. Cost is shown to vary with the quantity of output from, say, a factory, which it does. Moreover costs are calculated to be reduced by operating on a larger scale i.e. a bigger plant, which they may (though they may not). Hence economies of scale. The problem is that technology is treated as exogenous; and anyway it must be a secondary, if somewhat uncomfortable, consideration for a theory which exalts exchange above production. However, if there is no time in the theory, by definition there can be no change; costs vary only with quantities produced, "other things being

Conclusions

equal". Technological innovation is even more of a problem. No time, no change, no innovation. Other things are never equal. Time to descend into the real world, the one which everyone can recognise around them.

If we set aside the impositions of the classical theory, we can look at markets as they really are. First, markets have existed since time immemorial, long before economic theory intervened, ever since man decided that it was better to acquire by exchange than by force. That period covers about 95% of man's existence on earth. More recently he discovered that it was much easier if one could agree on a medium of exchange i.e. money in some form, because transactions could be more complicated and money could be kept for a rainy day, to everyone's advantage. More recently still, a mere 2500 years ago, markets became a focus for such heated exchange and debate that there emerged a new form of social organisation called democracy.

Markets have always been supervised, because they are full of people with all their human characteristics, not billiard balls. Ways of settling disputes have always been one of their features. Money is essential these days as never before, because otherwise you are faced with the problem of bartering TV sets for motor cars, or sheep, or any combination. Prices tend to emerge which are about the same, because people are not going to pay over the odds, and they naturally want to know how everyone else is doing. The mechanism does not have to be "perfect"; it works.

As for "equilibrium", consider the changes which have occurred in the balance of economic activity in the world over the last 20 years. Japan has risen from a minor economic power to a position as one of the strongest in the world. Others are following the same route. This can be construed as a continuation of the process by which from the beginning of the modern economic era in the eighteenth century one European power has succeeded to another, until in this century the USA succeeded them all. It might be thought of as the march of time. However the new arrivals have quite a different view of economic processes from the "perfection" of theory outlined above. Far from settling down to "equilibrium", the imbalances world-wide have grown.

Let us set aside the ideology and consider what we actually know. If time is not a variable in the classical economic process, it implies

The Scale and Scope of Economics

that the elements of its version of the economic process are treated as homogeneous through time; they run up and down the scale of output without changing their character. But conversion processes are certainly not homogeneous through time. They undergo a continual process of improvement through differentiation as the technology changes, both in existing installations and new ones. The qualitative nature of processes and products, which we call their scope, is continually changing with time. Economies of scale may still apply, but economic improvements resulting from this continual differentiation of products and processes is fundamentally more significant. The term "differentiation" in economics is not new; the global consequences for nations over time certainly are.

Economies of scope may also lead to increasing scale of operation. Increasing revenue which flows back from markets is reinvested to give even greater economies of scale and scope. The imbalances increase, not decrease with time. They cannot be matched by competitors through scalar reduction of "labour" costs, because economies of scope make increasingly better economic use of people. For those left behind in the race the cost of materials and energy inputs per unit of output may alone exceed the total unit costs of those who have economies of scale and scope; competitors cannot match them, even if their "labour" costs are zero. They form a competitive advantage which can be redressed only by investment in all the various aspects of conversion operations: people and equipment which transform inputs of information, materials and energy into outputs.

Technology is like a ratchet on the economic process, because once knowledge about transforming inputs into outputs has been obtained, and especially after it has been implemented, it does not disappear. There is no slipping back. Technological innovation moves the whole process forward notch by notch. Thus economies of scope confer permanent advantages on those who have them. This has been true since the beginning of time, from palaeolithic to neolithic, bronze age to iron age, and steel to rubber and plastics, synthetic fibres and now silicon.

Economies of scope are to be obtained from all the elements of the economic process which change with time, and hence are susceptible to improvement, whether as separate elements or in their configuration. They involve people, and their capacity to learn and

Conclusions

improve, and materials in all their different forms. Not least they require energy. All economies of scope are driven by energy. Nor do they arrive by chance; they are intended and planned for. They require organisation. Only money is homogeneous through time, because it is agreed and promised to be such. This is absolutely true of fiat money, quite true for gold, as long as it is not handled, and reasonably true for silver, provided you do not polish the oxide layer off too often. The people who use it, individuals, firms and institutions, are certainly not homogeneous through time.

All this is common sense, but it gives a quite different view of the economic process. The economic process consists of conversion processes in which materials are transformed through successive stages from raw inputs to finished products. They may pass from converter to converter through markets for intermediates. The final products are exchanged in markets and then consumed, which was the reason for their production in the first place. All exchanges take place through the medium of exchange, money, and the net revenue flowing back to a converter from the market tells him how to respond i.e. it acts as feedback. The conversion system cannot respond immediately to feedback because it involves materials and process energy, and may require a new organisation and investment in equipment. There is therefore a range of response times.

Services take place as exchanges outside this system and, although they may facilitate it, take no direct part until they feed back revenue into a conversion process i.e. they buy a product of a conversion process in a market.

It is much simpler to consider the economic system literally as a system, for that is what it is. Adam Smith thought of an economy as a system right back at the beginning of economics as a discipline, before the mathematical analysis of systems was in place, and before the market assumed theological proportions (1). Malthus wrote of economic systems in a more literal sense, but the mathematics of his assumptions led to particularly dismal conclusions (2). The analysis of this book is much more hopeful.

However that may be, the "perfect" market as a system is a non-starter; so must be the "equilibrium" which depends on it. Any "system" which relies on its parts to produce an optimum result for the whole solely by their independent actions cannot possibly work. It offends against the very first rule of systems, which is mathematical and homogeneous through time, and cannot be changed to suit preconceptions: you cannot optimise a whole system by optimising its parts; or in this case, a whole system cannot be optimised if its parts simply optimise their own positions. The reason lies in the interactions between them. It is not that the parts of the system, individuals, companies and institutions, lose their freedom to act, but rather that whatever one part does will react on the others, whether they know it or not. They are not billiard balls. At some level there has to be some common, openly acknowledged and understood co-ordination or co-operation or planning, or the whole system descends into chaos. The necessary condition for this is the free and public flow of unbiased information between all the economic and social subsystems of which the system itself is composed.

Time runs through all systems, whether explicitly or implicitly, because their interest for us lies in how they change in response to their environment. Markets and conversion processes can be usefully considered as systems for analytical purposes, because the small number of unbreakable rules give insight where the only alternative is verbiage. Money is a most important part of the economic system because it responds much faster than the energy-dependent parts. This is what enables it to be used as a feedback system for the whole system, rather like the nervous system in a human being. Moreover, these are systems which accumulate knowledge and learn from experience. in the long run they are capable of making increasingly better use of inputs to produce what they want. Those who do not learn are left behind.

None of this should come as any surprise on reflection. The economic system, indeed any social system, is in many respects just like the behavioural systems which occur in nature, though of course much more sophisticated, we like to think. Individuals of all species co-operate to protect themselves, procreate, nurture their young etc. Within these limits, the imperatives of survival, individuals are free to be individuals. Sometimes it is good to be free to act individually. At other times it is necessary, and may even be enjoyable to act collectively. What else is society?

The deficiencies of classical economics would not matter except to students, if they were not forced into practice by politicians. False

Conclusions

conclusions are drawn from flawed analyses, and imposed in the name of inevitability, while everyone is expected to wait for an automatic return to "equilibrium". Meanwhile planning, organisation, vision, skills, education, indeed all the real assets of a country which are its people, are scorned. The common sense of ordinary people is thrust aside in the rush back to the eighteenth century.

Times are changing. Great tides of information and energy flood across the globe every day, as never before. While they may be necessary to economic processes throughout the world, they are sweeping away old certainties and introducing instability, as we are all confronted with the world beyond our doorsteps, whether we like it or not. Millions of people, many of them young, are being denied the opportunity to take part in the economic processes which are the foundation of the societies in which they live, with what consequences for the future we can only guess. At the very best this can only be unhealthy, at worst ....

There is nothing inevitable in all this. The idea that the only thing to do is abdicate our responsibilities and let the economic process sort itself out is a counsel of despair rooted in the failings of classical economics. Economic systems are for the benefit of man, not vice versa; to coin a phrase, there are no economic ends.

Any fresh understanding which helps to break into cycles of decline should be welcomed, if not by experts, then by ordinary people, who know that old "solutions" are not working. I would be surprised if any of the great numbers of scientists and engineers and managers, and indeed anyone who is trying to push forward the frontiers of economic and social processes for the benefit of all, were to deny the force of what I hope are the commonsense arguments laid out here. Indeed many of them are themselves employed in the pursuit of economies of scope. Not that there are any tablets of stone, just room for open debate from which new and more fruitful directions can emerge. We should do it out of our own self interest, if nothing else, and above all, if we believe in the future, we owe it to our children.

REFERENCES

Chapter One - INTRODUCTION

1. See any standard economics textbook e.g. Richard G. Lipsey, An Introduction to Positive Economics, (Weidenfeld and Nicholson, London) or Paul A. Samuelson, Economics, (McGraw Hill)

2. See, for example, J. K. Galbraith, The New Industrial Estate (Pelican), or J. K. Galbraith and Nicole Salinger, Almost Everyone's Guide to Economics (Pelican Books).

3. For example, Joseph A. Schumpeter, The Theory of Economic Development.

4. A. C. Sturt, A Degree of Freedom, Churinga Publishing 1995.

5. Gerald M. Weinberg, An Introduction to Systems Thinking, (John Wiley and Sons, 1975).

6. Systems Thinking, Selected Readings ed. by F.E.Emery (Penguin Books).

7. Sir Arthur Eddington, The Nature of the Physical World, A Milestone of Scientific Thought, (Cambridge University Press and Comet Books, Collins), Chapters IV and V. A classic text containing the Gifford Lectures delivered in the University of Edinburgh in 1927.

Chapter Two - THE ECONOMIC PROCESS

1. G.M.Trevelyan, A Shortened History of England, Pelican), p389. There was a fuel famine in parts of England in the seventeenth century.

2 "Our society can be viewed as a complex machine for transforming high-grade energy, called fuel, into low-grade energy, called waste

References

heat, while extracting the energy required to produce the goods and services we call the GNP." National Science Foundation, quoted in Paul A. Samuelson, Economics, (McGraw Hill International Student Eleventh Edition) p168.

3. Paul A. Samuelson op. cit. p747 wrote that economics involves more than technology. Its laws must respect those of nature and physics i.e. the first law of thermodynamics which guarantees conservation of energy and more subtly, but no less consequential for economics, the second law of thermodynamics which requires that the total of entropy (or disorder) irreversibly increases.

    He thought this was why Vanderbilt University's Nicholas Georgescu-Roegen had argued that the long-run nature of economic equilibrium was not a regular pendulum motion and a steady-state GNP as the globe went through its seasons but the hour glass with its sands running down. He added that science can temporarily turn the glass over but the sands immediately start falling again. Producing the GNP speeds up the degradation of matter and usable energy.

4. Adam Smith, The Wealth of Nations, Book Two, Chapter III, Of the Accumulation of Capital or of Productive and Unproductive Labour.

Chapter Three - THE PERFECT MARKET AS A SYSTEM

1. Understanding Economics, The Manchester Economics Project, Project Head C. Giles, (Ginn and Co. Ltd., 18 Bedford Row, London), Section S5 etc.

2. Kenneth E. Boulding, Economic Analysis, Volume 1: Microeconomics, Harper and Row, International Student Reprint, Fourth Edition), pp 108-123, The Competitive Market.

3. Paul A. Samuelson, op. cit. Chapter 4, Supply and Demand: The Bare Elements, p62 Perfection of Competition as a Limiting Pole.

References

4. Richard G. Lipsey, Positive Economics, (Weidenfeld and Nicholson, Third Edition 1971), Chapter 32 Microeconomic Policy, p416 Market Imperfections.

5. Arthur M. Louis, The Stockmarket of the Future - Now Fortune October 29 1984 pp 89-92.

6. Understanding Economics, The Manchester Economics Project op. cit., Section 19

7. Paul A. Samuelson op. cit. Chapter 18 Synthesis of Monetary Analysis and Income Analysis, Appendix: Mechanisms of Monetarism and Income Determination.

8. W. Ross Ashby, An Introduction to Cybernetics, University Paperbacks, Methuen and Co. 1970 p50.

Chapter Four - THE MARKET SYSTEM IN THE REAL WORLD

1. Richard G. Lipsey op. cit. Chapter 32, Micro-economic Policy.

2. Paul A. Samuelson op. cit. Chapter 25, Maximum-Profit Equilibrium p 463.

3. Adam Smith op. cit. Chapter X, Part II, Of Wages and Profit in the Different Employments of Labour and Stock.

4. W. S. Jevons, Money and the Mechanism of Exchange, Appleton London 1875 p3: "There may be many people wanting, and many people possessed of those things wanted; but to allow an act of barter, there must be a double coincidence, which will rarely happen."

5. Richard G. Lipsey, op. cit. Chapter 12, The Dynamic Theory of Price.

6. Paul A. Samuelson, op. cit. Chapter 20, Determination of Price by Supply and Demand p381 Case 7, Dynamic Cobweb.

References

Chapter Five - THE COST BASIS OF ECONOMIC ACTIVITY

1. L. W. T. Stafford, Mathematics for Economists, Macdonald and Evans Handbook, Second Edition 1978 pp 126-8.

2. Paul A. Samuelson op. cit. Chapter 24, Analysis of Costs and Long-run Supply.

3. Richard G. Lipsey, op. cit. Chapter 18, The Theory of Costs p208, The Measurement of Opportunity Cost by the Firm.

4. Richard G. Lipsey op. cit. Chapter 29 Interest and the Return on Capital p376, The Present Value of Future Income.

Chapter Six - ECONOMIES OF SCOPE

1. Marshall, Alfred, Principles of Economics, Book IV, Chapter VIII Industrial organisation, Section 1 Mutual Debts of Biology and Economics: differentiation. See also his Economics of Industry, Book IV, Chapter VIII.

2. Adam Smith, The Wealth of Nations, Penguin 1974, p109.

3. William J. Abernathy, Kim B. Clark, Alan M. Kantrow, Industrial Renaissance, Basic Books Inc 1983, p63.

4. Hedley, Barry, Long Range Planning Vol. 9 No.6 December 1976, A Fundamental Approach to Strategy Development.

Chapter Seven - THE PROCESS OF TECHNOLOGICAL INNOVATION

1. Nathan Rosenberg, Cambridge University Press 1982 Inside the Black Box: Technology and Economics, p246.

2. Nathan Rosenberg, op. cit. p78.

References

3. Thomas J. Allen, The MIT Press Cambridge Massachusetts and London England 1979, Managing the Flow of Technology.

4. John Eatwell, Duckworth, British Broadcasting Corporation 1982, Whatever happened to Britain? p138.

5. Mansfield, J. Rapoport, A. Romeo, S. Wagner, and G. Beardsley, Social and Private Rates of Return from Industrial Innovations, Quarterly Journal of Economics, 91, (May 1977) pp 221-240.

6. Robert R. Nathan Associates, Net Rates of Return on Innovations, Report to the National Science Foundation (Washington DC, October 1978), Vols. 1 and 2.

7. Christopher Freeman ed., Long Waves in the World Economy, (Butterworths 1983).

Chapter Eight - ORGANISATION AND INNOVATION IN THE ECONOMIC PROCESS

1. M. J. Kearton, Adaptors and Innovators - Why New Initiatives Get Blocked, (Long Range Planning Vol. 17 No. 2 pp 137-143, 1984).

2. Gerald M. Weinberg, An Introduction to Systems Thinking, (John Wiley and Sons, 1975), p11.

3. E. F. Schumacher, Small is Beautiful - Economics as if People Mattered (Harper and Row, New York, 1973), p230, The Principle of Subsidiarity.

4. Tudor Rickards, Problem Solving through Creative Analysis (British Institute of Management: Gower Press 1974).

5. Brian Twiss, Managing Technological Innovation, (Longman 1974), Chapter 4, Creativity and Problem Solving.

6. Barry L. Schutler, Kristin Shannon and Alan Mosman, Community Problem Solving at the Neighbourhood Level, (Creativity Network

References

Vol. 1 No. 3, Tudor Rickards, Manchester Business School, Feb. 1975).

Chapter Nine - CONCLUSIONS

1. Adam Smith, The Wealth of Nations, (Penguin 1974) pp 12-13 Introduction by Andrew Skinner, Note 4. The Note says that Smith, the "father of economics", conceived of an economy as a system, which he defined as follows:

   "Systems in many respects resemble machines. A machine is a little system, created to perform, as well as to connect together, in reality, those different movements and effects which the artist has occasion for. A system is an imaginary machine, invented to connect together in the fancy those different movements and effects which are already in reality performed." Quote from Adam Smith: Principles which lead and direct Philosophical Enquiries: illustrated by the History of Astronomy (Oxford University Press edition p66).

   The Note goes on to say: "Smith in fact argued that the thinker would tend to produce systems in the sense just used, because of a natural dislike of the apparently unconnected and an equally natural preference for order.... He talks of 'our love of system' in his philosophical works."

2. Malthus wrote in The Essay on Population (1798) of:

   > Systems of Equality
   > Systems of Agriculture
   > Systems of Commerce and
   > Systems of Agriculture and Commerce Combined.

   (Author's Note: Malthus seems to have postulated in his systems that the supply of food could increase at best in less than arithmetic proportion, but that the numbers of the population must grow exponentially. If these hypotheses had been valid, the predictable outcome must indeed have been misery, tempered only by occasional famine and pestilence. However, fortunately for all,

References

neither the relationships nor the people who were expected to give rise to them turned out to be homogeneous through time).

Index

Accounting. *See* Organisation and Technological Innovation, budgets
Adam Smith
  division of labour. *See* Scope, Economies of, labour-related
  among pinmakers, 121
  economy as a system, 245
  invisible hand, 54
Added Value, 158
Agriculture. *See* Economic Process, farming
Atomistic Economic Behaviour, 241
Automation. *See* Scope, Economies of, capital-related
Bargaining Process. *See* Perfect Market
Barriers to Entry. *See* Costs
Biosphere. *See* Environment, Natural
Capital. *See* Scope, Economies of, capital-related
Centralisation. *See* Organisation
Chemical Industry, 129
  feedstock costs, 130
Cities. *See* Scope, Economies of, land-related
City of London, 135, 140
Classical Economics. *See* Neoclassical Economic Theory

Comparative Advantage, 157, 159, 187
Competitive Advantage and Disadvantage. *See* Costs
Conversion Processes, 58
  agriculture, 133
  costs/output curves. *See* Costs
  differentiation, 100, 197, 244
  division into stages, 121
  efficiency, 109, 127, 155
  energy. *See* Economic Process
  flowline representation, 47
  wear and tear, 48
  integrated, 130
  investment. *See* Systems, Economic
  metal strip production, 139
  output level, 108
  scale of. *See* Scale
  wear and tear, 101
Costs
  allocation by convention, 57, 237
  barriers to entry, 153, 154, 156, 198
  behavioural, 232
  break-even, 106, 112
  capital, savings, 129
  city dwellers, of, 135
  competitive advantage, 156, 198, 244
  formation, 157, 187

Index

endogenous, 115
exogenous, 115
externalised, 102
fixed operating, 106, 107, 110, 130
general costs/output curve, 107, 242
housing, 233
input, 100
   instantaneous, 100
labour, 244
marginal, 108
opportunity, 114, 116
output curves
   identical, 112
scale-related. *See* Scale
structures, 139
   oil price effect, 152
sunk, 101, 114
timing, 101
transport, 108
uncertainty, 116
variable operating, 104, 106, 108, 130
Costs:, 102
Counterfeiting, 159
Coupling. *See* Markets
Creativity, 17, 30, 123
Critical Mass. *See* Organisation and Technological Innovation
Decision-making. *See* Organisation, Section 8.5
investment, 158
Decoupling, Causal. *See* Markets
Defence, 98

Degrees of Freedom. *See* Perfect Market, Systems and Systems, Economic
Demand
   confounding in schedules, 25, 37
   schedules, 36
      limitations, 96
   schedules as vectors, 37
Democracy, 98, 243
Differentiation. *See* Conversion Processes, Markets, commodity and Scope
Discounted Cash Flow, 115
Economic Process. *See* Chapter Two
   agriculture. *See* farming, Markets and Scale
   business cycles. *See* Systems, Economic
   catalysts, 17, 67
   categories of functions, 15. *See* Figure 2.1
   chain, example of, 51
   competition, 109
   consumers, 66
   consumption, 10
   conversion processes, 19
      irreversibility, 23
   creativity. *See* Creativity
   decision-making, 30, 51, 87
   definition, 9, 245
   depreciation, 48
   destabilisation, 57
   development, 25
   diagram. *See* Figure 2.2

Index

dynamic physical analogue. *See* Systems, Economic, physical analogue
energy, 11, 15, 16, 50
  absence from neoclassical theory, 242
  costs, 26
  deficiency, 14, 30
  density, 12, 14, 143
  efficiency, 25, 158
  loss, 24
  resources, 25
  solar, 11, 13, 143
  stored, 14, 17
  transformation, 12, 15, 19, 61, 143
  waste materials, 24
evolution, 7, 149, 188
facilitators, 10, 16, 30, 96
failure, root causes of, 30
farming. *See* Chapter Two, Section 2.2
  agriculture, 113, 133
  flowline representation, 48, 97
  food, 12, 16
  growth, 30, 160
  harvest, 54, 101, 103, 108, 109
  imbalances, increasing with time, 244
  incentives, 16, 18, 28, 30, 67
individualism, historic, 239
investment. *See* Systems, Economic, investment
manpower, 12, 14, 17, 22, 50, 66
manufacturing, Chapter Two, Section 2.3, 13
markets. *See* Markets and Perfect Markets
money, 11, 18, 30, 37, 52, 58, 79, 243
  apples and pears, 102
  feedback system, 246
  flows, 234
  homogeneity through time, 245.
  notional value, 117
natural resources. *See* resources
network, 50, 97
oscillation, 93
new paradigm, 37
non-homogeneity through time, 116, 152
obsolescence, 48
organisation, 12, 13, 14, 17, 30. *See* also Organisation
production, 10
resources
  natural, 10, 14
  natural living, 11
  time and energy as scarce resources, 29
rules, 27
scope. *See* Scope
services, 16, 245
specialisation, 12, 13, 14
stocks, 13
systems. *See* Systems, Economic
time, in. *See* Time
tools, 11
utilities, 15

257

Index

Elasticity, 52, 153
Electricity
  grids, linking of, 139
  power generation, 138
Energy
  solar. *See* Economic Process, energy
Energy Content, Economic, 20
  build up, 22
  consumption, of, 16, 24
  production, of, 16
Energy Forms, 242. *See* also Economic Process
  charcoal, 14
  coal, 14
  costs, 26
  heat, light and power, 16
  oil. *See* Oil
  primary, 145
  sources of, 144
  special role. *See* Chapter Two, Section 2.5
Energy Intensity of GDP, 145
Engineering, 158
Entropy. *See* Systems and Systems, Economic
Environment, Natural, 9
  biosphere, 10
Equilibrium, Economic, 1, 8, 25, 36, 59, 62, 243
  energy loss, 7
  general, 25, 42
  perfect market, 54, 240
  static, 3
Evolution
  and economics. *See* Marshall

economic. *See* Economic Process
Experience Curves. *See* Scope, Economies of, capital-related
Farming. *See* Economic Process
Feedback. *See* Systems and Systems, Economic
Firm Size, 153
  bimodal, 154
Flexible Manufacturing Systems, 167
Fossil Fuels. *See* Energy Forms
Francis Bacon
  quotations, 9, 240
  on innovation, 161
Garden Centres, 138
Global Market, 191
Gold
  economic energy content, 37
  medium of exchange, 37
  product of conversion process, 37
Government
  market, outside, 98
  responsibility, 4
Growth. *See* Economic Process
Harvest, Economic. *See* Economic Process, harvest
Housing
  debt, 233
  high rise, improvement, 235
Incentives. *See* Systems, Economic, feedback

Index

Industrial Harvest. *See* Economic Process, harvest
Industrial Innovation, 2. *See* Technological Innovation
Information. *See* Markets, Perfect Market, Systems and Organisation
Information Technology, 148
Innovation. *See* Technological Innovation
  destabilisation of economic process, 57
  invention, difference from, 7
Invention, 162
Investment. *See* Systems, Economic
Japan
  approach to risk, 220
  competitive advantage, 190
  experience curves, 131
  flexible manufacturing systems, 129
  import quota on foreign cars, 190
  problem-solving, 223
  response times, 223
  rise of, 243
Keynes, 32
  quotations
    mathematical economics, 118
    non-homogeneity through time, 118
    systems, 31
Kondratieff, 193
Laissez-faire. *See* Markets:*laissez-faire*
Land. *See* Scope, Economies of
Language. *See* Scope, Economies of, labour-related and Scope, Diseconomies of
Law and Order, 98
Learning Systems. *See* Organisation and Systems, Economic
Less Developed Countries (LDCs), 146
Life Cycle. *See* Product Life Cycle
London Futures Exchange (LIFFE), 36
London Metal Exchange, 44
Malthus, 124, 245
Marginal Productivity, 124
Markets
  access, 18
  agriculture, 78
  bargaining process. *See* Perfect Market
  blackboards, 44, 59, 70
  cobweb behaviour, 92
  commodity differentiation, 66, 97, 100, 119, 155
  problems of definition. *See* imperfections
  common goods
  medium of exchange, 79, 95
  as a degree of freedom, 81
  networks, 93
  services, 94

Index

coupling by, 55, 96
decoupling, causal, 57
definition, 31, 33
development of, 12, 15
differentiation, 70
elasticity. *See* Elasticity
facilitators. *See* Economic Process
flaws in the mechanism of operation
   quantity of information, 69
   timing of information, 69
flowline representation, 46, 63, 97
historic, 59, 243
imperfections, 2, 44, 62, 241
   barter, 79
   bilateral trade, 81
   cartels, 63
   commodity
      definition, 64
      indivisibility, 64
   monopoly, 63
   monopsony, 63
   price guarantees, 78
   quotas, 77
   subsidies, 77
   tariffs, 77
information, 36, 44, 59, 61, 69, 70
information technology, 44
labour, 66, 97
laissez-faire, 32, 60
linked
   associated use, 68
   geographically, 68
   sequence in network, 68
   supplier, 69
medium of exchange. *See* common goods
network, 33, 54, 56
orthodox representation. *See* Supply and Demand
price
   as exchange value, 102
   oscillation, 69, 87
   signals, 82
product differentiation. *See* commodity
psychological constraints, 75
response times, 83. *See* Systems, Economic
services, 65, 97
speculation
   flowline representation, 74
static physical analogue, 58
stockmarkets, 44
stocks, 84
   flowline representation, 72, 84
submarket formation, 43
supervision, 243
ticker tapes, 44
trading
   flowline representation, 73
Marshall
   differentiation, as a parallel of evolution, 119, 244
Mathematical Representation
   underlying assumptions, 150

Index

Medium of Exchange, 97. *See* Markets, common goods and Systems, Economic, degrees of freedom
Mergers and Acquisitions, 158
Money. *See* Economic Process
NASDAQ, 45
National Industrial Pecking Order, 2, 191, 243
Neighbourhood Care, 130
Neoclassical Economic Theory, 32, 146, 240
   problems, 157, 159, 188, 199, 233, 235, 239
   political consequences, 246
   substitution in, 242
   technology as exogenous variable, 242
   time, absence of, 241
Net Revenue, 57
   calculated maximum, 108
   feedback, 84, 97, 155, 233, 244
   maximisation, 100, 101
   maximum in life cycle, 184
   potential, incentive to innovate, 233
Networks. *See* Scope, Economies of, land-related
New York Stock Exchange, 36, 45
Obsolescence. *See* Scope, Diseconomies of
OECD
   energy intensity of GDP, 145
   response times, 146
   unemployment, 193
Oil, 142, 144
   intensity of GDP, 146
   price
      increases in the 1970s, 140, 151
      scope effects, 141
   VLCCs, 142
Organisation, 8. *See* Chapter Eight. *See* also Economic Process
   accounting and, 237
   adaptation, 229
   architectures. *See* Section 8.4
   constraint on innovation, 228
   coordination matrix, 215
   hierarchies, 211
      interactions, sacrifice of, 211
      independent problem-solving groups, 222
      matrix, 214
   behavioural systems, 201, 236, 238, 246
      decomposition, 210
      economic costs, 231
   blackboards, 206
   centralisation, 159, 218
   communication, 203
   creative problem-solving. *See* Section 8.6
   critical mass, 229
   customer/contractor, 230, 238
   decision-making, 218. *See* Section 8.5

Index

choice between options, 218
difference from information flows, 237
definition, 200
division of labour, 207
environment, response to, 218
functional, 213
gatekeepers, 228
goals, 218, 225
groups
  learning, 200
  motivation, 220
  problem-solving, 221
individuals. *See* Section 8.1
  attitude to risk, 203
  creativity, 203
  free will, 203
  learning, 204
  motivation, 220
  non-homogeneity through time, 203
information. *See also* Information
  acquisition from environment, 217
  costs, 232
  flows, 200
    difference from decision-making, 237
    external, 210, 225, 228
    free, 238
    internal, 204, 210, 225, 228
  handling and interpretation, 205
  quantity to be processed, 207, 232, 238
  storage, 207
  systems. *See* Section 8.2
interactions, 204, 208, 225
  sacrifice of, 211, 215
  through coordination. *See* architectures
leadership, 220, 227
learning systems, 207, 216, 217, 237
levels of abstraction, 207
life cycle. *See* Product Life Cycle
management of change, 229, 236
matrix. *See* architectures
paradox of stability, 202
planning, 224
  horizon, 226
rates of change, 238
response times, 86, 205, 212, 219, 237
risks to, 219
scope effects, 218
size, 206
slack, 229
Subsidiarity, Principle of, 219
systems, as. *See* behavioural systems
task forces, 216
teams, 124, 236
technological innovation, in, 169. *See* Section 8.8
trust, 227, 236
yardsticks, 205, 207, 217

Index

Packaging. *See* Scope, Economies of, land-related
Pecking Order. *See* National Industrial Pecking Order
People
　role of, 7
Perfect Market
　access, freedom of, 33
　assumptions, 112
　　stochastic exchange, 233
　bargaining process, 38, 54, 189, 241
　blackboards, 38, 41, 42, 54, 241
　competition, 53
　conditions, 35, 60
　contradictions in hypothesis, 42
　definition, 33
　degrees of freedom. *See* blackboards
　　lack of, 41
　demand schedules, 36
　flaws
　　contribution to stability, 98
　　in the basic thesis, 62
　flowline representation, 34
　forecasting prices, 54
　impossibility, 97
　information
　　flows, 39
　　focus of, 34, 36
　　quantity of, 42, 241
　　role of, 37
　　stock of, 37
　interactions, 38, 42
　mechanism of operation, 34, 62
　network, 42
　number of participants, 42
　price
　　clearing, 36, 119
　　convergence process, 42
　　equilibrium, 36
　　formation, 34, 38
　product
　　homogeneity, 33
　　infinite divisibility, 33
　　quantity of information, 43
　　supply schedules, 36
　　timelessness, 36, 82
Planning. *See* Scope, Economies of
Poll Tax, 232
Population Distribution. *See* Scope, Economies of, land-related
Product Differentiation. *See* Markets, commodity
Product Life Cycle. *See* Section 7.6
　decline, 188, 198
　economies of scope in, 185, 186
　organisation, 202
　unit cost, point of minimum, 187
Research
　competitive advantage, 158
　contracting out, the non-learning system, 231
　costs, sunk, 182
　customer/contractor, 229

263

Index

market, invalid assumptions, 230
organisations, in, 229
Response Times. *See* Systems and Systems, Economic
Ricardo, 32, 190
Risks. *See* Organisation and Technological Innovation
  agricultural, 104
  conversion processes, 100
Say's Law, 51, 177
Scale, 15, 118
  agriculture, 103
  costs, 100, 103
  costs/output curve, 107
  diseconomies, 100, 112
  economies, 100, 110
    chemical plant, 111
    dangers of calculation, 112, 242
    geometric, 110
    information technology, effect of, 149
    limits to, 154
  scope, facilitation by, 13, 121, 197
Schumacher, 229
Scientific Knowledge
  accumulation of, 123
Scope, 15, 100. *See* Chapter Six
  agriculture, 12, 13
  changes. *See also* differentiation
    investment requirement, 137, 156, 157, 158, 187, 191
    physical separation processes, 141
  definition, 119, 120
  differentiation, 153
  diseconomies of. *See* Scope, Diseconomies of
  economies of. *See* Scope, Economies of scale
    facilitation of, 121, 244
    time, implicit in, 120
Scope, Diseconomies of
  agriculture, 134
  buildings, 128
  capital, 128
    destruction of, 132
  commuting, 136
  definition, 119
  environmental causes, 156
  land, 135
  language, 126
  obsolescence, 132, 234
  petrochemical plant, 129
  producer/consumer, 125
  railways, 128, 141
  schools, falling rolls, 137
  specialisation, 121
  supermarkets, 140
  time, 125
  tower blocks, 136
  transport, 136
Scope, Economies of, 244
  advantages, permanent, 244
  assets, change in the pattern of, 120
  buildings. *See* capital- and land-related

Index

capital-related, 133. *See* Section 6.2
  automation, 129
  buildings, 127
  design, 127
  deterioration and obsolescence, 132
  efficiency of conversion processes, 127
  experience curves, 131, 186
  extending capital, 131
  flexible manufacturing systems, 128
  process plant, 128
  product lifetime, 128
  shared assets, 128
definition, 119, 153, 156
energy -driven, 245
energy-related. *See* Section 6.4
  solar. *See* Economic Process, energy
firm size, implications for, 154
high rise flats, in, 235
information technology, effect of, 148
investment, through. *See* Scope, changes
irreversibility, 156, 244
labour-related. *See* Section 6.1
  creativity, 123
  division of labour, 121
  extension of time, 125
  language, 126
  specialisation, 121
  teams, 123
  technology, 122
land-related. *See* Section 6.3
  agriculture, 133
  buildings, 136
  cities, 135
  distance, 137
  financial institutions, 135
  networks, 139, 141
  packaging, 141
  population distribution, 135
  surface area, 134
language. *See* labour-related
life cycle, in. *See* Product Life Cycle
planning for, 157, 158, 226, 245
polarisation, 157
synergy, 124, 158
Services. *See* Economic Process and Markets
Silver. *See* Gold
Society, 98, 102, 110, 114, 246
  collective social provision, 98
South East Asia, 159, 198
State, The, 98
Statistics, 239
Strategy
  competitors, 225, 236
  management, 8, 117, 158
  national, 159
  objectives, 226
  pattern of resource allocation, 226
  plan, 228

Index

planning. *See* Section 8.7
  investments, sequence of, 226
  research, role of, 231
Supermarkets, 139
Supply
  confounding in schedules, 25, 37
  schedules, 36
    limitations, 96
  schedules as vectors, 37
Switzerland, 159
Synergy. *See* Scope, Economies of
Systems
  behavioural. *See* Organisation
  decomposition, 4
  definition, 3, 4
  degrees of freedom, 44
    lack of, 45
  differentiation, 5, 120
  economic. *See* Systems, Economic
  entropy, 5, 23, 48
  equilibrium, definition of, 7
  feedback, 6
  goals, 6
  hierarchy of subsystems, 4
  information, 5, 6
    free flow, 246
  inputs/outputs, 4
  learning. *See* Organisation and Systems, Economic
  open, 5
  response times, 87
  rules
    universal, 3
  whole/parts, 3, 201, 239, 246
  steady state, 7
  time, 6, 27
Systems, Economic
  behavioural. *See* Organisation
  business cycles, 92
  decomposition, 37
  degrees of freedom, 38, 39, 41
    lack of, 41
  medium of exchange, 95
  differentiation, 158. *See* Scope
  evolution parallel. *See* Marshall
  scope, changes of. *See* Scope
  dynamics, 58
  entropy, 48, 101, 132, 234
  examples, 3
  factory, 105
  feedback, 28, 38, 84. *See also* Systems
  incentives, 52, 58, 84, 233
  money, 246
  net revenue. *See* Net Revenue
  price, 52
  interactions, 38, 246
  oil price effect, 151
  investment, 59, 86, 120, 156
    changes of scope. *See* Scope, changes of
    concerted, 234

Index

to redress imbalances, 244
learning, 7, 59, 61, 97, 119, 120, 124, 145, 151, 153, 157, 244, 246
machines, 129
mathematical representation, 151
optimisation
  classical, 36
optimum size, 154
oscillation, 88, 93
physical analogue, 58
response times, 52, 57, 59, 97, 245
  examples, 89
  OECD, 146
  technological innovation, in, 167, 176, 197
statistical input, 239
steady state, 7, 25, 61
whole and parts, 115, 125
Technological Innovation. *See* Chapter Seven
budgets, repressive, 229
buildings, effect of layout, 168
bunching, 193, 198
capital
  annihilation, 183
  charge
    new differentiated product, 182
    new process, 178
  sunk, 178, 182, 189
competition, effect of. *See* Section 7.7
costs

  interactions, 194
  timing of, 184
critical mass, 196
cycles of, 193
definition, 2, 161, 228
  scope effect
    new differentiated product, 163
    new process, 162
destabilisation of economic process, 57
economic process, in, 7, 244
energy price increases, effects of, 183
energy use, and, 161
evolution of industrial base, 2, 119
facilitation by markets, 96
goal formation, 173
importance to economic development, 2
incentive to enter market
  new differentiated product, 181
  new process, 180
invention, distinction from, 162
materials, change of scope of
  design of components, 166
  elementary, 166
  spatial arrangements of components, 167
multiplier effect, 193
national upheaval, and, 196
need, perception of, 169
net benefit, 164, 192

267

Index

networks, opportunities arising from
  communications, 168
  electricity, 167
  organisation in. *See* Organisation
  processes. *See* Section 7.4.1
  products. *See* Section 7.4.2
  rates of change, 183, 196
    limiting, 183, 193, 198
  rates of return, 192, 198
  response times. *See* Systems, Economic
  risks
    buyers, 164
    innovator, 169, 174, 183, 229
    technological, 170, 177
  scope effect, 165
  scope effects on buyers and sellers, 165, 172, 176
  social benefits, 198
  stages of, 169, 171
  strategic management, 8
  systems interacting, 170, 197
    new system. *See* Figure 7.3
    process of. *See* Figure 7.2
  teams, 197
    multidisciplinary, 169
  unit costs of commodities, 163, 179
Technology, 30
  improvements, 25
  innovation. *See* Technological Innovation
  knowledge base, 15, 17
  accumulation, 122
  new, 2
  obsolescence, 122, 132
  ratchet on the economic process, 156, 244
Thomas Hobbes
  quotation, 9
Time
  conversion processes irreversibility, 23
  economic process, in, 11, 25, 48, 59
  absence from neoclassical theory, 241
  bargaining, 43
  homogeneity through, 116, 150, 158
  irreversibility, 27
  manufacturing, 13
  non-homogeneity through, 116, 119, 152, 158, 183, 244
  orthogonality, 37
  perfect markets, in, 46, 61, 119
  product life cycle. *See* Product Life Cycle
  response. *See* Systems and Systems, Economic
  scope, implicit in, 120
  shelf-life, 142
  systems, in, 6
Tower Blocks, 136
Transport, 137
  cities, in, 135
  costs, 108
  neighbourhood care, 130
  shipping containers, 142

Index

VLCCs, 142
UK, 191
Unemployment, 247

Wall Street, 135
Walras's auctioneer, 39